Let's grow together

KB276076

NE능률이
미래를
창조합니다.

건강한 배움의 고객가치를 제공하겠다는 꿈을 실현하기 위해
40년이 넘는 시간 동안 열심히 달려왔습니다.

앞으로도 끊임없는 연구와 노력을 통해
당연한 것을 멈추지 않고

고객, 기업, 직원 모두가 함께 성장하는 NE능률이 되겠습니다.

대한민국 고등학생 **10명** 중 **4.7** 명이 보는 교과서

영어 고등 교과서 점유율 1위
(7차, 2007 개정, 2009 개정, 2015 개정)

그동안 판매된
능률VOCA 1,100만 부

대한민국 박스오피스
**천만명을 넘은 영화
단 28개**

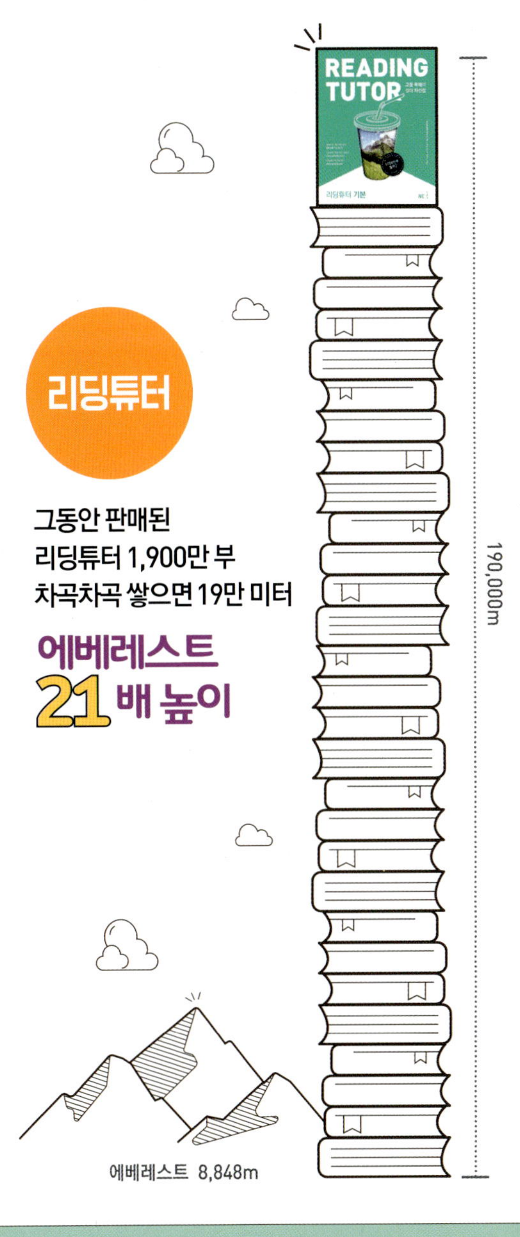

그동안 판매된
리딩튜터 1,900만 부
차곡차곡 쌓으면 19만 미터

**에베레스트
21 배 높이**

그래머존

그동안 판매된 450만 부의 그래머존을 바닥에 쭉 ~ 깔면

1000km 서울 - 부산 왕복가능

맞수

지은이	NE능률 영어교육연구소
선임연구원	전성호
연구원	선정아
영문교열	Olk Bryce Barrett, Nathaniel Galletta
디자인	송현아, 오솔길
맥편집	허문희
영업	한기영, 이경구, 박인규, 정철교, 김남준, 이우현
마케팅	박혜선, 남경진, 이지원, 김여진

맞수

맞춤형 **수**능영어
단기특강 시리즈

STRUCTURE

❶

01강 실전 모의고사

정답 및 해설 p. 2

1 대화를 듣고, 남자의 마지막 말에 대한 여자의 응답으로 가장 적절한 것을 고르시오.

① It was on last night at 6:00.
② I sleep for eight hours a day.
③ It starts at 8:00 this evening.
④ It's just another survival program.
⑤ It will be on TV for two and a half hours.

2 대화를 듣고, 그림에서 대화의 내용과 일치하지 <u>않는</u> 것을 고르시오.

3 대화를 듣고, 두 사람이 하는 말의 주제로 가장 적절한 것을 고르시오.

① 뷔페 식당의 인기 비결
② 뷔페 음식을 많이 먹는 방법
③ 뷔페 음식 메뉴의 선정 기준
④ 좋은 뷔페 식당을 고르는 법
⑤ 이윤 창출을 위한 뷔페 식당의 전략

4 대화를 듣고, 여자가 할 일로 가장 적절한 것을 고르시오.

① 손전등 찾기
② TV 켜기
③ 요가 수업 취소하기
④ 스마트폰 이용하기
⑤ 배터리 충전하기

5 대화를 듣고, 여자가 기부할 금액을 고르시오.

① $12
② $14
③ $22
④ $24
⑤ $34

6 다음을 듣고, 여자가 하는 말의 목적으로 가장 적절한 것을 고르시오.

① 새로운 전학생을 소개하려고
② 자원봉사 활동 자격을 공지하려고
③ 자원봉사자를 모집하려고
④ 해외 유학 시 겪을 수 있는 어려움을 알려주려고
⑤ 교환 학생 프로그램을 홍보하려고

7 대화를 듣고, 두 사람의 관계를 가장 잘 나타낸 것을 고르시오.

① 집주인 – 세입자
② 룸메이트 – 룸메이트
③ 고객 – 가구 배달원
④ 집주인 – 부동산 중개인
⑤ 거주자 – 이삿짐 운송업자

8 다음 표를 보면서 대화를 듣고, 여자가 선택할 항공편을 고르시오.

	Flight	Departure Date	Layover Location	Layover Time	Arrival Time
①	JC561	Monday	Salt Lake City	2 hours	4 p.m.
②	JC694	Monday	Los Angeles	4 hours	6 p.m.
③	AZ215	Tuesday	Salt Lake City	2 hours	8 p.m.
④	EM360	Tuesday	Los Angeles	4 hours	9 p.m.
⑤	EB806	Wednesday	Salt Lake City	2 hours	11 a.m.

9 특별 꽃꽂이 강좌에 관한 다음 내용을 듣고, 일치하지 <u>않는</u> 것을 고르시오.

① 총 4회 수업으로 진행된다.
② 부케 만들기를 배우는 초급자 과정이다.
③ 재료비는 수업료에 포함되어 있다.
④ 수업 후 남은 꽃들을 가져갈 수 있다.
⑤ 수강 신청은 웹사이트에서 할 수 있다.

10 다음 상황 설명을 듣고, James가 Fiona에게 할 말로 가장 적절한 것을 고르시오.

James: _______________________________________

① I didn't know you were still here.
② Please forgive me for forgetting our picnic today.
③ I'm sorry I'm late. I fell off my bike on my way here.
④ I'm so sorry that I couldn't call you to tell you I'd be late.
⑤ You should have told me that your phone battery ran out.

---

❶ 실전 모의고사

최신 수능 및 평가원 모의고사 출제 유형을 완벽히 반영한
12회의 실전 모의고사를 통해 수능 듣기에 대한 자신감을 얻을 수 있습니다.

NE Waffle

MP3 바로 듣기, 모바일 단어장 등 NE능률이 제공하는 부가자료를 빠르게 이용할 수 있는 통합 서비스입니다. 표지에 있는 QR코드를 스캔하여 한 번에 빠르게 필요한 자료를 이용하실 수 있습니다.

❷

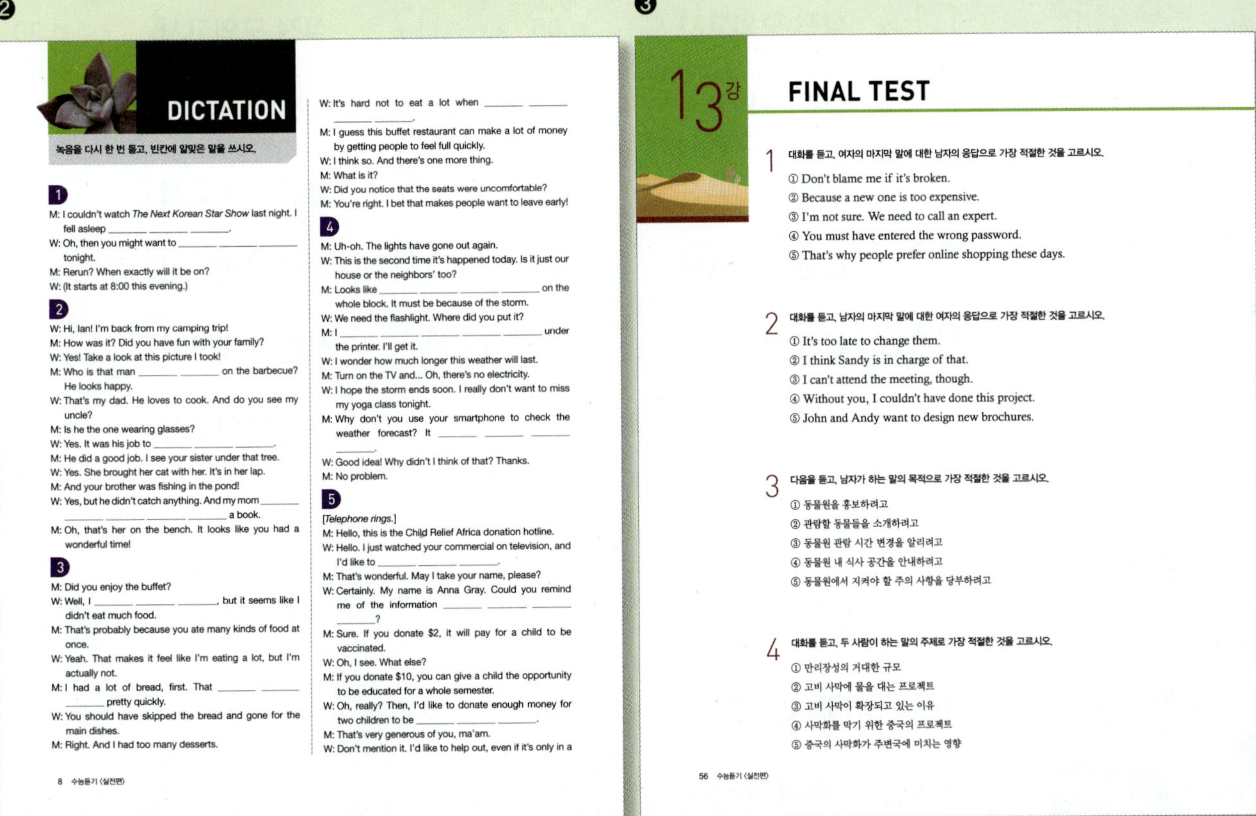

DICTATION

녹음을 다시 한 번 듣고, 빈칸에 알맞은 말을 쓰시오.

1

M: I couldn't watch *The Next Korean Star Show* last night. I fell asleep ___________ ___________ ___________.
W: Oh, then you might want to ___________ ___________ ___________ tonight.
M: Rerun? When exactly will it be on?
W: (It starts at 8:00 this evening.)

2

W: Hi, Ian! I'm back from my camping trip!
M: How was it? Did you have fun with your family?
W: Yes! Take a look at this picture I took!
M: Who is that man ___________ ___________ on the barbecue? He looks happy.
W: That's my dad. He loves to cook. And do you see my uncle?
M: Is he the one wearing glasses?
W: Yes. It was his job to ___________ ___________ ___________.
M: He did a good job. I see your sister under that tree.
W: Yes. She brought her cat with her. It's in her lap.
M: And your brother was fishing in the pond!
W: Yes, but he didn't catch anything. And my mom ___________ ___________ ___________ ___________ ___________ a book.
M: Oh, that's her on the bench. It looks like you had a wonderful time!

3

M: Did you enjoy the buffet?
W: Well, I ___________ ___________ ___________, but it seems like I didn't eat much food.
M: That's probably because you ate many kinds of food at once.
W: Yeah. That makes it feel like I'm eating a lot, but I'm actually not.
M: I had a lot of bread, first. That ___________ ___________ ___________ pretty quickly.
W: You should have skipped the bread and gone for the main dishes.
M: Right. And I had too many desserts.
W: It's hard not to eat a lot when ___________ ___________ ___________ ___________.
M: I guess this buffet restaurant can make a lot of money by getting people to feel full quickly.
W: I think so. And there's one more thing.
M: What is it?
W: Did you notice that the seats were uncomfortable?
M: You're right. I bet that makes people want to leave early!

4

M: Uh-oh. The lights have gone out again.
W: This is the second time it's happened today. Is it just our house or the neighbors' too?
M: Looks like ___________ ___________ ___________ ___________ on the whole block. It must be because of the storm.
W: We need the flashlight. Where did you put it?
M: I ___________ ___________ ___________ ___________ ___________ under the printer. I'll get it.
W: I wonder how much longer this weather will last.
M: Turn on the TV and... Oh, there's no electricity.
W: I hope the storm ends soon. I really don't want to miss my yoga class tonight.
M: Why don't you use your smartphone to check the weather forecast? It ___________ ___________ ___________ ___________.
W: Good idea! Why didn't I think of that? Thanks.
M: No problem.

5

[*Telephone rings.*]
M: Hello, this is the Child Relief Africa donation hotline.
W: Hello. I just watched your commercial on television, and I'd like to ___________ ___________ ___________.
M: That's wonderful. May I take your name, please?
W: Certainly. My name is Anna Gray. Could you remind me of the information ___________ ___________ ___________ ___________?
M: Sure. If you donate $2, it will pay for a child to be vaccinated.
W: Oh, I see. What else?
M: If you donate $10, you can give a child the opportunity to be educated for a whole semester.
W: Oh, really? Then, I'd like to donate enough money for two children to be ___________ ___________ ___________.
M: That's very generous of you, ma'am.
W: Don't mention it. I'd like to help out, even if it's only in a

❸

13강 FINAL TEST

1 대화를 듣고, 여자의 마지막 말에 대한 남자의 응답으로 가장 적절한 것을 고르시오.
① Don't blame me if it's broken.
② Because a new one is too expensive.
③ I'm not sure. We need to call an expert.
④ You must have entered the wrong password.
⑤ That's why people prefer online shopping these days.

2 대화를 듣고, 남자의 마지막 말에 대한 여자의 응답으로 가장 적절한 것을 고르시오.
① It's too late to change them.
② I think Sandy is in charge of that.
③ I can't attend the meeting, though.
④ Without you, I couldn't have done this project.
⑤ John and Andy want to design new brochures.

3 다음을 듣고, 남자가 하는 말의 목적으로 가장 적절한 것을 고르시오.
① 동물원을 홍보하려고
② 관람할 동물들을 소개하려고
③ 동물원 관람 시간 변경을 알리려고
④ 동물원 내 식사 공간을 안내하려고
⑤ 동물원에서 지켜야 할 주의 사항을 당부하려고

4 대화를 듣고, 두 사람이 하는 말의 주제로 가장 적절한 것을 고르시오.
① 만리장성의 거대한 규모
② 고비 사막에 물을 대는 프로젝트
③ 고비 사막이 확장되고 있는 이유
④ 사막화를 막기 위한 중국의 프로젝트
⑤ 중국의 사막화가 주변국에 미치는 영향

❷ DICTATION (듣기 집중 훈련)

앞에서 풀어본 문제들을 다시 한 번 들어보면서 핵심 어휘와 주요 표현을 익힐 수 있습니다.

❸ FINAL TEST

4회분의 FINAL TEST를 통해 앞에서 연습했던 각 유형들을 최종적으로 점검하고 수능 듣기에 자신 있게 대비할 수 있습니다.

CONTENTS

CHAPTER 01

CHAPTER 02

정답 및 해설 (책 속 책)

CHAPTER **01**

실전 모의고사

실전 모의고사

1 대화를 듣고, 남자의 마지막 말에 대한 여자의 응답으로 가장 적절한 것을 고르시오.

① It was on last night at 6:00.
② I sleep for eight hours a day.
③ It starts at 8:00 this evening.
④ It's just another survival program.
⑤ It will be on TV for two and a half hours.

2 대화를 듣고, 그림에서 대화의 내용과 일치하지 <u>않는</u> 것을 고르시오.

3 대화를 듣고, 두 사람이 하는 말의 주제로 가장 적절한 것을 고르시오.

① 뷔페 식당의 인기 비결
② 뷔페 음식을 많이 먹는 방법
③ 뷔페 음식 메뉴의 선정 기준
④ 좋은 뷔페 식당을 고르는 법
⑤ 이윤 창출을 위한 뷔페 식당의 전략

4 대화를 듣고, 여자가 할 일로 가장 적절한 것을 고르시오.

① 손전등 찾기
② TV 켜기
③ 요가 수업 취소하기
④ 스마트폰 이용하기
⑤ 배터리 충전하기

5 대화를 듣고, 여자가 기부할 금액을 고르시오.

① $12
② $14
③ $22
④ $24
⑤ $34

6 다음을 듣고, 여자가 하는 말의 목적으로 가장 적절한 것을 고르시오.

① 새로운 전학생을 소개하려고
② 자원봉사 활동 자격을 공지하려고
③ 자원봉사자를 모집하려고
④ 해외 유학 시 겪을 수 있는 어려움을 알려주려고
⑤ 교환 학생 프로그램을 홍보하려고

7 대화를 듣고, 두 사람의 관계를 가장 잘 나타낸 것을 고르시오.

① 집주인 – 세입자
② 룸메이트 – 룸메이트
③ 고객 – 가구 배달원
④ 집주인 – 부동산 중개인
⑤ 거주자 – 이삿짐 운송업자

8 다음 표를 보면서 대화를 듣고, 여자가 선택할 항공편을 고르시오.

	Flight	Departure Date	Layover Location	Layover Time	Arrival Time
①	JC561	Monday	Salt Lake City	2 hours	4 p.m.
②	JC694	Monday	Los Angeles	4 hours	6 p.m.
③	AZ215	Tuesday	Salt Lake City	2 hours	8 p.m.
④	EM360	Tuesday	Los Angeles	4 hours	9 p.m.
⑤	EB806	Wednesday	Salt Lake City	2 hours	11 a.m.

9 특별 꽃꽂이 강좌에 관한 다음 내용을 듣고, 일치하지 <u>않는</u> 것을 고르시오.

① 총 4회 수업으로 진행된다.
② 부케 만들기를 배우는 초급자 과정이다.
③ 재료비는 수업료에 포함되어 있다.
④ 수업 후 남은 꽃들을 가져갈 수 있다.
⑤ 수강 신청은 웹사이트에서 할 수 있다.

10 다음 상황 설명을 듣고, James가 Fiona에게 할 말로 가장 적절한 것을 고르시오.

James: _______________________________

① I didn't know you were still here.
② Please forgive me for forgetting our picnic today.
③ I'm sorry I'm late. I fell off my bike on my way here.
④ I'm so sorry that I couldn't call you to tell you I'd be late.
⑤ You should have told me that your phone battery ran out.

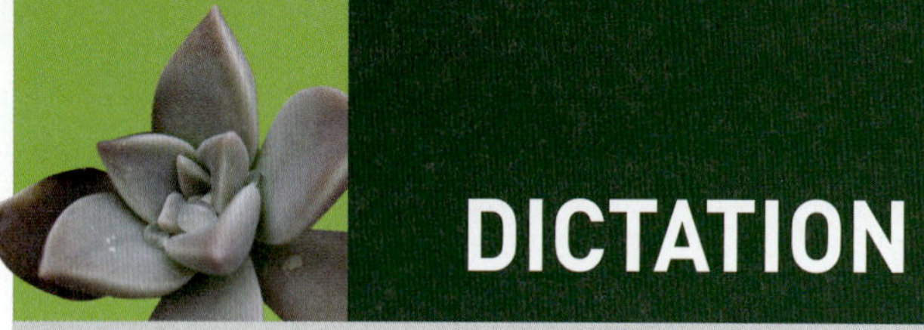

녹음을 다시 한 번 듣고, 빈칸에 알맞은 말을 쓰시오.

1

M: I couldn't watch *The Next Korean Star Show* last night. I fell asleep ________ ________ ________.

W: Oh, then you might want to ________ ________ ________ tonight.

M: Rerun? When exactly will it be on?

W: (It starts at 8:00 this evening.)

2

W: Hi, Ian! I'm back from my camping trip!

M: How was it? Did you have fun with your family?

W: Yes! Take a look at this picture I took!

M: Who is that man ________ ________ on the barbecue? He looks happy.

W: That's my dad. He loves to cook. And do you see my uncle?

M: Is he the one wearing glasses?

W: Yes. It was his job to ________ ________ ________.

M: He did a good job. I see your sister under that tree.

W: Yes. She brought her cat with her. It's in her lap.

M: And your brother was fishing in the pond!

W: Yes, but he didn't catch anything. And my mom ________ ________ ________ ________ ________ a book.

M: Oh, that's her on the bench. It looks like you had a wonderful time!

3

M: Did you enjoy the buffet?

W: Well, I ________ ________ ________, but it seems like I didn't eat much food.

M: That's probably because you ate many kinds of food at once.

W: Yeah. That makes it feel like I'm eating a lot, but I'm actually not.

M: I had a lot of bread, first. That ________ ________ ________ pretty quickly.

W: You should have skipped the bread and gone for the main dishes.

M: Right. And I had too many desserts.

W: It's hard not to eat a lot when ________ ________ ________ ________.

M: I guess this buffet restaurant can make a lot of money by getting people to feel full quickly.

W: I think so. And there's one more thing.

M: What is it?

W: Did you notice that the seats were uncomfortable?

M: You're right. I bet that makes people want to leave early!

4

M: Uh-oh. The lights have gone out again.

W: This is the second time it's happened today. Is it just our house or the neighbors' too?

M: Looks like ________ ________ ________ ________ on the whole block. It must be because of the storm.

W: We need the flashlight. Where did you put it?

M: I ________ ________ ________ ________ ________ under the printer. I'll get it.

W: I wonder how much longer this weather will last.

M: Turn on the TV and... Oh, there's no electricity.

W: I hope the storm ends soon. I really don't want to miss my yoga class tonight.

M: Why don't you use your smartphone to check the weather forecast? It ________ ________ ________ ________.

W: Good idea! Why didn't I think of that? Thanks.

M: No problem.

5

[*Telephone rings.*]

M: Hello, this is the Child Relief Africa donation hotline.

W: Hello. I just watched your commercial on television, and I'd like to ________ ________ ________.

M: That's wonderful. May I take your name, please?

W: Certainly. My name is Anna Gray. Could you remind me of the information ________ ________ ________ ________?

M: Sure. If you donate $2, it will pay for a child to be vaccinated.

W: Oh, I see. What else?

M: If you donate $10, you can give a child the opportunity to be educated for a whole semester.

W: Oh, really? Then, I'd like to donate enough money for two children to be ________ ________ ________.

M: That's very generous of you, ma'am.

W: Don't mention it. I'd like to help out, even if it's only in a small way.

6

W: Good morning students. Before starting class, I ________ ________ ________ ________. Entering a new school is always challenging, but doing so in a foreign country is even more difficult. As some of you may know, our high school will have several exchange students arrive next month. These students will need help ________ ________ ________ at our school and in our community. If any of you would like to volunteer to assist these students, please sign up in the teacher's room as soon as possible. Volunteers will be paired with exchange students who are the same age and gender. This is a great opportunity to help others while also ________ ________ ________ and friendships.

7

[Doorbell rings.]

W: Who is it?

M: Is this Ms. Murphy's house? I'm Michael Park. We spoke on the phone earlier today.

W: Ah, yes. Please come in. Thanks for coming over so quickly.

M: No problem. So, is this ________ ________ ________?

W: Yes, it's a one-room apartment.

M: Well, you don't have a lot of furniture. Will you ________ ________ ________ on the weekend?

W: I'd prefer to. How much does it cost on the weekend?

M: We're busy on weekends, so there's an extra fee.

W: Oh, really? Well, weekdays are fine, too. Could you give me an estimate of ________ ________ ________ ________ ________?

M: Hmm... For a pickup truck, a driver and two men to carry your furniture, it'll be $300.

W: That sounds reasonable.

M: Great. Let's arrange a time, and then we're all set.

8

[Telephone rings.]

M: Hello, you've reached Eagle Airlines. How can I help you?

W: Hi, I booked a flight to New York for next Thursday, but I would like to ________ ________ ________ ________ flight.

M: Sure. How about Wednesday morning?

W: Well, either Monday or Tuesday would be best.

M: ________ ________ ________ ________ in Salt Lake City or Los Angeles?

W: That would be fine. How long are the layovers?

M: Through Salt Lake City, it's two hours. Through Los Angeles, it's four hours.

W: Hmm… I would rather have ________ ________ ________ ________. What time do the flights arrive?

M: The Tuesday flights arrive at 8 and 9 p.m., and the Monday flights arrive at 4 and 6 p.m.

W: I see. I need some time to get to my hotel, so I had better take an earlier flight.

M: Okay. Then I have just the flight for you.

9

W: Whether you are looking to start a career as a florist or you are just an ________ ________, Flora Philadelphia can help you develop your skills in floral arts and design. We provide a vast array of specialized classes, and we are currently offering a special price for one of our introductory courses. The course ________ ________ ________ ________. In these classes, you will learn to put together beautiful wedding bouquets. The fee is only $200, with ________ ________ ________ ________ of $30 for each class. After the class, you can take the remaining materials home along with your own bouquet. ________ ________ ________ ________ this special offer, be sure to register on our website by April 10. If you have any questions, please call us at 555-6398. Don't miss this great opportunity!

10

M: After a busy semester at medical school, James has been looking forward to spending time with his girlfriend, Fiona. They have arranged to meet at the park for a romantic picnic. On his way to meet her, he happens to ________ ________ ________ ________ ________ her bike. By stopping to help her up, he makes himself ________ ________ ________ ________ for his date with Fiona. Unfortunately, he can't call her, as his phone's battery has run out. When he finally arrives at the park, he sees that Fiona ________ ________. In this situation, what would James most likely say to Fiona?

James: (I'm so sorry that I couldn't call you to tell you I'd be late.)

실전 모의고사

1 대화를 듣고, 여자의 마지막 말에 대한 남자의 응답으로 가장 적절한 것을 고르시오.

① Just check out all the club ads first.
② Rugby is my favorite sport, though.
③ Let's start warming up with some stretches.
④ How about going to a baseball game?
⑤ Sorry, but I'm already a member of another club.

2 대화를 듣고, 두 사람이 하는 말의 주제로 가장 적절한 것을 고르시오.

① 보행자의 안전 규칙
② 교통사고 후유증의 심각성
③ 올바른 스마트폰 사용법
④ 십 대들의 스마트폰 중독 현상
⑤ 보행 중 스마트폰 사용의 위험성

3 대화를 듣고, 남자가 할 일로 가장 적절한 것을 고르시오.

① 프린터 설치하기
② 새 프린터 사기
③ 새 전선 사기
④ 서비스 센터에 전화하기
⑤ 프린터 부품 교환하기

4 대화를 듣고, 여자가 지불한 금액을 고르시오.

① $5   ② $6   ③ $8   ④ $9   ⑤ $12

5 다음을 듣고, 남자가 하는 말의 목적으로 가장 적절한 것을 고르시오.

① 음식을 남기지 않도록 권고하려고
② 영양 섭취의 중요성을 강조하려고
③ 식당 자원봉사자를 모집하려고
④ 환경 보호 행사 참여를 독려하려고
⑤ 음식물 쓰레기 대책 마련을 촉구하려고

6 대화를 듣고, 여자가 남자에게 부탁한 일로 가장 적절한 것을 고르시오.

① 함께 IT 공부하기
② 커피 한 잔 갖다 주기
③ 웹사이트 디자인하는 것을 도와주기
④ 새로운 디자인 컨셉 정하기
⑤ 소프트웨어 사용법을 가르쳐주기

7 대화를 듣고, 그림에서 대화의 내용과 일치하지 <u>않는</u> 것을 고르시오.

8 다음 표를 보면서 대화를 듣고, 남자가 구입할 배낭을 고르시오.

Backpacks on Sale

	Model	Price	Color	Inner pockets	Size
①	A	$50	Blue	1	Medium
②	B	$65	Red	1	Medium
③	C	$70	Blue	4	Medium
④	D	$85	Black	2	Large
⑤	E	$95	Green	4	Large

[9-10] 다음을 듣고, 물음에 답하시오.

9 여자가 하는 말의 주제로 가장 적절한 것은?

① ideas for craft projects ② how artists see the world

③ a way to improve creativity ④ creative geniuses throughout history

⑤ the dangers of excessive imagination

10 연습 도구로 언급된 것은?

① a teacup ② a coin ③ a hat

④ a toy animal ⑤ flowers

DICTATION

녹음을 다시 한 번 듣고, 빈칸에 알맞은 말을 쓰시오.

1

W: I'd like to join the rugby club. What do you think?
M: I heard that their training is ________ ________ ________ the club sports.
W: Really? Um... I'm not sure which sports club ________ ________ ________, then.
M: (Just check out all the club ads first.)

2

M: What a nice dinner, darling. Did you...
W: Alan, a boy is crossing the road!
M: [*Tires screech.*] Wow, ________ ________ ________! Are you all right, honey?
W: Yes, and luckily so is that boy. I can't believe he walked into the street without looking.
M: He was making a common mistake.
W: What do you mean?
M: I mean he was using his smartphone ________ ________ ________.
W: Oh, yes. I see more and more people doing that these days. It's terrible!
M: I think so, too. It's frustrating when people use their smartphones in front of me on the sidewalk or in a hallway.
W: Well, it's ________ ________ when people casually walk into a busy street. Then it's dangerous!
M: I agree. It is a bad habit.

3

M: Wendy, have you ever ________ ________ ________ ________ before?
W: Sure. It's been a while, though.
M: Well, I just bought this printer, but I can't figure it out.
W: Hmm... It looks like you've already done the difficult part. Now you can just ________ ________ ________ ________.
M: I tried, but something's wrong. Maybe I'm plugging it in the wrong place.
W: No, that's the right place. Let me try. [*Pause*] That's strange.
M: Maybe I should call the customer service center.
W: Wait a minute. Here's the problem. The end of this cable is broken.
M: Oh, yeah. I'll take it back to the store to ________ ________ ________.
W: Okay. I'll help you finish setting it up later.
M: Thanks for your help.

4

M: Hello! Are you here for your usual morning coffee?
W: Yes, but ________ ________ ________ today. I'm getting one for a friend.
M: All right. Would you like anything to eat with those?
W: Hmm... These blueberry muffins ________ ________ ________. How much are they?
M: They're $2 each. They were just baked an hour ago.
W: Okay. I'll take three of those, then.
M: All right. The coffees are $3 each, plus you've got the three muffins for $2 each. Is that all?
W: Yes. Oh, and I have my frequent customer card. [*Pause*] Wow, that makes ten stamps.
M: In that case, you can ________ ________ ________ ________.
W: Oh, really? What a great surprise!
M: Here's your coffee and your muffins. Have a wonderful day.
W: Thanks. See you tomorrow!

5

M: Good afternoon. I want all of you to listen very carefully to what I have to say. The cooks in our cafeteria work very hard to prepare nice, healthy meals for all of you, but it has come to my attention that the amount of food that is ________ ________ ________ has been increasing. You are all young, and your bodies are still growing. So in order to ________ ________ ________ that your body needs, you need to make sure that you have plenty to eat. In addition, wasting food is ________ ________ ________ ________. When food waste is dumped in a landfill, it rots and produces methane, which is a greenhouse gas. So please try to do your part in helping to reduce the amount of food that is thrown away.

6

M: Hey, you look stressed out. What's wrong?

W: [*Sigh*] It's this web design software. It's _________ _________.

M: Which program are you using? Can I take a look?

W: Sure. I'm trying to use this one called Dreamweb.

M: Dreamweb? That's a pretty difficult program to use. I much prefer Webweaver.

W: Wait, you know about this stuff?

M: Sure. I _________ _________ _________ in college. Didn't you know that?

W: No, I thought you studied IT. So, could you _________ _________ _________ _________ _________?

M: Of course. What are friends for?

W: Thank you! You're the best.

M: But before I can do it, I'll need to know what kind of style you have in mind for your website.

W: Okay. Let's get some coffee and talk more about it.

M: Sounds good.

7

W: Let's make a poster for our school's music festival.

M: Good idea. Let's put the name of the festival at the very top _________ _________ _________.

W: Good! And let's write the date of the festival on the lower left side of the poster.

M: Okay. What about adding a picture of a band?

W: Sure! Let's put one _________ _________ _________. Should we put a singer between two guitarists, like this?

M: I think that looks good.

W: How about adding a drummer too?

M: Okay. Should we put him on the left side of the poster?

W: Well, I think it'll look better if we put him behind the singer.

M: Great. He looks perfect there.

W: Do you think we should include ticket price on the poster?

M: Sure. _________ _________ _________ the information about tickets on the lower right side?

W: Alright. It looks great now!

8

W: Look at this display. Don't you need a new backpack?

M: Yes. My new laptop doesn't _________ _________ _________ _________ _________.

W: Let's look at what's on sale. How much money can you spend?

M: I don't want to spend more than $90.

W: I see. How big does it need to be?

M: A medium- or large-sized one would be good.

W: Do you like this medium-sized red bag?

M: No way. I don't like the color red.

W: Then what about this medium-sized blue one? It is _________ _________.

M: I like blue. How many inner pockets does it have?

W: Just one. I think there would be enough space in it for your laptop and the rest of your stuff.

M: Actually, I need more than one pocket. It would help me _________ _________ _________ better.

W: Then I think it's pretty clear which bag is best for you.

9-10

W: Do you want to be creative? Then you should try to keep your imagination in excellent condition. All you need to do is _________ _________ _________ in a different way. To do this, just pick up an object and look at it carefully. Try not to think about what this object is used for in everyday life. Instead, focus on its size, shape, color, and texture. Use your imagination to think of other uses this object could have. For example, a teacup is usually just for _________ _________ _________, but how else could it be used? You could use it to hold coins, to dig a small hole on a beach, to make a hat for a toy animal, or to plant some flowers. When you do this exercise, try to come up with as many ideas as you can. Let your imagination _________ _________ _________.

실전 모의고사

1 대화를 듣고, 남자의 마지막 말에 대한 여자의 응답으로 가장 적절한 것을 고르시오.

① It's right next to the bookstore.
② You can get the right size there.
③ The discount doesn't apply on the weekend.
④ It has locations all over the world.
⑤ The store is open around the clock.

2 대화를 듣고, 두 사람이 할 일로 가장 적절한 것을 고르시오.

① 볼링 치러 가기　　　　② 미용실 가기
③ 영화 예약 시간 변경하기　　④ 영화 보러 가기
⑤ 치과 진료받기

3 대화를 듣고, 남자가 지불할 총 금액을 고르시오.

① $25　　② $27　　③ $29　　④ $30　　⑤ $36

4 대화를 듣고, 남자가 여자에게 부탁한 일로 가장 적절한 것을 고르시오.

① 남자의 여권 찾기　　　② 이메일 보내기
③ 노트북 챙기기　　　　④ 파일 저장하기
⑤ 일정표 출력하기

5 대화를 듣고, 두 사람의 관계를 가장 잘 나타낸 것을 고르시오.

① 영업 사원 – 고객　　　② 자동차 수리공 – 차 주인
③ 버스 운전 기사 – 손님　　④ 매장 관리인 – 직원
⑤ 접수원 – 환자

6 대화를 듣고, 여자가 장학금을 받을 수 <u>없는</u> 이유를 고르시오.

① 뒤늦게 신청해서　　　　② 학점이 낮아서
③ 봉사 활동 시간이 부족해서　　④ 거주 기간이 모자라서
⑤ 교육 프로그램을 이수하지 않아서

7　새 방송 프로그램에 관한 다음 내용을 듣고, 일치하지 <u>않는</u> 것을 고르시오.

① 회당 한 시간씩 총 8부작으로 구성되어 있다.
② 첫 방영일은 2월 15일 저녁 8시이다.
③ 여성들에 대한 남성들의 편견에 대해 토론한다.
④ 미혼 남성들을 위한 연애 비법 및 조언을 전달한다.
⑤ 진행자는 성공한 결혼 중매인이다.

8　대화를 듣고, 그림에서 대화의 내용과 일치하지 <u>않는</u> 것을 고르시오.

[9-10] 다음을 듣고, 물음에 답하시오.

9　여자가 하는 말의 주제로 가장 적절한 것은?

① the advantages of online shopping
② the benefits of offering free samples
③ marketing strategies for supermarkets
④ how to organize effective cooking classes
⑤ why customers are spending less money on groceries

10　언급된 전략이 <u>아닌</u> 것은?

① using social media　　　　② providing digital coupons
③ offering free cooking class　　④ providing free samples
⑤ showing reviews of products online

DICTATION

녹음을 다시 한 번 듣고, 빈칸에 알맞은 말을 쓰시오.

1

M: Mom, look! My sneakers are ___________ ___________. I need to buy new ones.

W: Well, I heard that there is ___________ ___________ ___________ at the new shoe store.

M: Great! Let's go there. Where is it located?

W: (It's right next to the bookstore.)

2

W: Do you have any plans for this afternoon?

M: No. I was supposed to ___________ ___________, but Henry canceled. How about you?

W: I'm going to a beauty shop. My hair needs a trim.

M: That doesn't sound very exciting.

W: I think you should get your hair cut, too. Let's go together.

M: No, thanks. I might go see that new Brad Pitt movie instead.

W: Has that movie ___________ ___________ ___________? I want to see it, too.

M: Then why don't you come with me to the theater?

W: But I've already made a hair appointment. Let's go see it together tomorrow!

M: No, I have to go to the dentist tomorrow.

W: Okay. I guess I can ___________ ___________ ___________ to tomorrow.

M: Good decision. Let's meet at four o'clock at the box office.

W: Sounds good.

3

M: These salads look ___________ ___________ ___________.

W: Yeah. We grew all the vegetables and fruit in our salad ourselves.

M: I see. How much are these ricotta cheese salads?

W: The large salads are 9 dollars each and the small ones 7 dollars each.

M: Well, it sounds too expensive.

W: It's because ___________ ___________ ___________ ___________. They're very healthy.

M: Okay. Let me have a large one. And the potato salads look great, too.

W: Yeah, they're organic. They are 6 dollars each.

M: Hmm… three potato salads, please. How much are these sauces?

W: They're 3 dollars a bottle.

M: Great. I'll take one bottle, please. I think that's all. Ah, I have a 10% ___________ ___________. Can I use it?

W: Sure.

4

W: Do you have everything ready for your business trip, George?

M: Well, I'm nearly done packing. But I think I've forgotten something.

W: Try to think. [*Pause*] Did you ___________ ___________ ___________ and ticket?

M: Yeah, I put them in a separate bag. Oh, now I remember. Are you on the computer right now?

W: Yes, dear. I'm sending an email to Jenny.

M: Can you ___________ ___________ my business trip schedule for me?

W: Sure. Where can I find the schedule?

M: I saved it on the desktop.

W: Okay. Oh, ___________ ___________ ___________ pack your laptop this time.

M: I've already packed it. And now I'm ready to go.

5

M: Good afternoon. How can I help you?

W: I hear a grinding sound whenever I ___________ ___________ ___________.

M: That could be serious. Is it an old car?

W: No. I bought it a little over a year ago.

M: I think I should inspect the brakes to see ___________ ___________ ___________ that sound.

W: Do you have time to do that this afternoon?

M: Sure. I can get started in about thirty minutes. Do you mind waiting?

W: Not at all. I am free all afternoon.

M: Okay. Just ___________ ___________ ___________ ___________ and leave your key with me.

W: Do you have a pen I could borrow?

M: Here you are. And help yourself to some coffee in the waiting area.

6

M: May I help you?

W: Hi. This is Diana Dunstet. I got an email saying that my community volunteer scholarship application was rejected, but it doesn't explain why.

M: Hmm... Did you ________ ________ ________?

W: Yes. I know the required grade average is at least a B, but mine is an A!

M: Yes, I see that here. You also had to perform at least 100 hours of local volunteer service, which you've done.

W: Right! I help out every Saturday at the animal shelter. What else?

M: You have to ________ ________ ________ ________ ________ for at least one year.

W: Oh, no! I must have missed that when I was reading the program requirements.

M: Well, the good news is that you'll ________ ________ next semester.

W: That's a relief! I'll definitely reapply then. Thanks for the information.

7

M: This spring, Channel Five will bring you eight one-hour episodes of Brenda Stone's new show, *Tough Love*. It starts on Sunday, February 15, at 8 p.m. This new series is for all the really great men out there who can't ________ ________ why they are still single. In it, New York matchmaker Brenda Stone teaches single men about ________ ________ ________ ________ ________. She also tells them truthfully why they don't impress women when they go on a date. Brenda's honest advice has made her America's ________ ________ ________. She has the courage to tell men not what they want to hear, but what they need to hear in order to find love.

8

[*Cell phone rings.*]

M: Hi, honey. Did you arrive at the airport safely?

W: Yes. I'm sorry that I ________ ________ ________ for a whole week.

M: That's all right. It's a business trip, so just focus on your work.

W: Thank you. But I was in such a rush that I didn't complete some household chores.

M: Tell me what they are, and I'll handle them.

W: Good. First, I think I forgot to ________ ________ ________.

M: Yes. There are lots of dishes in the sink.

W: And please take out the trash. The trash can is already full.

M: Oh, right. I meant to take it out earlier.

W: If you would, please straighten up the table, too. It's too messy.

M: No problem.

W: Also, please close the veranda doors. It's supposed to rain tonight.

M: Don't worry. I can take care of it all. By the way, should I ________ ________ ________ ________ from the veranda?

W: No, I already did that, so you don't have to worry about it.

9-10

W: Good afternoon everyone, and welcome to the Northeast Marketing Association's annual meeting. Studies show that online shopping is decreasing the amount of money customers are spending on groceries. Today, I'd like to ________ ________ ________ that can help you get more customers to visit your stores' locations. All stores should make use of social media. Share pictures of store displays and provide digital coupons to customers. Free cooking classes are also very popular. I suggest that you offer weekly or monthly cooking or baking classes. Customers will come to your stores to learn a new recipe, and most will purchase ingredients for it at your stores to make the dishes at home. Another great strategy is to offer ________ ________ ________ free samples throughout your stores. Tasting a product makes customers more likely to purchase it. It also gives customers ________ ________ ________ ________ your stores, as free samples of freshly cooked food are not part of the online shopping experience.

실전 모의고사

1 대화를 듣고, 남자의 마지막 말에 대한 여자의 응답으로 가장 적절한 것을 고르시오.

① I need to find the invitation first.
② I can't wait to go to the wedding.
③ I don't have time to take pictures.
④ Oh, that's right. I forgot about that!
⑤ I don't know where your cell phone is.

2 대화를 듣고, 두 사람이 하는 말의 주제로 가장 적절한 것을 고르시오.

① 악수의 기원
② 악수의 중요성
③ 여러 나라의 인사법
④ 악수할 때의 예절
⑤ 다양한 손동작의 의미

3 대화를 듣고, 남자가 지불할 총 금액을 고르시오.

① $5.50　　② $6.50　　③ $7.00　　④ $7.50　　⑤ $8.00

4 다음을 듣고, 남자가 하는 말의 목적으로 가장 적절한 것을 고르시오.

① 선인장을 키울 때 주의 사항을 당부하려고
② 물을 좋아하는 식물의 종류를 소개하려고
③ 식물이 주는 심리적 안정 효과를 알리려고
④ 실내에서 키우기 쉬운 화초를 소개하려고
⑤ 식물의 건강 상태를 파악하고 관리하는 법을 알리려고

5 대화를 듣고, 두 사람의 관계를 가장 잘 나타낸 것을 고르시오.

① 비서 – 상사
② 수리공 – 손님
③ 세탁소 직원 – 손님
④ 호텔 직원 – 투숙객
⑤ 여행사 직원 – 관광객

6 대화를 듣고, 남자가 할 일로 가장 적절한 것을 고르시오.

① 새 옷 쇼핑하기 ② 스피커 시연해 보기
③ 가전 코너 둘러보기 ④ 판매원 찾기
⑤ 매장 밖에서 기다리기

7 대화를 듣고, 여자가 상품을 받을 수 <u>없는</u> 이유를 고르시오.

① 배송지가 누락되어서 ② 재고가 없어서
③ 주문 오류가 발생해서 ④ 배송이 지연되어서
⑤ 배송 중 상품이 파손되어서

8 eggplant에 관한 다음 내용을 듣고, 일치하지 <u>않는</u> 것을 고르시오.

① 인도가 원산지이며, 유럽으로 전파되었다.
② 15세기 이전에는 주로 장식용으로 사용되었다.
③ 예전에는 독성이 있다고 생각하여 먹지 않았다.
④ 거위 알을 닮은 열매에서 그 이름이 유래했다.
⑤ 지방이 없고 비타민과 미네랄이 풍부하다.

[9-10] 다음을 듣고, 물음에 답하시오.

9 남자가 하는 말의 주제로 가장 적절한 것은?

① the cancellation of an event
② why the school festival is postponed
③ the list of school clubs and activities
④ raising money in support of local bands
⑤ the information on a schedule change

10 언급된 행사가 <u>아닌</u> 것은?

① a band performance ② a breakdancing performance
③ a short play ④ a quiz contest
⑤ a bazaar

DICTATION

녹음을 다시 한 번 듣고, 빈칸에 알맞은 말을 쓰시오.

1

M: Hurry up, Emily. We're going to be ________ ________ ________ ________.

W: I know, but I can't find the invitation. There's a map on it.

M: Didn't you take ________ ________ ________ ________ with your cell phone?

W: (Oh, that's right. I forgot about that!)

2

W: What are you watching, Tom?

M: It's a documentary about the ways ________ ________ ________ ________ around the world.

W: That sounds interesting.

M: It sure is. Did you know that the handshake was started by the ancient Greeks?

W: No. Is that true?

M: Yes. They used it as ________ ________ ________ of friendliness, hospitality, and trust.

W: But I heard that it was started by ancient Egyptian pharaohs.

M: That's another theory. Anyway, most experts agree that the modern handshake started in medieval Europe.

W: Wow, it's been quite a long time.

M: Yes. Kings and knights would extend their hands to each other as a demonstration that they did not possess concealed weapons.

W: Oh! I guess it's a more casual gesture today.

M: Right. Most people don't carry weapons, but the action still ________ ________ ________ ________ of two people.

3

W: Hi. Can I ________ ________ ________?

M: Yes, I'd like a hamburger and French fries, please.

W: That'll be $5. Would you like to add anything to drink with that?

M: Yes. I will have a cola, please.

W: A cola costs $1. But if I add everything together as a set, you can get the cola for just 50¢.

M: Oh, actually I have a coupon for a free drink.

W: All right. Then the cola is free. Is there anything else?

M: Hmm... How much does it cost to ________ ________ ________ ________?

W: Side salads cost $2.

M: Okay, then I'll add one of those to my order.

W: All right. Your order ________ ________ ________ ________.

4

M: Have you ever had one of your plants die and did not know the reason? Many people don't notice that a plant is not healthy until it is ________ ________ ________ ________ it. Basically, plants need water and sunlight to survive. But too much of either can kill them. If your plant's leaves begin ________ ________ and the soil is moist, this is a sign that your plant is overwatered. And you should decrease how often you water it. Some plants like cacti love lots of direct sunlight, but other plants cannot tolerate this. If your plant becomes pale and loses its color, it should probably be moved to an ________ ________ ________ ________.

5

W: Good evening. How can I help you?

M: I'd like to stay an extra couple of days.

W: Sure. How many days do you want to ________ ________ ________ by?

M: Well, the conference ends on the fifth, but I'm going to stay until the seventh.

W: Okay. Please tell me your room number and your name.

M: It's 405, and my name is Christopher Hill.

W: Okay. Let me ________ ________ ________ ________. [*Pause*] That'll be fine.

M: Good. Oh, by the way, the Internet in my room doesn't work, and I need to check my email before tomorrow's meeting.

W: Oh, I'm sorry for the inconvenience. I'll get ________ ________ ________ ________ right away. Is there anything else I can do for you?

M: Oh, yes. I almost forgot. Is my laundry ready?

W: Sure, let me just get it for you.

M: Thanks.

6

M: Chloe, I've been looking for you for a long time. What are you doing over here?

W: I'm ________ ________ ________ something.

M: Wireless earbuds? You already have a pair.

W: No, a Bluetooth speaker.

M: Oh, cool. We could listen to music together at home.

W: Exactly. I'm waiting for a salesperson to come over. I have some questions about the speakers.

M: All right. Well, I'll ________ ________ the sportswear department for a while.

W: Okay, but I'm worried that we won't have ________ ________ ________ ________ a washing machine.

M: Then I'll check out the home appliance section first. Just call me when you finish shopping.

W: All right. I won't be long.

7

[*Telephone rings.*]

M: You've reached True Fashion Clothing. How can I help you?

W: I ordered a T-shirt from your website last week, but I still haven't received it.

M: Oh. Are you sure you wrote down the correct address?

W: Yes. I'm sure. And nothing on the website said the T-shirts were ________ ________ ________ at that time.

M: Do you have the order confirmation number?

W: Yes, it's K59-001.

M: Okay. [*Pause*] Our computer system says that the order ________ ________ ________.

W: Did the delivery company pick it up from the warehouse?

M: Yes, but there may be ________ ________ ________ ________ because the orders are pouring in these days.

W: Hmm... Then when might I receive it?

M: It should arrive by Friday. I'm really sorry for the delay.

8

W: Do you like eggplant? It's a popular vegetable around the world. The plant originally ________ ________ ________ and spread to Europe through Africa. What many people don't know, however, is that before the 15th century the plant was mostly ornamental. People were afraid to eat eggplant because they believed it ________ ________ ________. The name eggplant originated from the fruits of some plants grown in Europe in the 1700s, which were yellow or white and resembled goose eggs. Though it is not rich in any specific vitamin or mineral, eggplant ________ ________ ________ ________. It is also easy to cook and has a thick texture, which makes it great as a main dish or as an addition to dishes like pasta. Why not have eggplant for dinner tonight?

9-10

M: Good morning, everyone. Thank you for coming to the Georgia High School Annual Festival. I know many of you were expecting the festival to begin with a performance by the school band. Unfortunately, the band is currently ________ ________ ________ ________. Therefore, we've pushed their performance back to 2:00 p.m. Instead, the festival will open with an amazing breakdancing performance by the school's dance club. After that, there will be a short play by the drama club that you ________ ________ ________ ________. At 1:00 p.m., you can participate in the quiz contest, which is sure to be a lot of fun. The winner will even receive a gift certificate to Shrimp City. One hour later, the band will be ready to perform. Also, don't forget to visit the booths arranged all over the school. I hope you all enjoy the festival. And remember, all the money that is raised will be used to ________ ________ ________ in our city!

실전 모의고사

1 대화를 듣고, 남자의 마지막 말에 대한 여자의 응답으로 가장 적절한 것을 고르시오.

① Happy New Year to you, too!
② I observe the lunar New Year's holiday.
③ No, I couldn't solve any of the problems.
④ Yes, I'm planning to learn how to play the drums.
⑤ Yes, I meet with my family for dinner on New Year's eve.

2 대화를 듣고, 여자의 마지막 말에 대한 남자의 응답으로 가장 적절한 것을 고르시오.

① It will make the room smell really nice.
② Do you want me to give you a suggestion?
③ I received a guitar as my birthday present.
④ How about preparing for the party together?
⑤ I can't decide where we should throw the party.

3 대화를 듣고, 두 사람이 하는 말의 주제로 가장 적절한 것을 고르시오.

① 새의 암수 구별법
② 새가 짝짓기를 하는 시기
③ 새가 노래하는 이유
④ 새가 먹이를 구하는 방법
⑤ 노래를 많이 하는 새의 종류

4 대화를 듣고, 남자가 할 일로 가장 적절한 것을 고르시오.

① 식당 예약하기
② 선물 고르기
③ 졸업식 참석하기
④ 표 예매하기
⑤ 뮤지컬 함께 보기

5 대화를 듣고, 여자가 지불할 금액을 고르시오.

① $240   ② $270   ③ $300   ④ $324   ⑤ $360

6 대화를 듣고 남자가 여자에게 부탁한 일로 가장 적절한 것을 고르시오.

① 운전하기 　　　　　　　　　② 내비게이션 시스템 켜기
③ 연료 채우기 　　　　　　　　④ 길 묻기
⑤ 물 사다 주기

7 대화를 듣고, 두 사람의 관계를 가장 잘 나타낸 것을 고르시오.

① 승객 – 버스기사 　　　　　　② 수리공 – 고객
③ 운전기사 – 사장 　　　　　　④ 경찰관 – 버스기사
⑤ 경비원 – 직원

8 다음 열차 시간표를 보면서 대화를 듣고, 남자가 구매할 열차표를 고르시오.

Weekend Schedule — Trains to Chicago

	Number	Type	Depart	Arrive	Cost
①	213	Express	3:30 p.m.	4:45 p.m.	$7.50
②	175	Local	4:00 p.m.	5:55 p.m.	$9.50
③	325	Local	5:00 p.m.	6:55 p.m.	$9.50
④	634	Express	5:45 p.m.	7:00 p.m.	$15.00
⑤	478	Local	6:00 p.m.	7:55 p.m.	$8.50

[9-10] 다음을 듣고, 물음에 답하시오.

9 여자가 하는 말의 주제로 가장 적절한 것은?

① misconceptions about home remedies
② reasons home remedies are widely used
③ increased concerns about home remedies
④ the use of home remedies in various countries
⑤ the effect of home remedies on modern medicine

10 언급된 음식이 <u>아닌</u> 것은?

① chicken soup 　　　② ginger tea 　　　③ an egg
④ apple juice 　　　　⑤ vinegar

DICTATION

녹음을 다시 한 번 듣고, 빈칸에 알맞은 말을 쓰시오.

1

M: New Year's Day ______ ______ ______!
W: Yes, I'm very excited to greet the new year.
M: Do you have ______ ______ ______ ______?
W: (Yes, I'm planning to learn how to play the drums.)

2

W: Harry, did you ______ ______ ______ to Claire's birthday party?
M: Yes. I bought an aroma candle for her. What are you going to bring to the party?
W: Actually, ______ ______ ______ ______.
M: (Do you want me to give you a suggestion?)

3

M: It's such a nice day for a walk in the park. Oh, look at the bright colors on that bird.
W: Wow, it's really beautiful. There are so many birds here today, and they're singing so loudly.
M: It's nice to hear birds singing. But do you know ______ ______ ______?
W: Is it to express how they feel?
M: No. Actually, male birds mostly sing ______ ______ ______. It's an important mating ritual.
W: How do the females decide which male to choose?
M: They pick the one that sings the most.
W: Is that because they are impressed by how the male sings?
M: No. Actually, the singing shows that the male has a lot of food and will be a good mate.
W: I don't understand. How is singing ______ ______ ______?
M: Well, if a bird is singing a lot, that means he doesn't have to spend much time searching for food.
W: Ah, I see. That's really interesting.

4

W: Thanks for this fabulous dinner, Dad!
M: ______ ______ ______! And there's another present for you to open as well.
W: Another one? I can't believe it!
M: Here it is! Congratulations on graduating!
W: Thank you! I wonder what's in this envelope. [Pause] Wow, ______ ______ ______ ______!
M: Well, I know you love musicals. And I heard that's the most popular one these days.
W: That's right. I've wanted to see it, but I couldn't because it's too expensive.
M: Great. Why don't you go with your best friend? There are two tickets.
W: I have a better idea. Why don't we see it together? That would be ______ ______ ______ ______.
M: How considerate! Thank you, honey.
W: Don't mention it. You're the best, Dad!

5

M: Hi, can I help you with anything?
W: Yes, I'm a new member here, and I would like to sign up for some exercise classes.
M: That's a great idea. Right now we have yoga classes and aerobics classes.
W: Yoga sounds good. How often ______ ______ ______ ______?
M: There is one class that meets three days a week and another that meets five days a week.
W: How much do they cost?
M: The five-day-a-week class ______ ______ ______ ______, and the three-day-a-week class is $20 cheaper.
W: All right. I think I will go with the three-day-a-week option.
M: Also, if you register for a full three months, you can get a 10 percent discount.
W: That sounds like ______ ______ ______. I will go ahead and do that.

6

W: We've been driving around this area for over an hour.
M: I don't understand. The campsite is definitely around

here somewhere.

W: Hmm. Why don't you ________ ________ ________ ________ system?

M: Unfortunately, it's broken. Oh, I think the campsite is down this road.

W: Are you kidding? We went down that road before. I think we need to ask someone for help.

M: Wait a minute. I'm sure I can find it...

W: ________ ________ ________ ________, we're almost out of gas.

M: Oh! Let's stop off at a gas station and ________ ________ ________ ________ ________ gas.

W: We really should. And we can ask for directions there.

M: Good idea! Could you get a bottle of water while I ask for directions?

W: Sure.

7

M: Excuse me, ma'am. What are you doing?

W: Oh, my! You scared me. I didn't know there was anyone else in the garage.

M: I ________ ________ ________ ________ the cars during the night shift here. So, what were you doing?

W: I ________ ________ ________ ________ ________ ________. I was trying to reach through the window and unlock the door.

M: I see. Is this your car?

W: Well, no. This is a company car. I work for a company called Business Limousine Service.

M: I see. I can help you, but before that, can I see your ID?

W: Sure. Here it is. I belong to the marketing team.

M: [*Pause*] Okay. Just wait here for a moment. I'll ________ ________ ________ ________ from the office.

W: Thank you for your help.

8

W: Good afternoon, sir. How can I help you?

M: I need to catch a train to Chicago tomorrow evening. Can I see a schedule?

W: Certainly, sir. Here's our weekend schedule.

M: Thank you. My appointment is at eight, so I'd like to get there ________ ________ ________ ________.

W: Okay. This express train will get you there on time.

M: Yes, but $15 is a lot of money for a one-way ticket.

W: In that case, why not take a local train? This one ________ ________ ________ ________.

M: Yes, I suppose so. But why is express train number 213 ________ ________ ________ ________?

W: It runs before our peak rush-hour period, so the price is lower.

M: I see. But it gets me there too early. I'll take this local train.

W: Okay, sir. Here's your ticket.

9-10

W: Wherever you go in the world, you will find home remedies for various illnesses. While they might not all be medically proven, these methods have been used for a long time to treat all kinds of problems. For example, chicken soup is ________ ________ ________ ________ in the United States. One study showed that it actually is effective in reducing the symptoms of respiratory illnesses. In Japan, though, a cold might be ________ ________ ________ ________. This stimulates blood circulation, which will help your body recover faster. If you get a headache in China, someone might recommend a traditional egg rub, in which the head, face, and neck are rubbed with a warm, freshly-cooked egg. In Germany, sunburns are sometimes treated with apple cider vinegar. Vinegar is also commonly used in Russia and Ukraine ________ ________ ________ ________. This method involves soaking a cotton bed sheet in a mixture of vinegar and water and using it to wipe down the ill person's body.

실전 모의고사

1 대화를 듣고, 남자의 마지막 말에 대한 여자의 응답으로 가장 적절한 것을 고르시오.

① We'd better wear masks then.
② I hope it stops raining soon.
③ I agree. Let's stay home.
④ We have so much food to eat.
⑤ We don't have to worry about it.

2 대화를 듣고, 남자가 할 일로 가장 적절한 것을 고르시오.

① 선물 사기
② 파티 장소 알아보기
③ 반지 고르기
④ 인터넷 검색하기
⑤ 여동생에게 전화하기

3 대화를 듣고, 남자가 지불할 금액을 고르시오.

① $4.50   ② $5.00   ③ $5.40   ④ $8.00   ⑤ $10

4 다음을 듣고, 여자가 하는 말의 목적으로 가장 적절한 것을 고르시오.

① 신제품을 소개하려고
② 직원들의 노고를 치하하려고
③ 제품의 문제점을 지적하려고
④ 신제품 출시 지연을 알리려고
⑤ 예정된 모임 날짜를 변경하려고

5 대화를 듣고, 남자가 생각보다 낮은 성적을 받은 이유를 고르시오.

① 시험을 잘 못 봐서
② 보고서를 제출하지 않아서
③ 결석을 많이 해서
④ 수업 태도가 나빠서
⑤ 조별 활동에 소극적이어서

6 대화를 듣고, 두 사람의 관계를 가장 잘 나타낸 것을 고르시오.

① 약사 – 손님
② 의사 – 환자
③ 집주인 – 세입자
④ 간호사 – 환자
⑤ 이삿짐 센터 직원 – 고객

7 Rise Up for the Rainforest 행사에 관한 다음 내용을 듣고, 일치하지 <u>않는</u> 것을 고르시오.

① 행사는 지리학 선생님의 생각으로 시작되었다.
② 학생들은 자신이 조사한 내용에 대해 발표를 했다.
③ 학생들은 열대 우림에 관한 다큐멘터리를 제작했다.
④ 학생들은 열대 우림이 입은 피해를 알리는 포스터를 만들었다.
⑤ 학생들은 학교 웹사이트에 포스터를 올렸다.

8 대화를 듣고, 그림에서 대화의 내용과 일치하지 <u>않는</u> 것을 고르시오.

9 대화를 듣고, 여자의 의견으로 가장 적절한 것을 고르시오.

① 주제를 뒷받침하는 내용을 추가하라.
② 작문할 때 결론을 먼저 쓰며 시작하라.
③ 하나의 글에서 제기하는 주장은 일관되어야 한다.
④ 주제와 관련된 자료를 충분히 조사해야 한다.
⑤ 단락의 개수는 글의 완성도에 큰 영향을 미치지 않는다.

10 대화를 듣고, 남자의 마지막 말에 대한 여자의 응답으로 가장 적절한 것을 고르시오.

Woman: ___________________________________

① You should have told me much earlier.
② That's why we should travel to Europe together.
③ Great. I'll ask my friends if we can visit their house.
④ Well, I really don't have any interest in Rome or Paris.
⑤ If we tell them our problem, they'll let us stay with them.

DICTATION

녹음을 다시 한 번 듣고, 빈칸에 알맞은 말을 쓰시오.

1

M: Are you ________ ________ our picnic?
W: I am, but there is ________ ________ ________
   in the air.
M: There is. We shouldn't breathe it in, but I don't want to
   cancel our plans.
W: (We'd better wear masks then.)

2

M: Sally, what are you doing?
W: I'm looking for the perfect gift for my parents' wedding
   anniversary.
M: Why don't you just ________ ________ ________ for
   them like last year?
W: No, that would be too predictable. I want to do
   something special this year.
M: Then what about making rings for them? That's what my
   sister is doing for her boyfriend.
W: Oh, that's a good idea. But I'm not sure I can do that.
M: Don't worry. I heard that some shops offer that kind of
   class. You can ________ ________ ________ ________.
W: I'm not good at finding things online. Do you happen to
   know any good places?
M: Well, I don't, but I'm sure my sister does. I'll ________
   ________ ________ ________.
W: Thanks. My parents will be impressed by my present.
M: I'm sure they will. There's something special about a
   handmade gift.

3

M: Hi. Do you have any batteries? I can't find them.
W: Oh, we keep all our batteries behind the counter. What
   kind do you need?
M: Just standard AAA batteries for a remote control.
W: All right. ________ ________ ________ packs of two.
   Each pack is $2.50.
M: Well, actually my remote control requires three batteries.
W: We also have packs of ten. Those cost $10.00 each.
M: I don't need that many batteries. Just give me ________

________ ________ ________.
W: Certainly, sir. Do you have a membership card? You can
   get a 10% discount if you have one.
M: Yes, I do. But I ________ ________ ________ ________.
W: No problem. Just tell me your phone number.
M: Okay.

4

W: Hello, everyone. I would just like to ________ ________
   ________ regarding the release of our new laptop. As I'm
   sure you all know, this is a truly revolutionary product,
   and I am very proud of all the hard work that has gone
   into developing it. Unfortunately, due to some minor
   technical problems, we need to delay the product's
   release for one month. ________ ________ ________
   ________ is no longer October 10—it is now November
   10. This extra time is necessary in order to make sure
   the product meets the highest standards. I believe
   that these minor issues ________ ________ ________
   ________ and our new laptop will be a huge success.
   Thank you for your time and attention.

5

M: Hi, Professor Smith. Can we talk?
W: Sure, Justin. Have a seat.
M: Thanks. I saw my grade for the biology lecture course.
W: Yes, I ________ ________ ________ this morning.
M: Honestly, I'm pretty disappointed.
W: You thought you would receive a better grade?
M: Yes. I did well on the tests and got a good grade on my
   report too.
W: Yes, but grades ________ ________ ________ more than
   that.
M: Yes, but I had perfect attendance and a good attitude
   too.
W: Actually, I received negative reports from the other
   members of your group. They said you weren't active
   enough. That influenced your grade.
M: I didn't know group work counted toward grades.
W: Students only get a good grade if they ________
   ________ ________ in group work.
M: Okay. I understand.

6

W: Hello, sir. Can I help you?
M: Yes, I think ________ ________ ________ ________. I

have a sharp pain in my spine.

W: What happened? Did you fall down?

M: No, I injured it moving some heavy furniture. I just moved to a new apartment.

W: Well, put this pain relief patch on your back. It will ________ ________ ________. And you should take this medicine, too.

M: How often do I need to take it?

W: You should take one tablet 30 minutes after each meal.

M: Thanks a lot. I hope these work.

W: They will definitely ________ ________ ________ ________ for now. But if the pain persists, you'd better go see a doctor.

M: Okay, thanks.

7

M: Good morning. I'd like to tell you about a recent event my class took part in called "Rise Up for the Rainforest." The event was our geography teacher's idea. She wanted our lessons on endangered ecosystems to really mean something to us. So, she asked each student to research a rare plant or animal species found in the rainforest. Each of us then ________ ________ ________ ________ to the class. After that, we watched several documentaries about the endangered ecosystems of the world's rainforests. We then ________ ________ to inform people of the damage being done to the rainforests. We scanned them and ________ ________ to our school website for everyone to see. It was a really great event, and we learned a lot.

8

[*Telephone rings.*]

W: Hello?

M: Hi, Susan. It's Mark. I'm going to be late to the studio because I was in a minor traffic accident.

W: Oh, no! Are you all right?

M: Yes, I'm fine. I just want to confirm that ________ ________ ________ for the filming.

W: Okay. Well, I just set up the square table in the middle of the room with four chairs around it.

M: Good. Are the checkered curtains in front of the window tied back?

W: Yes. I also ________ ________ ________ ________ on the wall.

M: Great. Did someone hang the chandelier from the ceiling?

W: Yeah. That's all ________ ________ ________. And the round picture is hanging up on the wall to the left.

M: Excellent. I think that's everything. I will probably be at the studio in about an hour.

W: Okay. See you soon.

9

W: Hi Marcus. Did you ________ ________ ________ for English class?

M: Not yet. I have been working on it, but my essay is too short.

W: Did you begin by writing a thesis, like Mr. Alden suggested in class?

M: I did. I think my thesis is very good.

W: How many paragraphs did you write?

M: Three paragraphs: introduction, body, and conclusion.

W: I think you should try writing two more body paragraphs. This will ________ ________ ________ ________ and more effective.

M: Three body paragraphs? How can I do that?

W: You should choose three topics that support your thesis.

M: And should I write one body paragraph for each topic?

W: Yes. Write a paragraph for each topic. Explain how each topic ________ ________ ________ in your thesis.

M: That is a great method. I will try that.

10

M: So, what do you think about my plan for our trip to Europe?

W: I agree that Paris, Rome, and Vienna are good choices.

M: Good! Is there anything you want to change about the plan?

W: Well, I ________ ________ ________ London to the list. I really want to go there.

M: But that would make our trip longer and increase its cost.

W: I know, but I have some friends there that I'd really like to visit. We can stay at their home.

M: Oh, really? That would certainly ________ ________ ________ ________.

W: I think it will cut down our food costs, too.

M: All right. If that's what you really want, I'm ________ ________ ________.

W: (Great. I'll ask my friends if we can visit their house.)

실전 모의고사

1 대화를 듣고, 남자의 마지막 말에 대한 여자의 응답으로 가장 적절한 것을 고르시오.

① Sorry, but our business hours are over.
② Well, I think you'd look better in black.
③ Oh, okay. I'll check if your size is in stock.
④ Yes, I will be right back with a smaller size.
⑤ Yes, you can receive a small discount today.

2 대화를 듣고, 여자의 의견으로 가장 적절한 것을 고르시오.

① 요가는 건강 유지에 도움이 된다.
② 컴퓨터 게임을 과도하게 하면 건강에 해롭다.
③ 중요한 일을 우선적으로 처리해야 한다.
④ 활력을 얻기 위해서 충분한 수면을 취해야 한다.
⑤ 구체적인 목표와 계획을 세워야 한다.

3 대화를 듣고, 남자가 할 일로 가장 적절한 것을 고르시오.

① 물리 수업 듣기
② 할머니 댁 방문하기
③ 스터디 모임 취소하기
④ 이메일 보내기
⑤ 학습 자료 출력하기

4 다음을 듣고, 남자가 하는 말의 목적으로 가장 적절한 것을 고르시오.

① 축제 일정 변경을 안내하려고
② 행사 물품 후원을 부탁하려고
③ 성공적인 축제 개최를 축하하려고
④ 학교 축제의 자원봉사자를 모집하려고
⑤ 노래 자랑 대회 참가 자격을 공지하려고

5 대화를 듣고, 여자가 여행을 갈 수 <u>없는</u> 이유를 고르시오.

① 몸이 아파서
② 비용이 비싸서
③ 일이 바빠서
④ 휴가가 부족해서
⑤ 다른 약속이 있어서

6 대화를 듣고, 두 사람의 관계를 가장 잘 나타낸 것을 고르시오.

① 운전 기사 – 승객
② 교수 – 학생
③ 입학 상담원 – 지원자
④ 도서관 사서 – 학생
⑤ 대학생 – 대학교 투어 참가자

7 Gina Lee에 관한 다음 내용을 듣고, 일치하지 <u>않는</u> 것을 고르시오.

① 〈Two Days〉로 여우주연상을 받았다.

② 지금까지 두 편의 영화를 찍었다.

③ 〈Midnight〉은 다음 주에 개봉될 예정이다.

④ 다양한 TV 프로그램에 출연했다.

⑤ 자신의 노래를 담은 앨범을 녹음 중이다.

8 대화를 듣고, 그림에서 대화의 내용과 일치하지 <u>않는</u> 것을 고르시오.

[9-10] 다음을 듣고, 물음에 답하시오.

9 남자가 하는 말의 주제로 가장 적절한 것은?

① how to make a good first impression

② problems with trusting first impressions

③ why your clothing style should represent you

④ reasons that people care about their appearance

⑤ how to relax before meeting someone for the first time

10 언급된 요소가 <u>아닌</u> 것은?

① appearance　　② clothes　　③ a sense of humor

④ smile　　⑤ a positive attitude

DICTATION

녹음을 다시 한 번 듣고, 빈칸에 알맞은 말을 쓰시오.

1

M: ________ ________ ________ ________ this sweater?

W: Sure. That is our best-selling item these days. We also have it in black.

M: I like this blue one. Do you have a larger size? It ________ ________ ________ ________.

W: (Oh, okay. I'll check if your size is in stock.)

2

W: Hi Tony, I didn't see you in yoga class this morning.

M: Yeah, I couldn't wake up. I ________ ________ ________ your energy.

W: I think we have the same amount of energy.

M: Really? Then why do you always ________ ________ ________ ________?

W: I think we just make different choices.

M: I don't think so. I wanted to go to yoga. I just couldn't.

W: Why couldn't you wake up?

M: I was up late playing computer games online.

W: So, what is more important to you, yoga or computer games?

M: Well, yoga. My health is a priority.

W: Right. So you should have chosen to go to bed early. When you have many things that need to be done, do the most important things first.

M: I understand. I will accomplish more if I ________ ________ what is important.

3

[*Telephone rings.*]

W: Hello?

M: Hi, Marcy. It's Calvin from your physics class. I'm just ________ ________ ________ ________ about our study group tonight.

W: Oh, thanks. I had totally forgotten. What time do we meet?

M: We're meeting at seven o'clock at the public library.

W: Really? Sorry, but I'm not going to ________ ________ ________ ________.

M: Why? What's wrong?

W: I'm at my grandmother's house now. It'll take a little time to get there.

M: Oh, really? But what about the material you prepared for tonight?

W: Don't worry. I saved it on my USB memory stick.

M: What a relief! If you send it to me by email, I will print everything out for you ________ ________.

W: Thanks. I'll do it right now. Please tell the others I'll be late.

M: Okay. See you later.

4

M: As you know, our school's festival is held in June. This year's festival will be held from June 10 through 14. We think it will be ________ ________ ________. A highlight of the festival every year is the outdoor singing contest on the last day. All students are welcome to participate in it, and I'd like to remind you that ________ ________ ________ ________. We need people to help set up the stage and guide visitors. With your help we can ________ ________ ________ ________ for everyone. If you'd like to help out at the festival, visit our volunteer sign-up meeting. It will be held Tuesday, May 5, at 7:00 p.m. in the school library. All volunteers get free T-shirts sponsored by a popular sports brand. Please help us make this year's festival another hit!

5

[*Telephone rings.*]

W: Hello, Ira.

M: Hey, Victoria. I'm calling to ask you something. Have you ever visited Germany?

W: I've been there once. Why?

M: I ________ ________ ________ ________ on the Internet on a trip to Berlin.

W: Really? It sounds wonderful. I want to go back someday.

M: Would you like to join me?

W: Wow! I would love to go to Berlin with you. How much does it cost?

M: It's $1,350 per person, and the hotels and a round-trip flight ________ ________.

W: That's not bad. What are the dates of the trip?

M: It's the second week in September. Can you go?

W: Oh, no. I won't be able to go with you because of work.

M: Can't you ________ ________ ________? I don't want to miss this opportunity.

W: Sorry, Ira. September is an extremely busy time for my firm.

6

M: The next stop on our tour is the Lockwood Library.

W: Wow! It looks really old.

M: It is. In fact, it is the oldest building on campus.

W: Do students still study there?

M: Of course. I was actually there last night ________ ________ for a history paper.

W: Do you have to write a lot of papers at this university?

M: Well, a lot more than you have been doing in high school.

W: I'm worried that I won't be able to ________ ________ ________.

M: Adjusting to college life is not easy. But if you work hard, you'll be able to handle it.

W: Was it difficult for you?

M: Honestly, the first semester was really challenging. But then I ________ ________ ________ the changes. Now I love studying here.

W: That's good.

M: Yes. Now, shall we move on to the next point of interest? Please follow me, everyone.

7

W: Tonight's guest is a talented young actress named Gina Lee. Last year, Ms. Lee ________ ________ ________ ________ ________ for her work in the romantic comedy, *Two Days*. Since that time, she has appeared in two more films. The most recent is a big change from the comedies in which she previously appeared. It's called *Midnight*, and in it she plays a vampire. *Midnight* will be officially ________ ________ ________, but it has already won awards at several film festivals. Besides appearing in movies, Ms. Lee has also appeared on various television sitcoms and is currently ________ ________ ________ of her own songs. Let's give a warm welcome to Gina Lee!

8

W: And here is my room.

M: Wow! It looks really nice! Look at the blanket ________ ________ ________ ________! It doesn't seem like your style.

W: Well, it's not. My mom just bought it for me.

M: I see. Oh, is this the teddy bear I bought you on your last birthday?

W: That's right. It's always on my bed. I really like it.

M: I'm glad to hear that. Oh, you have a lot of books on the bookshelf on your desk.

W: Yeah, I like to read books. I'm also ________ ________ ________.

M: That's why you put this world map on the wall.

W: Yeah, because I'm thinking about traveling around the world someday. I want to play my guitar for people all around the world.

M: That's awesome! So, is this guitar ________ ________ ________ yours? Can you play a song for me now?

W: Sure.

9-10

M: Do you think first impressions are important? Well, according to experts, it takes just ________ ________ ________ for someone to evaluate you. In this short time, a person is able to form a lasting opinion about you based on your appearance and ________ ________ ________ ________. This makes first encounters extremely important. So, when meeting somebody, make sure you ________ ________ ________. Consider how appropriate your clothes and style are for different environments and events. For example, wear fresh, stylish clothes to a job interview or a first date. In addition to your overall style, a friendly smile will help put the other person at ease. When the time comes for conversation, remember to project ________ ________ ________ ________ ________, even if you find yourself struggling with nervousness. Don't forget to ask people questions about themselves to keep the conversation going.

실전 모의고사

1 대화를 듣고, 남자의 마지막 말에 대한 여자의 응답으로 가장 적절한 것을 고르시오.

① About a month ago.
② It's not a serious injury.
③ Of course you can visit her.
④ You need to wait until next Monday.
⑤ She won't come back until you apologize.

2 대화를 듣고, 그림에서 대화의 내용과 일치하지 <u>않는</u> 것을 고르시오.

3 대화를 듣고, 남자가 할 일로 가장 적절한 것을 고르시오.

① 전공 서적 구입하기
② 책 교환하기
③ 화학 수업 듣기
④ 학생 회의 참석하기
⑤ 회의 후 전화하기

4 대화를 듣고, 여자가 지불할 금액을 고르시오.

① $9
② $10
③ $12
④ $23
⑤ $30

5 대화를 듣고, 남자가 부모님을 배웅할 수 <u>없는</u> 이유를 고르시오.

① 발표를 준비해야 해서
② 상사와 회의가 있어서
③ 해외 여행 중이어서
④ 학회에 참석해야 해서
⑤ 항공편이 변경되어서

6 대화를 듣고, 두 사람의 관계를 가장 잘 나타낸 것을 고르시오.

① 호텔 지배인 – 투숙객　　　　　② 가구 판매원 – 고객

③ 부동산 중개인 – 고객　　　　　④ 중고 가구점 주인 – 구매자

⑤ 인테리어 디자이너 – 집주인

7 대화를 듣고, 소풍에 관해 두 사람이 언급하지 <u>않은</u> 것을 고르시오.

① 소풍 장소　　　② 소풍 프로그램　　　③ 참여 인원

④ 안전 대책　　　⑤ 점심 장소

8 다음 표를 보면서 대화를 듣고, 남자가 무선 스피커를 구입할 곳을 고르시오.

Bestprice.com

	Store	Price	Shipping	Warranty
①	E-World	$75.00	Free	Yes
②	Sound and More	$70.00	$7.99	No
③	Stereo Company	$69.00	$9.99	Yes
④	Tech Town	$95.00	Free	Yes
⑤	All about Music	$90.00	Free	Yes

9 기말고사에 관한 다음 내용을 듣고, 일치하지 <u>않는</u> 것을 고르시오.

① 이번 달 22일에 치러질 예정이다.　　② 50개의 객관식 문항으로 구성된다.

③ 시험은 교과서에서 출제된다.　　　　④ 재시험 대상자는 30일에 발표된다.

⑤ 학기 전체 성적의 40%를 차지한다.

10 다음 상황 설명을 듣고, Grace가 여자에게 할 말로 가장 적절한 것을 고르시오.

Grace: _______________________________________

① You've changed a lot since high school.

② You've mistaken me for somebody else.

③ You look exactly like an old friend of mine.

④ I'm disappointed that you don't recognize me.

⑤ Do you remember that woman from high school?

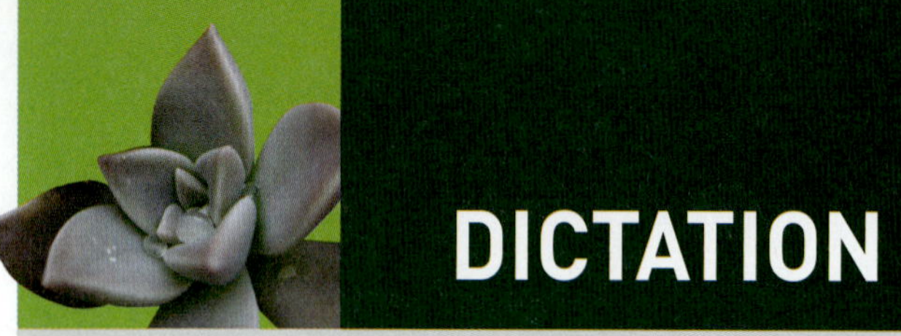

녹음을 다시 한 번 듣고, 빈칸에 알맞은 말을 쓰시오.

1

M: I need to see Professor Jang today. I ________ ________ ________ to ask her.

W: Don't you know that she's in the hospital? She was in a car accident.

M: Really? I ________ ________ ________. When will she come back?

W: (You need to wait until next Monday.)

2

W: I'm so excited. I can't believe the exhibition is this weekend.

M: ________ ________ ________. Now we need to make a final check to see if everything is ready.

W: Okay. Did you put the banner on the wall?

M: You mean the one that says "The 7th School Art Exhibition"? Yes, I already did.

W: Well done. How about the sculpture?

M: I placed it ________ ________ ________ ________ the gallery.

W: Good. But why are these paintings still on the floor?

M: Oh! I forgot to hang them on the wall. I'll do it tomorrow morning.

W: Okay. I'll help you. And I ________ ________ ________ ________ ________ on the table here.

M: Oh, they look nice! Now I'll just put this plant by the door.

W: Perfect. I think we're almost ready for the exhibition.

3

W: Oh, I don't believe it!

M: What's wrong?

W: I just realized that I ________ ________ ________ ________ yesterday.

M: What did you buy?

W: I bought a book called *Chemistry Masters*, but I should have bought *Chemistry Matters*.

M: Yes. I made the same mistake. The titles are so similar.

W: Well, what should I do? This book was expensive.

M: I'm sure the university bookstore will ________ ________

________ it. In fact, I'm going there now. Why don't you come with me?

W: I can't. I have a student council meeting in a few minutes. I think I'd better exchange it this afternoon.

M: Well, I can ________ ________ ________ ________. Do you have the receipt?

W: Yes, here it is. Thank you so much.

M: No problem. Just call me after finishing the meeting.

4

W: Good morning. Do you ________ ________?

M: Yes, we do. How many pages does the book have?

W: Well, it has 112 pages now, but I only need 100 of them bound.

M: Do you want them in color or in black and white?

W: How much for color?

M: 30 cents per page.

W: Really? What about black and white?

M: Just 10 cents per page. If you'd like, you can select certain pages for color and ________ ________ ________ ________ in black and white.

W: That sounds like a good idea. Let me see... I only really need these 10 pages done in color.

M: All right. So, 90 pages in black and white and 10 in color, right?

W: That's right.

M: Okay. It'll ________ ________ ________ 2 p.m.

5

[*Telephone rings.*]

W: Hello?

M: Hey, Tracy. It's John.

W: Hi, John. What's up?

M: Well, I need to ________ ________ ________ ________.

W: All right. What is it?

M: ________ ________ ________ taking Mom and Dad to the airport next week?

W: I thought you were going to take them. Are you still busy trying to finish that big presentation?

M: No, actually I gave the presentation yesterday. It went so well that my boss wants to send me to Hawaii ________ ________ ________ ________.

W: Congratulations! That's fantastic!

M: Yeah, but the conference is next week. I have to fly there the day before Mom and Dad leave.

W: I see. Well, in that case, I will take Mom and Dad to the airport.

M: Thanks, Tracy.

6

M: So, what do you think of this one?

W: Hmm. It's a little small, but __________ __________ __________.

M: The owner told me that she'll be leaving the refrigerator here.

W: Oh, that's good to know.

M: Yes. And you can get rid of the old furniture if you want, and __________ __________ __________ instead.

W: Maybe that's what I'll do. What's the view like?

M: Come and take a look out the window. You can see the mountains over there, and the air around here is just wonderful.

W: Oh, it's lovely! [*Pause*] How about the bedroom?

M: It needs a new coat of paint, but it's nice enough, as you can see.

W: Yes, it is. Well, __________ __________ __________ __________ enough. I'll take it.

M: Good. You won't regret it.

7

W: Hey, did you notify your students of the outing __________ __________ __________ __________?

M: Of course. They're all excited to go to Balboa Park.

W: That's good. My students are also very excited. By the way, is it true that we're going to __________ __________ __________ __________ at the park?

M: Yes. Some of my students already started practicing for it.

W: That's great. I think there will be about 300 students going.

M: That's what I heard. I hope they're all careful. We don't want any accidents.

W: Right. I don't think there will be any problems, though. So, where will we have lunch?

M: We'll have lunch near the lake.

W: Okay. Then, we have to make sure all the students __________ __________ __________ __________.

M: Yes, there is no place to buy lunch near the lake.

W: Well, it will be an exciting day.

M: Yes, I'm sure it will.

8

W: Hi, Elton. What are you doing?

M: I'm looking for the best place to buy new wireless speakers.

W: I see. It looks like Tech Town is __________ __________ __________.

M: True, but I pay attention to shipping charges and whether there's a warranty, __________ __________ just looking at the base price.

W: Oh, you don't want to buy speakers without a warranty.

M: Of course not! And Tech Town ships its products for free.

W: Okay. But look at these. They have __________ __________ __________ __________ __________, too.

M: Do they? Oh, and the prices are much cheaper.

W: Well then, use the site that has a lower price.

M: Okay.

9

W: Good afternoon, class. Your final exam will be on the 22nd of this month in room 213. The exam will have 50 multiple-choice questions. In terms of content, __________ __________ __________ chapters 10 through 20 in the textbook. I will finish grading the exams by the 30th. So you can come to me on that day to __________ __________ __________ __________. Be sure to study hard, because if you fail the exam, you will not have an __________ __________ __________ it. It is worth 40 percent of your grade for the semester, and if you fail the class, you will have to take it again. If you have any questions, you can come and ask me any time before the exam.

10

M: One day while walking down the street, Grace saw a woman she went to high school with. They had been friends at one time, but __________ __________ __________ __________ since graduation. Grace immediately recognized her old classmate and said hello. The woman smiled politely, but she __________ __________ __________ __________ __________. Grace assumed her friend didn't recognize her because she had changed so much over the years. But after Grace told the woman who she was, she realized that she had made a mistake. It turned out that the woman was __________ __________ __________ __________. In this situation, what would Grace most likely say to the woman?

Grace: (You look exactly like an old friend of mine.)

실전 모의고사

1 대화를 듣고, 여자의 마지막 말에 대한 남자의 응답으로 가장 적절한 것을 고르시오.

① She deserves the award.
② You mean the tall girl with glasses?
③ I didn't know how to say this to you.
④ Cheer up! You did your best, after all.
⑤ She always focuses on her teachers' lessons.

2 대화를 듣고, 여자의 의견으로 가장 적절한 것을 고르시오.

① 교사는 학생들을 엄격하게 훈육해야 한다.
② 교사는 항상 창의적인 교수법을 개발해야 한다.
③ 보상이 학생들에게 동기를 부여하는 최고의 방법이다.
④ 학업 성적을 높이기 위해 어느 정도 스트레스가 필요하다.
⑤ 더 높은 기준을 설정함으로써 더 좋은 결과를 만들 수 있다.

3 대화를 듣고, 남자가 할 일로 가장 적절한 것을 고르시오.

① 음식 차리기   ② 좌석 안내하기
③ 지하실 정리하기   ④ 의자 가져오기
⑤ 참석 인원 세어보기

4 대화를 듣고 남자가 지불할 금액을 고르시오.

① $13.50   ② $15.00   ③ $16.50   ④ $21.60   ⑤ $24.00

5 다음을 듣고, 남자가 하는 말의 목적으로 가장 적절한 것을 고르시오.

① 신입 회원을 환영하려고   ② 클럽의 기념일을 축하하려고
③ 회원들의 클럽 활동 참여를 독려하려고   ④ 행사의 세부 일정을 알리려고
⑤ 기념일 행사에 대한 제안을 요청하려고

6 대화를 듣고, 두 사람의 관계를 가장 잘 나타낸 것을 고르시오.

① 사진작가 – 배우 ② 소설가 – 영화감독 ③ 기자 – 소설가
④ 평론가 – 배우 ⑤ 기자 – 영화감독

7 Field Trip에 관한 다음 내용을 듣고, 일치하지 <u>않는</u> 것을 고르시오.

① 학생들은 견학 후에 시험을 본다. ② 견학을 마치고 다시 학교로 돌아온다.
③ 학생들은 점심 도시락을 가져와야 한다. ④ 견학 시 시설물 사진 촬영이 가능하다.
⑤ 견학 신청 시 부모님의 동의서가 필요하다.

8 대화를 듣고, 남자의 마지막 말에 대한 여자의 응답으로 가장 적절한 것을 고르시오.

Woman: _______________________________________

① In that case, you should see a dentist.
② Okay, I'll think about when I want to go.
③ You need to stop thinking and just go.
④ I'm glad that you finally found a better dentist.
⑤ Would you like to reschedule your appointment?

[9-10] 다음을 듣고, 물음에 답하시오.

9 남자가 하는 말의 주제로 가장 적절한 것은?

① why animals have dreams
② how dreams affect animals
③ animals' ability to have dreams
④ the interpretation of animals' dreams
⑤ how animals' dreams differ from humans

10 꿈을 꿀 때 하는 행동으로 언급되지 <u>않은</u> 것은?

① breathing faster ② making noises
③ moving their legs ④ shaking their heads
⑤ moving their eyes

DICTATION

녹음을 다시 한 번 듣고, 빈칸에 알맞은 말을 쓰시오.

1

W: Hi, David. Did you ________ ________ ________ about Jenny?

M: The news that she has the best grades in the class this semester?

W: Right. How could she ________ ________ ________?

M: (She always focuses on her teachers' lessons.)

2

W: Hi Tom, how are your students doing this semester?

M: A lot of my students are getting low test scores.

W: I had the same problem during my first year as a teacher.

M: Really? Did you change your teaching methods?

W: I didn't change how I taught. I changed ________ ________ ________ my students.

M: Did you become stricter?

W: No, I ________ ________ ________ for my students. I let them know that I expected them to do well on my tests.

M: Didn't the students just feel stressed?

W: Not at all. If you let students know that you believe in their abilities, they will ________ ________ ________ as well.

M: So, by setting higher standards, I can give my students more confidence.

W: Right. And they'll do better on their tests.

M: Thanks. I'll try that.

3

M: Wow, our party is a big success!

W: I know. ________ ________ ________ so many people to come.

M: Well, I think we should serve the food now. Let's ask everyone to take a seat.

W: Um, wait. I think there's going to be a problem.

M: What kind of problem?

W: We only have 30 chairs, but there are ________ ________ ________ that.

M: Don't worry. We have lots of folding chairs in the basement.

W: Great. Do you want me to ________ ________ ________?

M: No, I'll do it. How many do we need?

W: Well... I'm not sure.

M: Walk around and see how many people are here, and then let me know.

W: Sure. Hold on a second.

4

W: Thanks for shopping at Food World. Your total is $21.60.

M: $21.60? I'm sorry, but I think you've ________ ________ ________. That seems too high.

W: Let me check the receipt. You purchased three cartons of milk, right?

M: That's right. And they cost $2 each.

W: Yes, that's correct. And you also ________ ________ ________ ________.

M: I have two. I believe they cost $4.50 each.

W: Yes, that's correct. Oh, I see my mistake. I charged you for four pizzas. Sorry about that.

M: That's okay. And did you ________ ________ ________ 10% from the total for my coupon?

W: Let's see. Yes, your discount was applied correctly.

M: Okay. So what's the correct total?

W: Please wait one moment while I check.

M: Sure. No problem.

5

M: Before we end today's meeting, I'd like to remind everyone that our club ________ ________ ________ its ten-year anniversary at the end of next month. I believe this will be a great opportunity for all of us to get together and think back on all the good times we've had together. Nothing has been planned yet or even decided on at this point, so we are ________ ________ ________ ________ you might have. As long as it's within our budget, we'll consider any proposals. You can send them to me by email or simply ________ ________ ________ on a piece of paper. I'll see everybody next week.

6

M: Thank you for the tour of your studio.

W: You're welcome. It was my pleasure.

M: Can we sit somewhere for a while now and talk about ________ ________ ________?

W: Of course. Have a seat right here.

M: Thank you. Your last project was a great success and brought you a lot of fame.

W: Yes, that was a real surprise. The reviews it received were very good.

M: That's true. My newspaper gave it ________ ________ ________. And the public loved it.

W: Yes, they did. I think I make films that the average person can enjoy.

M: So what's next for you?

W: I'm ________ ________ ________ ________ for a couple of weeks. Then I'll get back to work!

7

W: Good afternoon, students. Next Monday, we will be taking a field trip to a local recycling center. There, you will learn all about how the recycling process works. You will be ________ ________ ________ ________ after the field trip, so be sure to bring a notebook and a pen to take notes. We will be leaving at 10 a.m., traveling by bus to the center, and returning to school at approximately 4 p.m. ________ ________ ________ ________, but you are welcome to bring snacks if you wish. You are also permitted to bring cameras and to photograph the facilities. All students attending the field trip are required to return ________ ________ ________ signed by a parent by Thursday.

8

M: Ouch! Ooh, that hurts!

W: What's the matter, Aaron?

M: I have a terrible toothache. It's so painful.

W: Then you should go to the dentist right away. Have you ________ ________ ________ ________?

M: No. I keep putting it off.

W: Why on earth are you doing that? That kind of pain won't ________ ________ ________ ________, you know.

M: I know. But I really dread going to the dentist.

W: Well, so does everyone else, Aaron.

M: I think I hate it more than most people. I'm serious.

W: What's the reason you hate it so much?

M: I don't know. I just ________ ________ ________ ________ ________ whenever I think about it.

W: (You need to stop thinking and just go.)

9-10

M: Dreaming is an activity most people experience during sleep. But people are not the only creatures ________ ________ ________. Some scientists have also observed dreaming behavior in sleeping animals. Personally, I've noticed that when my dog is asleep, he sometimes seems to be having a dream. He moves his legs as if he were walking around or ________ ________ ________. He also makes some strange noises. Sometimes he gets so excited that he wakes himself up! Of course, people do similar things during sleep. Sleeping people's eyes move behind their closed eyelids, and people ________ ________ while sleeping. Animals do the exact same things. They also move their legs and make sounds, just like I've noticed my dog doing. Scientists don't know what animals dream about yet, but I hope they discover a way to find out. It would be really interesting if we could know what animals were dreaming about.

실전 모의고사

1 대화를 듣고, 남자의 마지막 말에 대한 여자의 응답으로 가장 적절한 것을 고르시오.

① Oh, certainly not. Go ahead.
② Sorry, but I changed my mind.
③ There's no problem with this chair.
④ Why do you have to remind me of that?
⑤ Sorry, but you are not allowed to take it with you.

2 대화를 듣고, 여자의 의견으로 가장 적절한 것을 고르시오.

① 인턴사원 근무는 취업의 필수 요건이다.
② 다양한 삶의 경험을 가져야 한다.
③ 자격증을 많이 취득하는 것이 도움이 된다.
④ 유력한 구직자는 흔히 시험 점수가 높다.
⑤ 고용주는 지원자의 봉사 활동 경력을 중요하게 여긴다.

3 대화를 듣고, 두 사람이 매니저를 만나려는 이유를 고르시오.

① 예정된 행사가 취소되어서
② 근무 일정을 변경해야 해서
③ 아르바이트 면접을 봐야 해서
④ 추가 인력 보충이 필요해서
⑤ 매장 이전에 대해 상의를 해야 해서

4 대화를 듣고, 여자가 지불할 금액을 고르시오.

① $25　　② $30　　③ $35　　④ $40　　⑤ $45

5 대화를 듣고, 남자가 여자에게 부탁한 일로 가장 적절한 것을 고르시오.

① 남자의 어머니를 만나 뵙기
② 꽃 주문하기
③ 꽃가게에 같이 가기
④ 출장 일정 변경하기
⑤ 생신 파티 준비하기

6 대화를 듣고, 두 사람의 관계를 가장 잘 나타낸 것을 고르시오.

① 기자 – 작가
② 배우 – 작가
③ 배우 – 영화감독
④ 영화감독 – 투자자
⑤ 기자 – 투자자

7 대화를 듣고, 그림에서 대화의 내용과 일치하지 <u>않는</u> 것을 고르시오.

8 다음 상황 설명을 듣고, Fred가 Alice에게 할 말로 가장 적절한 것을 고르시오.

Fred: _______________________________________

① Get up, Alice. Let's keep walking.

② Watch out for the glass. It's sharp!

③ Stop joking around, Alice. It isn't funny.

④ You shouldn't have removed your shoes.

⑤ Wait here, Alice. I'm going to go get help.

[9-10] 다음을 듣고, 물음에 답하시오.

9 여자가 하는 말의 주제로 가장 적절한 것은?

① the secret to happiness

② how to reduce stress in daily life

③ alternative ways to express emotions

④ maintaining good relationships with others

⑤ what causes us to be annoyed and disturbed

10 언급된 방법이 <u>아닌</u> 것은?

① learn to say "no"　　② avoid stressful situations

③ express your feelings　　④ look on the bright side

⑤ share your troubles with others

DICTATION

녹음을 다시 한 번 듣고, 빈칸에 알맞은 말을 쓰시오.

1

M: Excuse me. _____________ _____________ _____________ _________?
W: Not these two.
M: Then do you _________ _________ I take one?
W: (Oh, certainly not. Go ahead.)

2

W: Hi Alex, what are you working on?
M: This is a practice test for the TOEIC exam. I want to _________ _________ _________ _________.
W: Are you already thinking about _________ _________ _________?
M: Yes. I will graduate from college next year. It is hard to find a good job, so I want to have good qualifications.
W: Having high test scores is important, but I found that there are more important things employers consider.
M: Do you mean doing things like volunteering?
W: Volunteer work helps. But the best applicants have a variety of life experiences.
M: I see. Maybe I should apply for an internship.
W: That is a great idea. But don't just focus on internships. Any real life experience will give you _________ _________ _________ _________.
M: That is great advice. Thank you.

3

W: Oh, next week's schedule is terrible.
M: _________ _________ _________ _________?
W: Well, next Monday is the high school football team's championship game.
M: Right. We're supposed to get some extra workers for that, aren't we?
W: No, there aren't _________ _________ _________ _________. That's the problem.
M: No way! All the students will come here for ice cream afterward. How can two of us handle all of them?
W: I think we should talk to our manager.

M: I agree. He said he was _________ _________ _________ _________ some part-time people.
W: He must have forgotten about it. I heard he has been very busy recently because he is moving to a new house.
M: I'll talk to him right now.

4

W: Hi. I want to _________ _________ _________ _________. How much will it cost?
M: It will be five dollars for the battery. Hmm... I think you'd better change this watchband, too.
W: Right. It's so old. So how much are these ones here?
M: The gold ones are $30 and the silver ones are $20.
W: I'll _________ _________ _________ _________, please.
M: All right. This will just take a few minutes. [*Pause*] Hmm... That's strange.
W: What's wrong?
M: I changed the battery, but your watch still doesn't work. I think it's broken.
W: Oh, dear. So, you mean I have to _________ _________ _________?
M: Yes. The repair charge would be $10.
W: Okay. Please repair it for me. When can I pick it up?
M: It'll be ready in a day. You can pay then.
W: Thanks.

5

W: Are you okay? You look worried.
M: I am. Next Thursday is my mother's birthday.
W: So? What's the problem?
M: I'll be in Singapore on _________ _________ _________ from next Monday to Friday.
W: I see. Well, you could ask a flower shop to deliver a bunch of flowers to your mother on her birthday.
M: Yes, that is a great idea. I can _________ _________ _________ before I leave. Do you know any good flower shops?
W: Sure. I pass a lovely flower shop every day on my way home from work.
M: Good. You probably know more about flowers than I do. Can you _________ _________ _________?
W: Of course I can!
M: Thanks. That's really nice of you.

6

W: Thanks for coming, Mr. Song. So, you're interested in ________ ________ ________?

M: That's right. I think it would be a creative use of my money.

W: Yes. And ________ ________, too.

M: Please tell me about the film you're currently working on.

W: Well, it's a love story set in the future. Here's a copy of the script.

M: I'll look it over. Do you really think this kind of film will be popular?

W: Yes. You know, romantic movies are the big trend in theaters these days.

M: I know. Have you decided on any actors to ________ ________ ________?

W: Not yet. But I've been talking to some popular celebrities.

M: Well, I'm very interested. Let's talk again after I read this.

7

M: Thank you for bringing me to this new coffee shop. It is lovely.

W: I agree. I wasn't expecting such a modern interior.

M: I like the big rectangular table over there.

W: You mean the one beneath the chandelier hanging from the ceiling?

M: Yes. ________ ________ ________ like that would be nice for dinner parties.

W: I'm impressed by the fast service, too.

M: Well, it helps that there are ________ ________ ________ ________.

W: Right. Anyway, we should get going.

M: Pass me your coffee cup. Customers have to put dirty dishes on the shelf over there, where the trays are stacked up.

W: Okay. Thanks. I'm going to find a restroom.

M: No problem. I'll meet you ________ ________ ________ ________ with the cakes and pies to the right of the counters.

W: All right. I'll be right back.

8

M: Fred and his younger sister, Alice, were at the beach. They ________ ________ ________ along the shore when Alice screamed. At first, Fred thought that she was joking around, but he soon realized that something was seriously wrong. Alice sat on the ground and held her right foot with both of her hands. Fred saw that Alice's foot was bleeding, and he noticed a piece of broken glass ________ ________ ________ ________ ________. Alice was crying, and Fred could tell that she was ________ ________ ________ ________ ________. Fred looked around and saw a lifeguard stand in the distance. In this situation, what would Fred most likely say to Alice?

Fred: (Wait here, Alice. I'm going to go get help.)

9-10

W: Good evening, ladies and gentlemen. Today I am going to talk to you about something that we all face in our daily lives. No matter who you are, there are things that happen that ________ ________ ________ ________. To minimize these stressful situations, it's important to know your limits and learn how to politely say "no." You won't let people down if you are honest with them about what you can handle. Also, try to avoid situations that stress you out. For example, if you always end up in a traffic jam, look for an alternative route. In addition, it's very important to ________ ________ ________. If you keep your emotions hidden inside, the issues that are troubling you will never get resolved. Finally, do your best to ________ ________ ________ ________, and try to view challenging situations as opportunities for personal development. These simple things can help you live a happier, more peaceful life.

실전 모의고사

1 대화를 듣고, 여자의 마지막 말에 대한 남자의 응답으로 가장 적절한 것을 고르시오.

① You know I have a fear of heights.
② I didn't know you can't ride a bike.
③ Come on up! Check out the nice view.
④ Then let's go on one of the smaller rides.
⑤ It was the most horrible thing I've ever seen.

2 다음을 듣고, 여자가 하는 말의 목적으로 가장 적절한 것을 고르시오.

① 박물관 웹사이트의 개설을 알리려고
② 외국인에게 한국의 자연을 알리려고
③ 사찰 체험 프로그램을 홍보하려고
④ 한국 불교의 특징을 설명하려고
⑤ 절에서 지켜야 하는 예절을 소개하려고

3 대화를 듣고, 두 사람이 하는 말의 주제로 가장 적절한 것을 고르시오.

① 칭찬의 중요성
② 토론 주제 선정 시 유의점
③ 어색한 분위기를 깨는 방법
④ 학회에서의 적절한 매너
⑤ 회사 내 소통이 필요한 이유

4 대화를 듣고, 남자가 할 일로 가장 적절한 것을 고르시오.

① 학교에 데려다주기
② 선생님께 전화하기
③ 찬장 정리하기
④ 병원에 데려다주기
⑤ 약 가져다주기

5 대화를 듣고, 현수막을 다시 제작하는 이유를 고르시오.

① 인쇄 회사가 실수를 저질러서
② 축제가 미루어져서
③ Jason이 회의에 참석하지 않아서
④ Jason이 주문을 잘못해서
⑤ 인쇄 회사가 제작 비용을 더 요구해서

6 대화를 듣고, 여자가 남자에게 부탁한 일로 가장 적절한 것을 고르시오.

① 어머니 마중 나가기
② 비행기 예약하기
③ 회의에 참석하기
④ 문자 메시지 보내기
⑤ 도넛 사기

7 대화를 듣고, 두 사람의 관계를 가장 잘 나타낸 것을 고르시오.

① 사진작가 – 모델
② 광고주 – 배우
③ 영화감독 – 배우
④ 디자이너 – 모델
⑤ 운동선수 – 코치

8 다음 표를 보면서 대화를 듣고, 남자가 지원할 인턴직을 고르시오.

	Internship	Paid	Industry	Type of Work	Location
①	A	Yes	Advertising	Doing research	Uptown
②	B	Yes	Tourism	Doing research	Uptown
③	C	Yes	Advertising	Doing research	Downtown
④	D	No	Tourism	Answering phones	Downtown
⑤	E	Yes	Advertising	Answering phones	Uptown

9 No Uniform Day에 관한 다음 내용을 듣고, 일치하지 <u>않는</u> 것을 고르시오.

① 학생들은 사복을 입을 수 있다.
② 기금 마련을 위한 특별 공연이 있다.
③ 참가자들은 문구류를 기부해야 한다.
④ 장기자랑 및 책 교환 행사가 진행된다.
⑤ 선생님들도 참여가 가능하다.

10 다음 상황 설명을 듣고, Andrea가 남편에게 할 말로 가장 적절한 것을 고르시오.

Andrea: ____

① I think we should replace our old car.
② There is no excuse for illegal parking.
③ Since I'm the better driver, I'll drive us to work.
④ Remember to fasten your seat belt when you drive.
⑤ You shouldn't exceed the speed limit on the freeway.

DICTATION

녹음을 다시 한 번 듣고, 빈칸에 알맞은 말을 쓰시오.

1

W: Look at the height of that roller coaster!
M: I know, but it's not ________ ________ ________ it looks.
W: Even so, I don't really ________ ________ ________ it.
M: (Then let's go on one of the smaller rides.)

2

W: Having worked in the Korean tourism industry for over seven years, I have found one experience to be at the top of most foreign visitors' lists. That experience is the temple stay program, a cultural experience designed to help people ________ ________ ________ ________ of Korean Buddhism. Taking part in a temple stay gives you the opportunity to ________ ________ and chanting, as well as the chance to take part in a communal Buddhist ________ ________. Other activities you may choose include making lotus lanterns, learning about tea ceremonies, and playing folk games. To ________ ________ ________ in the program, please visit the official website.

3

W: Welcome back, Jim. How was the conference?
M: It was okay, but I had ________ ________.
W: That's normal. I used to have that problem too.
M: Oh? What do you do to break the ice now?
W: I usually talk about the weather or compliment the other person's clothes.
M: Really? But don't you think those topics could be ________ ________ ________?
W: Not really. Many people like to start conversations this way.
M: I see. What should I talk about after that part of the conversation ends?
W: Well, there will always be food at a conference. Comment on it, and give the person ________ ________ ________.
M: That's a good idea. It sounds like you're a communication expert.

W: Thanks. Just remember to pick topics that both of you are familiar with.

4

M: Good morning, honey. Come and have your breakfast.
W: I don't feel like eating, Dad. I don't feel good.
M: What's wrong, Fiona? You look pale.
W: I think I've caught a cold. I have a fever.
M: Oh, dear. ________ ________ ________ ________ today. If you want, I'll call your teacher and tell her you're too sick to attend school.
W: No, you don't have to. It's not that serious. Do we have any medicine for a cold?
M: There's some in the kitchen cupboard. Sit down and ________ ________ ________ ________.
W: Oh, thanks, Dad.
M: But are you sure you're okay with just the medicine? Why don't you go to the doctor's office before school? I'll drive you there.
W: No, don't worry, Dad. I'll be okay if I ________ ________ ________.
M: Okay, honey. I'll be right back.

5

W: Hello, Jason. How are ________ ________ ________ ________?
M: Not so good. The banners we ordered have the wrong dates on them.
W: That's terrible. The printing company will have to reprint them. Can they have new banners printed ________ ________ for the festival?
M: I just called them. They can print them in time, but there is another problem.
W: What is that?
M: They said that if we want them to reprint the banners, we will have to pay again.
W: Why should we pay for their mistake?
M: Actually… I gave them the wrong information when I ________ ________ ________.
W: What? I told you the dates in last week's meeting.
M: I know. I must have misremembered.
W: Weren't you taking notes?
M: I didn't think I needed to.
W: That is unacceptable, Jason.

6

[*Cell phone rings.*]
M: Hello?
W: Hi, honey. It's me. I called to ask you a favor.
M: Oh, what is it?
W: As you know, I'm ________ ________ ________ ________ your mom from the airport after work.
M: Yes. Are you worried you can't make it?
W: Don't worry. I can. But I forgot the terminal number and flight number.
M: Well, you can ________ ________ ________.
W: I know, but I'm about to go into a meeting, so I don't have time.
M: Do you want me to ________ ________ ________ ________ ________ containing that information?
W: Yes, please. That's what I was going to ask you to do.
M: No problem. Oh, and try to arrive on time.
W: Okay. And I'll pick up some doughnuts on the way. I know she doesn't like airplane food.

7

M: That looks like a perfect spot. If you stand right there, then I can get the mountain in the background.
W: Wait a second! I'll go there. [*Pause*] Here?
M: That looks great. Let's get started with a picture ________ ________ ________.
W: Okay. How about this pose?
M: It looks good. I can see the jacket really well. Now can you turn to the side a little bit?
W: Like this?
M: That's perfect. I'll ________ ________ ________ ________ from this angle.
W: Should we get some with me tossing snow up in the air?
M: Sure, that's a good idea. And ________ ________ ________ ________ ________ so it looks like you're really having fun.
W: Can you still see the jacket?
M: Yeah. The company's going to be very happy with these.
W: I bet the whole winter catalogue is going to look great!

8

W: Hey, Sam. Are you ________ ________ ________ ________ this summer?
M: Yeah. Actually, I am looking at my options right now.
W: Oh, which one do you think you will apply for?

M: I'm not sure yet. I ________ ________ ________ one that is paid.
W: Of course. But it's more important to have an internship that's related to your major.
M: I guess you're right. I should probably go for an advertising internship then.
W: And the type of work you do is important as well.
M: Well, doing research would be ________ ________ ________ ________ ________ answering phones.
W: And what about the location?
M: It would take a long time to commute uptown.
W: Then you'd better stay downtown. It would be much more convenient.
M: Right. It looks like I know which internship to apply for!

9

W: Good morning, students and staff. I'd like to talk to you about our upcoming "No Uniform Day." It is for both fun and for fundraising. On that day, none of you have to wear your school uniforms. Instead, you can ________ ________ ________ ________ to school. In return, you must donate some nice new stationery items to our school charity, the Green Street Orphanage. We will also have ________ ________ ________ in the afternoon, such as a talent contest and book swap. Teachers, remember you can also take part! ________ ________ ________ formal clothes, please wear a casual outfits. I hope all of you will take an active part in this event.

10

M: Andrea and Danny have been married for three years, and both of them work at the same marketing firm. Since they live and work together, they often ________ ________ ________ each other to work. On several recent occasions, Andrea has noticed that her husband forgets to ________ ________ ________ ________ while driving. She, on the other hand, always makes sure that she fastens her seat belt. She believes that doing so is very important, as it can keep a person safe in case of an accident. She is worried about what would happen if her husband ________ ________ ________ a car crash. In this situation, what would Andrea most likely say to her husband?
Andrea: (Remember to fasten your seat belt when you drive.)

실전 모의고사

1 대화를 듣고, 여자의 마지막 말에 대한 남자의 응답으로 가장 적절한 것을 고르시오.

① Either is fine by me.
② My watch is half an hour slow.
③ I prefer watching movies alone.
④ Why don't we watch it with Sarah?
⑤ I'm sorry, I cannot go to the movies.

2 대화를 듣고, 남자의 마지막 말에 대한 여자의 응답으로 가장 적절한 것을 고르시오.

① I just want to pay in cash.
② I need to receive a full refund.
③ I purchased it with my credit card.
④ I don't think the color looks good on me.
⑤ Because I want to give this skirt to my sister.

3 대화를 듣고, 여자의 의견으로 가장 적절한 것을 고르시오.

① 개를 보살피는 데에 비용이 많이 든다.
② 개를 키우는 것은 많은 책임을 요구한다.
③ 강아지 종류별 특징과 성격을 알아봐야 한다.
④ 입양에 앞서 남자의 생활 패턴을 고려해야 한다.
⑤ 애완동물을 키우기 위해 주인은 소정의 교육을 받아야 한다.

4 대화를 듣고, 남자가 할 일로 가장 적절한 것을 고르시오.

① 노트북 컴퓨터 빌려주기　　　　② 영화 함께 보기
③ TV 소리 줄이기　　　　④ 컴퓨터 수리하기
⑤ 컴퓨터 프로그램 설치하기

5 다음을 듣고, 남자가 하는 말의 목적으로 가장 적절한 것을 고르시오.

① 유전공학의 이점을 알리려고　　　　② 유전자 복제 과정을 설명하려고
③ 인간 복제의 위험성을 경고하려고　　　　④ 새로운 유전공학 기술을 발표하려고
⑤ 유전자 복제에 대한 관심을 촉구하려고

6 대화를 듣고, 두 사람의 관계를 가장 잘 나타낸 것을 고르시오.

① 손님 – 집주인　　　　　　　　② 기자 – 박물관 직원

③ 관광객 – 관광 안내원　　　　　④ 세입자 – 건물 관리인

⑤ 손님 – 부동산 중개인

7 대화를 듣고, 여자가 지불할 금액을 고르시오.

① $27　　　② $45　　　③ $47　　　④ $50　　　⑤ $55

8 다음 상황 설명을 듣고, Steve의 어머니가 Steve에게 할 말로 가장 적절한 것을 고르시오.

Steve's mother: _______________________________

① It's never too early to start healthy habits.

② I think you should just take it easy for now.

③ I'm glad you're taking good care of yourself.

④ You should not spend all your money on food.

⑤ Too much exercise can harm your health.

[9-10] 다음을 듣고, 물음에 답하시오.

9 남자가 하는 말의 주제로 가장 적절한 것은?

① a history of women's running

② the schedule change of an event

③ information about the marathon race

④ reasons why running is good for our health

⑤ the rules that marathon runners should follow

10 행사에 관해 언급된 사항이 <u>아닌</u> 것은?

① location and date

② how to register

③ registration fee

④ prize money

⑤ how to cancel registration

DICTATION

녹음을 다시 한 번 듣고, 빈칸에 알맞은 말을 쓰시오.

1

W: Sam, would you like to _________ _________ _________ _________ on Sunday?

M: Sure. What movies are showing now?

W: There is an action movie and a romantic comedy. Which would you _________ _________ _________?

M: (Either is fine by me.)

2

M: Did you _________ _________ _________ for this skirt?

W: Yes, here you are.

M: Thanks. Could you tell me why you want to _________ _________ _________?

W: (I don't think the color looks good on me.)

3

M: Hi Marcy. I am thinking about _________ _________ _________.

W: Have you ever owned a dog before?

M: No. How hard could it be? Dogs just need food, water, and exercise, right?

W: I'm afraid not. Being a dog owner is a lot of work.

M: What kind of work?

W: Dogs need a lot of care: trimming their nails, weekly baths, and daily brushing of their fur and teeth.

M: Okay. That's a lot of grooming. But it doesn't sound so bad.

W: Also, dogs need attention. You can't be _________ _________ _________ for too long.

M: So, I would have to come home right after work every evening?

W: Yes. You will always need to think about _________ _________ _________ first.

M: Well, maybe I should think more about this.

W: That's a good idea.

4

W: Mark, what are you watching?

M: It's a new movie directed by Christopher Jones. I just downloaded it.

W: Wow. I've been waiting for it.

M: Why don't you watch it with me?

W: I'd love to, but the reason I came here is to _________ _________ _________ _________.

M: Oh, is it too loud? I'll turn it down.

W: No, that's not it. Actually, my computer's not working, and I _________ _________ _________ _________.

M: Do you need some help with it?

W: Yes. _________ _________ _________.

M: Okay, I'll help you. You know, I know a lot about computers.

W: You're the best, Mark.

5

M: As scientists continue to discover more and more about genetics and DNA, the process of cloning animals is becoming more common. Many people believe that it's only a matter of time before we _________ _________ _________ _________ as well. But many other people, including myself, feel this would be a disastrous step _________ _________ _________ _________. While I acknowledge that there may be some scientific benefits to cloning humans, there are too many risks to even consider it. It seems as though _________ _________ _________ far outweigh the benefits.

6

M: Excuse me. What is this building here?

W: Ah, that's _________ _________ _________. It's estimated to be 3,000 years old.

M: Wow, that's old. What are those big statues near the entrance?

W: Those are golden lions. They are supposed to guard the temple.

M: How interesting! Is it possible to go inside?

W: Yes, but there is a small fee. The money is used to maintain the temple.

M: I see. Will you come with us?

W: Of course. I'll _________ _________ _________ _________

________ inside the temple. And there are a few things you need to be aware of.

M: Oh, are there some rules?

W: Yes. You're not allowed to take photographs inside the temple. And you have to ________ ________ ________.

M: Okay.

7

M: Good morning. Welcome to the Modern Art Museum. How can I help you?

W: Hello. ________ ________ ________ ________ ________?

M: They are $10 for adults and $5 for children.

W: Good. I will buy two adult tickets and two child tickets. I also have a coupon. May I use this?

M: Let me see… Yes, you can get a 10 percent discount on all tickets.

W: That's great.

M: Today we are also ________ ________ ________ ________ that your family can take part in. You can make art using clay.

W: That sounds fun. Is it included in the admission fee?

M: No. Passes for the workshop are $5 per person, and the ________ ________ ________.

W: Okay. I'll buy four passes.

M: So two child tickets, two adult tickets, and four passes for the workshop?

W: Right. Here is my card and the coupon.

8

W: Steve is a middle school student. Recently, his mother began to ________ ________ ________ ________. Steve only enjoys watching sports and playing computer games at home. He doesn't like going outside or exercising at all. In fact, lately he has been spending many sunny days just sitting on the sofa, watching TV. He also eats a lot of ________ ________ between meals, like potato chips and candy bars. When his mother mentioned her concerns, Steve pointed out that he isn't overweight and has had no health problems. But his mother is worried that it is just a matter of time before ________ ________ ________. In this situation, what would Steve's mother most likely say to Steve?

Steve's mother: (It's never too early to start healthy habits.)

9-10

M: The annual Peace Square Run, a special event for ________ ________, is open to all women in their twenties. The race is seven kilometers long and attracts runners from all over the world. It was started in 2005 and has been held every year since then. Last year more than 5,000 contestants participated. The event will take place on May 26 at 6:30 p.m., beginning at Peace Square, located near World Cup Stadium. All runners ________ ________ ________ ________ the race should visit the event's website to register. There is a $20 fee for registration, and all registrations must be completed before April 16. If you want to ________ ________ ________, you must do so before April 30 at 6 p.m. Registrations can be cancelled through the website or ________ ________ ________ ________ ________ by phone by dialing 234-8282. Allow three to five days after cancellation for your refund to be processed.

*Check What You've
Learned So Far*

CHAPTER 02

FINAL TEST

FINAL TEST

1 대화를 듣고, 여자의 마지막 말에 대한 남자의 응답으로 가장 적절한 것을 고르시오.

① Don't blame me if it's broken.
② Because a new one is too expensive.
③ I'm not sure. We need to call an expert.
④ You must have entered the wrong password.
⑤ That's why people prefer online shopping these days.

2 대화를 듣고, 남자의 마지막 말에 대한 여자의 응답으로 가장 적절한 것을 고르시오.

① It's too late to change them.
② I think Sandy is in charge of that.
③ I can't attend the meeting, though.
④ Without you, I couldn't have done this project.
⑤ John and Andy want to design new brochures.

3 다음을 듣고, 남자가 하는 말의 목적으로 가장 적절한 것을 고르시오.

① 동물원을 홍보하려고
② 관람할 동물들을 소개하려고
③ 동물원 관람 시간 변경을 알리려고
④ 동물원 내 식사 공간을 안내하려고
⑤ 동물원에서 지켜야 할 주의 사항을 당부하려고

4 대화를 듣고, 두 사람이 하는 말의 주제로 가장 적절한 것을 고르시오.

① 만리장성의 거대한 규모
② 고비 사막에 물을 대는 프로젝트
③ 고비 사막이 확장되고 있는 이유
④ 사막화를 막기 위한 중국의 프로젝트
⑤ 중국의 사막화가 주변국에 미치는 영향

5 대화를 듣고, 두 사람의 관계를 가장 잘 나타낸 것을 고르시오.

① 교수 – 학생
② 기자 – 교수
③ 면접관 – 지원자
④ 직장 상사 – 직원
⑤ 심리 상담사 – 학생

6 대화를 듣고, 여자가 남자에게 부탁한 일로 가장 적절한 것을 고르시오.

① 공부하는 것을 도와주기
② 커피 만들어 주기
③ 제과점에 데려다 주기
④ 간식 만들어주기
⑤ 도넛 사다 주기

7 대화를 듣고, 그림에서 대화의 내용과 일치하지 <u>않는</u> 것을 고르시오.

8 대화를 듣고, 남자가 야구를 보러 가지 <u>않는</u> 이유를 고르시오.

① 친구의 이사를 도와야 해서
② 몸이 좋지 않아서
③ 야구를 싫어해서
④ 날씨가 좋지 않아서
⑤ 푯값이 비싸서

9 대화를 듣고, 여자가 지불할 금액을 고르시오.

① $70   ② $75   ③ $80   ④ $81   ⑤ $90

10 대화를 듣고, 송년회에 관해 두 사람이 언급하지 <u>않은</u> 것을 고르시오.

① 음식   ② 공연   ③ 대표 연설
④ 장소   ⑤ 복장 규정

11 박물관 안내에 관한 다음 내용을 듣고, 일치하지 <u>않는</u> 것을 고르시오.

① 인류 문화사 관련 전시품들이 있다.
② 방문객들을 위한 무료 안내 책자가 제공된다.
③ 3개 국어로 음성 안내 투어가 제공된다.
④ 방문객들을 위한 음료가 1층에서 제공된다.
⑤ 박물관 내부에 기념품 가게가 있다.

12 다음 표를 보면서 대화를 듣고, 여자가 구독할 잡지를 고르시오.

	Magazine	Genre	Free Gift	Price (1 Year)
①	*Trendsetter*	Fashion	a travel cup	$100
②	*The Weekly Recipe*	Cooking	a teapot	$100
③	*Your Design*	Fashion	a comb	$120
④	*Food Today*	Cooking	a package of flour	$120
⑤	*Money Issues*	Economics	two smartphone cases	$150

13 대화를 듣고, 여자의 마지막 말에 대한 남자의 응답으로 가장 적절한 것을 고르시오.

Man: ___________________________________

① I'll call you when the key is ready.
② That's fine. I know you need to hurry.
③ No. I made a mistake, so this one is free.
④ Sure. It's a good idea to have a spare key.
⑤ No. I'm afraid we don't have a machine.

14

대화를 듣고, 남자의 마지막 말에 대한 여자의 응답으로 가장 적절한 것을 고르시오.

Woman: _______________________________________

① I started drinking coffee during my first year in university.

② You should ask your doctor if you can take the test again.

③ If you tell the truth, I'm sure that everyone will understand.

④ Just try to reduce the amount of coffee you drink each week.

⑤ There's a great coffee shop around the corner from my house.

15

다음 상황 설명을 듣고, Marie가 남편에게 할 말로 가장 적절한 것을 고르시오.

Marie: _______________________________________

① I'm sorry, but can you help me out?

② Just tell your boss you can't stay late.

③ I think everything is ready for the party.

④ Don't worry. I can take care of it myself.

⑤ I'm so busy that I can't come to the party.

[16-17] 다음을 듣고, 물음에 답하시오.

16

여자가 하는 말의 주제로 가장 적절한 것은?

① ways to safely lose weight

② ways to lower one's blood pressure

③ the benefits of blood pressure medication

④ the dangers associated with high blood pressure

⑤ how a doctor can help you live a healthier lifestyle

17

언급된 방법이 <u>아닌</u> 것은?

① losing weight　　② regular exercise

③ a healthy diet　　④ avoiding sodium

⑤ nutritional supplements

FINAL TEST

1 대화를 듣고, 남자의 마지막 말에 대한 여자의 응답으로 가장 적절한 것을 고르시오.

① Yes, I made a good decision.
② Right. You will do well on the exam.
③ Well, it wouldn't hurt you to think positively.
④ I should have thought about the midterm.
⑤ I think you need to make more of an effort.

2 대화를 듣고, 여자의 마지막 말에 대한 남자의 응답으로 가장 적절한 것을 고르시오.

① In that case, let's call and make a reservation.
② Don't worry. You will really like the sushi here.
③ Actually, I was thinking of a different restaurant.
④ I think some people are almost finished. Let's wait.
⑤ That's strange. I guess it's not as popular as I thought.

3 다음을 듣고, 남자가 하는 말의 목적으로 가장 적절한 것을 고르시오.

① 낙서 방지법을 설명하려고
② 정부에 법률 변경을 요청하려고
③ 경찰관들의 근무태만을 고발하려고
④ 새로운 환경 미화 정책을 소개하려고
⑤ 낙서행위의 철저한 단속을 촉구하려고

4 대화를 듣고, 남자의 의견으로 가장 적절한 것을 고르시오.

① 사업주는 자신의 분야에서 전문가여야 한다.
② 사업 규모를 늘리려면 과감한 투자가 필요하다.
③ 철저한 준비 없이 사업을 시작하면 낭패를 보기 쉽다.
④ 창업을 준비할 때 자신만의 차별화 전략을 세우는 것이 중요하다.
⑤ 다른 사람들의 실패에서 배울 점을 찾는 것은 성공을 위한 좋은 방법이다.

5 대화를 듣고, 두 사람의 관계를 가장 잘 나타낸 것을 고르시오.

① 작가 – 감독　　　　　　　② 소설가 – 독자

③ 서점 직원 – 고객　　　　　④ 동호회 회장 – 회원

⑤ 도서관 사서 – 출판업자

6 대화를 듣고, 그림에서 대화의 내용과 일치하지 <u>않는</u> 것을 고르시오.

7 대화를 듣고, 여자가 할 일로 가장 적절한 것을 고르시오.

① 전등 수리하기　　　　　　② TV 드라마 시청하기

③ 전력 회사에 신고하기　　　④ 전력 회사 연락처 찾기

⑤ 휴대전화 배터리 교체하기

8 대화를 듣고, 남자가 휴대전화를 사용하지 <u>못한</u> 이유를 고르시오.

① 집에 두고 와서　　　　　　② 배터리가 닳아서

③ 도난당해서　　　　　　　　④ 충전 중이어서

⑤ 친구에게 빌려줘서

9 대화를 듣고, 여자가 지불할 금액을 고르시오.

① $90　　　② $100　　　③ $110　　　④ $125　　　⑤ $130

10 대화를 듣고, 가구 박람회에 관해 언급되지 <u>않은</u> 것을 고르시오.

① 개최 장소 ② 참가 업체 수
③ 출품된 가구의 종류 ④ 특별 행사
⑤ 입장료

11 현장 학습에 관한 다음 내용을 듣고, 일치하지 <u>않는</u> 것을 고르시오.

① 8시까지 학교로 와야 한다.
② 점심은 미술관 근처 공원에서 먹는다.
③ 필기도구를 준비해야 한다.
④ 보고서는 다음 주 월요일에 제출해야 한다.
⑤ 미술관 입장료를 가져와야 한다.

12 다음 표를 보면서 대화를 듣고, 두 사람이 선택할 자동차를 고르시오.

	Car Name	Type	Sunroof	Navigation System	Price
①	Volt	SUV	No	Yes	$25,000
②	Pilot	Sedan	Yes	No	$27,000
③	Road Trip	SUV	No	Yes	$29,000
④	Expert	Sedan	No	Yes	$30,000
⑤	Superior	SUV	Yes	Yes	$32,000

13 대화를 듣고, 여자의 마지막 말에 대한 남자의 응답으로 가장 적절한 것을 고르시오.

Man: _______________________________________

① Thanks for understanding my feelings.
② You'll have to make sure you study harder.
③ Well, you didn't have to tell me your score.
④ I don't agree with you. It's complete nonsense.
⑤ Maybe next time I should prepare for the exam with you.

14 대화를 듣고, 남자의 마지막 말에 대한 여자의 응답으로 가장 적절한 것을 고르시오.

Woman: ____

① Don't worry. You don't have to buy new one.

② You can bring it when you pick up your camera.

③ We will notify you when it is ready to be picked up.

④ Unfortunately, your camera will not be ready in time.

⑤ I'm sorry, but we don't offer a warranty on this product.

15 다음 상황 설명을 듣고, Mandy가 Greg에게 할 말로 가장 적절한 것을 고르시오.

Mandy: ____

① Why have you been exercising at the gym?

② I don't think you've gained weight recently.

③ I'm so proud of you for keeping your resolution.

④ If you keep getting up early, it will get easier soon.

⑤ I found it hard to keep in shape during the semester.

[16-17] 다음을 듣고, 물음에 답하시오.

16 여자가 하는 말의 주제로 가장 적절한 것은?

① some of history's greatest inventors

② inventions that were created by accident

③ the secret to inventing something useful

④ the careful planning needed to invent things

⑤ inventions that have become very popular

17 언급된 발명품이 <u>아닌</u> 것은?

① potato chips   ② ice cream cones

③ waffles   ④ Velcro

⑤ Popsicles

1 대화를 듣고, 남자의 마지막 말에 대한 여자의 응답으로 가장 적절한 것을 고르시오.

① He doesn't like T-shirts.
② I prefer the men's pants.
③ I don't like either of them.
④ This yellow one doesn't suit me.
⑤ I want to exchange this pink striped one.

2 대화를 듣고, 여자의 마지막 말에 대한 남자의 응답으로 가장 적절한 것을 고르시오.

① I stayed there for five days.
② I'll be back in a couple of weeks.
③ I bought some souvenirs for you.
④ I'm totally exhausted from this trip.
⑤ I just came back on Sunday evening.

3 다음을 듣고, 여자가 하는 말의 목적으로 가장 적절한 것을 고르시오.

① 핼러윈의 다양한 놀이를 추천하려고
② 교내 핼러윈 특별행사를 소개하려고
③ 핼러윈 복장을 만드는 법을 설명하려고
④ 핼러윈 활동 시 안전수칙을 안내하려고
⑤ 어린이 안전 사고의 위험성을 경고하려고

4 대화를 듣고, 남자의 의견으로 가장 적절한 것을 고르시오.

① 대인 관계에서 첫인상은 매우 중요하다.
② 습관을 바꾸는 데는 많은 노력이 필요하다.
③ 때와 장소에 맞는 옷차림을 갖추어야 한다.
④ 다른 사람의 시선을 신경 쓸 필요는 없다.
⑤ 꾸준한 자기 관리는 현대인에게 필수적이다.

5 대화를 듣고, 두 사람의 관계를 가장 잘 나타낸 것을 고르시오.

① 의사 – 환자 ② 형사 – 용의자
③ 사장 – 직원 ④ 자동차 판매원 – 고객
⑤ 경찰관 – 운전자

6 대화를 듣고, 그림에서 대화의 내용과 일치하지 <u>않는</u> 것을 고르시오.

7 대화를 듣고, 남자가 할 일로 가장 적절한 것을 고르시오.

① 가격 할인해 주기 ② 샌들 추천해 주기
③ 샌들 교환해 주기 ④ 샌들 주문해 주기
⑤ 샌들 배송해 주기

8 대화를 듣고, 여자가 직장을 다닐 수 <u>없는</u> 이유를 고르시오.

① 동료들과 사이가 안 좋아서 ② 일이 힘들어서
③ 상사가 괴롭혀서 ④ 회사가 멀어서
⑤ 급여가 적어서

9 대화를 듣고, 남자가 지불할 금액을 고르시오.

① $270 ② $285 ③ $295 ④ $300 ⑤ $315

10 대화를 듣고, carpool의 장점에 관해 언급되지 <u>않은</u> 것을 고르시오.

① 편의성　　　　　　　　② 연료비 절감
③ 환경 보호　　　　　　　④ 출근 시간 단축
⑤ 동료와의 친분 도모

11 cricket에 관한 다음 내용을 듣고, 일치하지 <u>않는</u> 것을 고르시오.

① 수비 팀은 11명의 선수로 구성되어 있다.
② 영국에서는 야구보다 인기가 더 많다.
③ 야구보다 훨씬 전에 행해졌다.
④ 최초로 고안한 사람의 이름에서 명칭을 따왔다.
⑤ 대부분의 사람들은 영국 경기라고 생각한다.

12 다음 표를 보면서 대화를 듣고, 두 사람이 구입할 소파를 고르시오.

Holiday Sale on All Sofas

	Model	Size (number of people)	Price	Sofa material	Color
①	A	2	$500	Fabric	White
②	B	4	$650	Fabric	Black
③	C	4	$760	Leather	Black
④	D	6	$890	Leather	White
⑤	E	6	$920	Leather	Black

13 대화를 듣고, 남자의 마지막 말에 대한 여자의 응답으로 가장 적절한 것을 고르시오.

Woman: ________________________________

① I was a little upset at being scolded.
② I promise that I'll try to make fewer mistakes.
③ I'll apologize to my coworkers for leaving early.
④ When people yell at me, it makes me feel stressed.
⑤ Well, if people are complaining, I guess I should watch my temper.

14

대화를 듣고, 여자의 마지막 말에 대한 남자의 응답으로 가장 적절한 것을 고르시오.

Man: ____

① Thank you for the useful information.

② I'm so grateful to the lost and found staff.

③ If I were you, I would buy a new cell phone.

④ I'm really sorry for causing such a big mistake.

⑤ Yes, you need to report the lost item right away.

15

다음 상황 설명을 듣고, Lucy가 Tara에게 할 말로 가장 적절한 것을 고르시오.

Lucy: ____

① Don't worry. You're going to be fine.

② I already told you about the school reunion.

③ I'm so happy to be able to attend your wedding.

④ Your high school friends will attend your wedding.

⑤ I'm so sorry, but I have prior engagement that day.

[16-17] 다음을 듣고, 물음에 답하시오.

16

여자가 하는 말의 주제로 가장 적절한 것은?

① the problems of barter exchange

② how currency developed over time

③ the benefits of bartering goods directly

④ the advantages of using digital currency

⑤ why precious metals became used as coins

17

언급된 물건이 <u>아닌</u> 것은?

① apples   ② seashells

③ rocks   ④ metals

⑤ paper

FINAL TEST

1 대화를 듣고, 남자의 마지막 말에 대한 여자의 응답으로 가장 적절한 것을 고르시오.

① It should be at the end of this aisle.

② You really like to read, don't you?

③ Yes. He is one of my favorite artists.

④ I didn't expect you to like Pablo Picasso.

⑤ Okay. Can you put this book on the top shelf?

2 대화를 듣고, 여자의 마지막 말에 대한 남자의 응답으로 가장 적절한 것을 고르시오.

① Well, I did work very hard this year.

② I don't remember the last time I saw you.

③ You tried hard. Maybe you will win it next year.

④ Congratulations! Everybody thinks you deserve it.

⑤ It will be good to have some new employees this year.

3 다음을 듣고, 여자가 하는 말의 목적으로 가장 적절한 것을 고르시오.

① 비행기 연착을 알리려고

② 비행기 탑승을 촉구하려고

③ 수하물 분실에 대해 사과하려고

④ 게이트 변동 사항을 공지하려고

⑤ 비행기 탑승 절차를 안내하려고

4 대화를 듣고, 여자의 의견으로 가장 적절한 것을 고르시오.

① 감정이 격할 때는 말을 아껴야 한다.

② 친구와 다투는 것은 자연스러운 일이다.

③ 바람직하지 않은 교우관계는 피해야 한다.

④ 약속을 지키는 것은 교우관계에 있어서 중요하다.

⑤ 부정적인 감정을 허용되는 방식으로 표현하는 것이 좋다.

5 대화를 듣고, 두 사람의 관계를 가장 잘 나타낸 것을 고르시오.

① 기자 – 건축가
② 사회자 – 감독
③ 면접관 – 지원자
④ 심사위원 – 예술가
⑤ 아나운서 – 박물관장

6 대화를 듣고, 그림에서 대화의 내용과 일치하지 <u>않는</u> 것을 고르시오.

7 대화를 듣고, 여자가 할 일로 가장 적절한 것을 고르시오.

① 강습 일정 확인하기
② 수영 강습 신청하기
③ 수영장 이용에 따른 추가 비용 내기
④ 수영장 구역 떠나기
⑤ 수영 모자 쓰기

8 대화를 듣고, 남자가 쇼핑을 갈 수 <u>없는</u> 이유를 고르시오.

① 다른 약속이 생겨서
② 이미 옷을 구입해서
③ 돈을 절약해야 해서
④ 몸이 좋지 않아서
⑤ 친구 집에 들러야 해서

9 대화를 듣고, 여자가 지불할 금액을 고르시오.

① $40   ② $46   ③ $50   ④ $53   ⑤ $56

10 대화를 듣고, 출간 파티에 관해 언급되지 <u>않은</u> 것을 고르시오.

① 사인 행사   ② 행사 장소   ③ 기자 간담회
④ 질의응답 시간   ⑤ 추첨 행사

11 North City 예술 축제에 관한 다음 내용을 듣고, 일치하지 <u>않는</u> 것을 고르시오.

① 올해로 3회째를 맞는 행사이다.   ② 지역 예술가들의 작품이 이틀 동안 전시된다.
③ 일부 도로들은 차량이 통제된다.   ④ 국제 무용단들의 공연이 예정되어 있다.
⑤ 일요일 저녁에 불꽃놀이 행사가 열린다.

12 다음 표를 보면서 대화를 듣고, 두 사람이 머무를 호텔을 고르시오.

	Hotel	Location	Shuttle Service	Price per Night	Free Breakfast
①	Sunflower Hotel	Gimpo	Yes	$150	Yes
②	Riverside Hotel	Seoul	Yes	$200	No
③	Fifth Avenue Hotel	Seoul	Yes	$300	Yes
④	Hotel Empire	Seoul	No	$200	Yes
⑤	City Center Hotel	Gimpo	Yes	$100	No

13 대화를 듣고, 남자의 마지막 말에 대한 여자의 응답으로 가장 적절한 것을 고르시오.

Man: _______________________________________

① You should have taken more driving lessons.
② Just try to have more confidence in yourself.
③ You can choose another instructor if you want.
④ Why don't you use public transportation instead?
⑤ Just write down your answers slowly and carefully.

14 대화를 듣고, 남자의 마지막 말에 대한 여자의 응답으로 가장 적절한 것을 고르시오.

Woman: _______________________________________

① You should get more organized.

② I guess you forgot to bring the book.

③ I don't think you copied all 20 pages.

④ That's why we need to work on our report.

⑤ It's good to know you are going to get a daily planner.

15 다음 상황 설명을 듣고, 코치가 Becky에게 할 말로 가장 적절한 것을 고르시오.

Coach: _______________________________________

① Even the best players lose a game sometimes.

② You should do your best to achieve good results.

③ If you hadn't gotten hurt, you would have done well.

④ Eventually, you'll have a chance to display your skills.

⑤ Next time, you should ask me before making a decision.

[16-17] 다음을 듣고, 물음에 답하시오.

16 남자가 하는 말의 목적으로 가장 적절한 것은?

① how to keep the brain healthy

② the importance of diet and exercise

③ the brain's role in the aging process

④ activities that can help you feel young

⑤ recent scientific discoveries about aging

17 언급된 활동이 <u>아닌</u> 것은?

① doing regular exercise

② getting enough sleep

③ eating foods with omega-3 fatty acids

④ maintaining an ideal body weight

⑤ activities you do with your hands

지은이

NE능률 영어교육연구소

NE능률 영어교육연구소는 혁신적이며 효율적인 영어 교재를 개발하고
영어 학습의 질을 한 단계 높이고자 노력하는 NE능률의 연구조직입니다.

맞수 수능듣기 〈실전편〉

펴 낸 이	주민홍
펴 낸 곳	서울특별시 마포구 월드컵북로 396(상암동) 누리꿈스퀘어 비즈니스타워 10층
	㈜NE능률 (우편번호 03925)
펴 낸 날	2020년 10월 5일 개정판 제1쇄
	2023년 9월 15일 제4쇄
전　　화	02 2014 7114
팩　　스	02 3142 0356
홈 페 이 지	www.neungyule.com
등 록 번 호	제1-68호
I S B N	979-11-253-3479-8
정　　가	10,000원

NE 능률

고객센터

교재 내용 문의 : contact.nebooks.co.kr (별도의 가입 절차 없이 작성 가능)
제품 구매, 교환, 불량, 반품 문의 : 02-2014-7114
☎ 전화문의는 본사 업무시간 중에만 가능합니다.

NE능률 교재 MAP

아래 교재 MAP을 참고하여 본인의 현재 혹은 목표 수준에 따라 교재를 선택하세요.
NE능률 교재들과 함께 영어실력을 쑥쑥~ 올려보세요!
MP3 등 교재 부가 학습 서비스 및 자세한 교재 정보는 www.nebooks.co.kr 에서 확인하세요.

수능

맞수

맞춤형 **수**능영어
단기특강 시리즈

수능듣기
실전편

정답 및 해설

NE 능률

맞수

맞춤형 **수**능영어
단기특강 시리즈

수능듣기
실전편

정답 및 해설

1 ③	2 ④	3 ⑤	4 ④	5 ④
6 ③	7 ⑤	8 ①	9 ③	10 ④

1 정답 ③

남: 어젯밤에 〈The Next Korean Star Show〉를 못 봤어. 시작하기 전에 잠들어 버렸거든.
여: 아, 그럼 오늘 저녁에 하는 재방송을 보고 싶겠다.
남: 재방송? 정확히 언제 하는데?
여: <u>오늘 저녁 8시에 시작해.</u>

어휘 | rerun 재방송 **|문제|** survival 생존

문제해설 | TV 프로그램을 놓친 남자가 정확한 재방송 시간을 묻고 있으므로, 이에 대한 여자의 응답으로 ③번이 가장 적절하다.
① 그건 어젯밤 6시에 했어.
② 난 하루에 여덟 시간을 자.
④ 그건 그저 또 하나의 서바이벌 프로그램일 뿐이야.
⑤ 그건 텔레비전에 두 시간 반 동안 방영될 거야.

2 정답 ④

여: 안녕, Ian! 나 캠핑 여행에서 돌아왔어!
남: 어땠어? 가족들이랑 재미있었니?
여: 응! 내가 찍은 이 사진 좀 봐봐!
남: 그릴 위의 고기를 뒤집고 있는 저 남자는 누구야? 행복해 보여.
여: 우리 아빠야. 아빠는 요리하는 것을 정말 좋아하시거든. 그리고 우리 삼촌도 보이니?
남: 안경 끼신 분이니?
여: 응. 텐트를 조립하는 게 삼촌의 일이었어.
남: 정말 잘하셨다. 저 나무 아래 네 여동생이 보여.
여: 응. 그 애는 고양이를 데려왔어. 그녀의 무릎 위에 있지.
남: 그리고 네 남동생은 연못에서 낚시하고 있었구나!
여: 응, 하지만 그는 아무것도 잡지 못했어. 그리고 우리 엄마는 여행 내내 책을 읽으셨지.
남: 아, 벤치에 계신 저분이구나. 너 즐거운 시간을 보낸 것 같다!

어휘 | flip 홱 뒤집다 hamburger 햄버거; *햄버거용 다진 고기 barbecue 바비큐 (파티); *(바비큐용) 석쇠, 그릴 assemble 모이다; *조립하다 lap 무릎 pond 연못

문제해설 | 남동생은 연못에서 낚시하고 있었다고 했으므로, 대화의 내용과 일치하지 않는 것은 ④번이다.

3 정답 ⑤

남: 뷔페 잘 먹었니?
여: 음, 정말 배가 부르긴 한데, 음식을 많이 먹은 것 같진 않아.
남: 한번에 많은 종류의 음식을 먹었기 때문일 거야.
여: 응. 그게 많이 먹는 것처럼 느끼게 하지만, 실제로 난 그렇지 않거든.
남: 난 처음에 빵을 많이 먹었어. 그래서 배가 정말 빨리 불렀어.
여: 넌 빵을 건너뛰고 메인 요리로 갔어야 했어.
남: 맞아. 그리고 난 후식을 너무 많이 먹었어.
여: 리필이 무료라면, 많이 먹지 않기가 힘들지.
남: 이 뷔페 식당은 사람들의 배를 빨리 부르게 해서 돈을 많이 벌 수 있을 것 같아.
여: 나도 그렇게 생각해. 그리고 한 가지 더 있어.
남: 뭔데?
여: 의자가 불편하다는 거 눈치챘니?
남: 네 말이 맞아. 그게 사람들이 빨리 나가고 싶게 만드는 것이 틀림없어!

어휘 | at once 한번에 skip 빼다, 건너뛰다 main dish 주요리, 메인 요리 dessert 디저트, 후식 refill (음식물의) 다시 청한 몫, 리필 uncomfortable 불편한 bet 틀림없다, 분명하다

문제해설 | 두 사람은 이윤을 얻기 위해 손님들의 배를 빨리 부르게 하는 여러 가지 방법을 쓰고, 불편한 의자를 배치하는 뷔페 식당의 전략에 대해 이야기하고 있다.

4 정답 ④

남: 이런. 불이 또 나갔어.
여: 오늘 정전이 된 게 이번이 두 번째야. 우리 집만 그런 거야, 아니면 이웃집들도 그런 거야?
남: 모든 구역의 전기가 나간 것 같아. 폭풍우 때문인 게 틀림없어.
여: 우리는 손전등이 필요해. 그것을 어디에 두었니?
남: 프린터 아래 있는 서랍 안에 넣어 뒀어. 내가 가져올게.
여: 난 이런 날씨가 얼마나 더 오래 지속될지 궁금해.
남: TV를 켜면… 아, 전기가 안 들어오는구나.
여: 폭풍우가 곧 끝나면 좋겠는데. 난 오늘 밤 요가 수업을 정말 빠지고 싶지 않아.
남: 네 스마트폰을 사용해서 일기예보를 확인해 보는 게 어때? 그건 배터리로 작동되잖아.
여: 좋은 생각이야! 왜 내가 그 생각을 못 했을까? 고마워.
남: 천만에.

어휘 | go out (불 등이) 꺼지다, 나가다 power 힘; *전력, 전기 flashlight 손전등 drawer 서랍 last 계속되다, 지속하다 electricity 전기 weather forecast 일기예보

문제해설 | 남자가 스마트폰을 이용하여 일기예보를 확인해 보는 게 어떠냐고 말하자 여자가 좋은 생각이라고 했으므로, 여자는 스마트폰을 이용할 것이다.

5 정답 ④

[전화벨이 울린다.]
남: 여보세요, Child Relief Africa 기부 상담 전화입니다.

여: 여보세요. 제가 방금 TV에서 광고를 봤는데, 기부를 하고 싶어
　　서요.
남: 훌륭하시네요. 성함 좀 알려주시겠어요?
여: 그럼요. 제 이름은 Anna Gray예요. 광고에 나온 정보를 저에
　　게 다시 한번 알려주시겠어요?
남: 물론이죠. 만약 2달러를 기부하시면, 한 명의 아이가 백신 접종
　　을 받는 데 쓰이게 됩니다.
여: 아, 그렇군요. 또 뭐가 있죠?
남: 만약 10달러를 기부하시면, 한 명의 아이에게 한 학기 내내 교
　　육을 받을 수 있는 기회를 주실 수 있습니다.
여: 아, 그래요? 그럼, 전 두 명의 아이들이 백신 접종을 받고 교육
　　을 받을 수 있을 만큼 충분한 돈을 기부하고 싶어요.
남: 정말 관대하시네요, 부인.
여: 별말씀을요. 제가 조금이나마 도움이 되면 좋겠네요.

어휘 | relief 구제, 구원 donation 기부, 기증(*v.* donate) hotline
상담 전화 commercial 광고 방송 remind A of B A에게 B를 상기
시키다 feature 특색으로 삼다 vaccinate 백신[예방] 주사를 맞히다
opportunity 기회 educate 교육하다 semester 학기 generous 관
대한, 아량 있는

문제해설 | 여자는 두 명의 아이들이 백신 접종을 받을 수 있고($2×2),
교육을 받을 수 있는($10×2) 돈을 기부하겠다고 했으므로, 여자가 기
부할 금액은 24달러이다.

6 정답 ③

여: 학생 여러분 좋은 아침이에요. 수업을 시작하기 전에 간단하게
　　알릴 것이 있습니다. 새로운 학교에 들어가는 것은 언제나 쉽지
　　않은 일인데, 외국에서 그렇게 하는 것은 훨씬 더 어렵죠. 여러
　　분 몇몇이 알고 있듯이, 우리 고등학교에 다음 달에 교환 학생
　　몇 명이 도착할 것입니다. 이 학생들은 우리 학교와 우리 공동체
　　생활에 적응하면서 도움이 필요할 겁니다. 여러분 중 누가 자원
　　해서 이 학생들을 돕고 싶다면 최대한 빨리 교무실에서 신청하
　　세요. 자원봉사자들은 같은 연령과 동성인 교환 학생과 짝을 이
　　루게 될 겁니다. 이건 특별한 추억과 우정도 만들고 다른 사람을
　　도울 수 있는 절호의 기회입니다.

어휘 | brief 짧은, 간단한 announcement 소식, 발표 challenging
힘든, 어려운 foreign country 외국 exchange student 교환 학생
adjust to …에 적응하다 community 공동체 volunteer 자원봉사하
다; 자원봉사자 assist 돕다 sign up 참가하다, 가입하다 pair 짝짓다

문제해설 | 여자는 교환 학생들이 학교 생활에 적응할 수 있도록 도와줄
자원봉사자를 모집하고 있다.

7 정답 ⑤

[초인종이 울린다.]
여: 누구세요?
남: 여기가 Murphy 씨 댁인가요? 저는 Michael Park인데요. 우
　　리는 오늘 아까 전화 통화를 했었죠.

여: 아, 네. 들어오세요. 이렇게 빨리 와 주셔서 고맙습니다.
남: 별말씀을요. 그럼, 이 방뿐인가요?
여: 네, 이곳은 원룸 아파트예요.
남: 음, 가구는 많이 없네요. 주말에 이사 가세요?
여: 전 그러고 싶어요. 주말에는 비용이 얼마나 드나요?
남: 저희가 주말에는 바빠서, 추가 비용이 있어요.
여: 아, 그래요? 음, 주중에도 괜찮아요. 비용이 얼마나 들지 견적을
　　내주시겠어요?
남: 음… 소형 트럭 한 대, 운전기사 한 명과 가구 나르는 사람 두 명
　　이면, 300달러가 되겠네요.
여: 적당한 것 같네요.
남: 좋아요. 시간을 정하고 나면 모든 준비가 끝납니다.

어휘 | furniture 가구 fee 수수료, 요금 estimate 추정; *견적(서)
pickup truck 소형 트럭 carry 나르다, 운반하다 reasonable (가격이)
적당한 arrange 정하다, 준비하다 set 준비된

문제해설 | 여자는 원룸 아파트에서 이사를 가려고 하고, 남자는 이사할
때 드는 비용을 계산하는 것으로 보아, 거주자와 이삿짐 운송업자 간의
대화임을 알 수 있다.

8 정답 ①

[전화벨이 울린다.]
남: 안녕하세요, Eagle 항공사입니다. 어떻게 도와 드릴까요?
여: 안녕하세요, 다음 주 목요일 뉴욕행 비행기를 예약했는데, 더 빠
　　른 항공편으로 바꾸고 싶어서요.
남: 네. 수요일 오전은 어떠세요?
여: 음, 월요일이나 화요일이 가장 좋을 것 같아요.
남: 솔트레이크시티나 로스엔젤레스에서 환승하는 건 괜찮으세요?
여: 괜찮을 것 같아요. 경유 시간이 얼마나 되나요?
남: 솔트레이크시티를 경유하는 것은 2시간이에요. 로스엔젤레스를
　　경유하는 것은 4시간이고요.
여: 음… 경유 시간이 좀 더 짧은 게 좋겠어요. 비행기가 몇 시에 도
　　착하나요?
남: 화요일 비행기는 밤 8시와 9시에 도착하고, 월요일 비행기는 오
　　후 4시와 6시에 도착해요.
여: 알겠습니다. 호텔에 도착하는 데 시간이 좀 걸려서, 더 일찍 출
　　발하는 비행기를 타는 게 좋겠어요.
남: 네. 그러면 고객님에게 딱 맞는 항공편이 있네요.

어휘 | reach 닿다; *(전화로) 연락하다 book 예약하다 switch to …로
바꾸다 transfer 갈아타다 layover 중간 하차, 경유 **|문제|** departure
출발 location 위치, 장소

문제해설 | 여자는 월요일이나 화요일 비행기 중 경유 시간이 짧은 솔트
레이크시티에서 환승하고 더 일찍 출발하는 것을 타고 싶다고 했으므로,
여자가 선택할 항공편은 ①번이다.

9 정답 ③

여: 여러분이 플로리스트로서의 경력을 시작하기를 고려하고 있든,

그냥 열정적인 원예 애호가이든지 간에 Flora Philadelphia가 여러분의 화예 디자인 기술을 개발하는 데 도움을 줄 수 있습니다. 저희는 다양한 전문 강좌를 제공하며, 현재 입문 강좌 중 하나를 특별가로 제공해 드리고 있습니다. 이 강좌는 네 번의 수업으로 이루어져 있습니다. 이 수업들에서, 여러분은 아름다운 결혼식 부케를 만드는 방법을 배우게 됩니다. 수강료는 단지 200달러이며, 각 수업마다 30달러의 추가 재료비가 듭니다. 수업 후에 여러분만의 부케와 남은 재료를 집으로 가져가셔도 됩니다. 이 특별 혜택을 누리시려면, 4월 10일까지 반드시 저희 웹사이트에서 등록하셔야 합니다. 질문이 있으시면, 555-6398로 전화해 주세요. 이 좋은 기회를 놓치지 마세요!

어휘 | look to …을 고려해 보다 enthusiastic 열성적인 gardener 정원사 floral 꽃으로 만든 an array of 다수의 vast (수·양이) 막대한 specialized 전문적인 offer 제공하다; (보통 짧은 기간 동안의) 할인 introductory 서두의; *입문자들을 위한 consist of …로 구성되다 put together …을 만들다 additional 추가적인 material 재료 take advantage of …을 활용하다 register 등록하다

문제해설 | ③ 각 수업에 추가로 재료비 30달러가 부가된다고 했다.

10 정답 ④

남: 의과 대학에서의 바쁜 한 학기 후에, James는 그의 여자 친구인 Fiona와 함께 시간을 보내기를 고대해 왔다. 그들은 낭만적인 소풍을 위해 공원에서 만나기로 했다. 그녀를 만나러 가는 도중에, 그는 한 여자가 자전거에서 넘어지는 것을 우연히 보게 된다. 그녀를 부축하려고 멈춰 서느라 그는 Fiona와의 데이트에 30분을 늦는다. 불행히도, 그의 전화기의 배터리가 떨어져서, 그는 그녀에게 전화를 할 수 없다. 그가 마침내 공원에 도착했을 때, 그는 Fiona가 화가 난 것을 본다. 이런 상황에서, James가 Fiona에게 할 말로 가장 적절한 것은 무엇인가?
James: 내가 전화해서 늦을 거라고 말하지 못해서 정말 미안해.

어휘 | medical school 의과 대학 fall off …에서 떨어지다 help … up …를 도와 일으키다 run out 다 떨어지다[되다] annoyed 짜증이 난

문제해설 | James는 Fiona를 만나러 가는 길에 자전거 사고를 당한 사람을 도와주다 늦었지만, 전화기의 배터리가 떨어져서 전화를 하지 못해 Fiona가 화가 난 상황이므로, James가 Fiona에게 할 말로 ④번이 가장 적절하다.
① 네가 아직 여기에 있을 줄 몰랐어.
② 내가 오늘 우리의 소풍을 잊은 걸 용서해 줘.
③ 늦어서 미안해. 여기 오는 길에 자전거에서 넘어졌거든.
⑤ 넌 나한테 네 전화 배터리가 떨어졌다고 말했어야 해.

1. before it started / watch the rerun
2. flipping hamburgers / assemble the tent / spent the whole trip reading

3. do feel full / filled me up / the refills are free
4. the power is out / put it in the drawer / runs on a battery
5. make a donation / featured in the commercial / vaccinated and educated
6. have a brief announcement / adjusting to life / making special memories
7. the only room / be moving out / how much it will cost
8. switch to an earlier / Do you mind transferring / a shorter layover time
9. enthusiastic gardener / consists of four classes / an additional materials fee / To take advantage of
10. see a woman fall off / half an hour late / is annoyed

02강 실전 모의고사　　　　　pp. 10-11

1 ①	2 ⑤	3 ⑤	4 ④	5 ①
6 ③	7 ⑤	8 ③	9 ③	10 ①

1 정답 ①

여: 나 럭비 동아리에 가입하고 싶어. 어떻게 생각해?
남: 그곳의 훈련이 모든 스포츠 동아리 중에서 가장 힘들다고 들었어.
여: 정말? 음… 그럼 어떤 스포츠 동아리가 나한테 가장 잘 맞을지 모르겠네.
남: 일단 모든 동아리 광고를 먼저 확인해 봐.

어휘 | tough 힘든, 어려운 suit (…에게) 맞다 **|문제|** warm up 준비 운동을 하다 stretch 스트레칭

문제해설 | 여자가 어떤 스포츠 동아리를 골라야 할지 모르겠다고 했으므로, 이에 대한 남자의 응답으로 ①번이 가장 적절하다.
② 그렇지만 럭비는 내가 가장 좋아하는 운동이야.
③ 스트레칭으로 준비 운동을 시작하자.
④ 야구 경기를 보러 가는 게 어때?
⑤ 미안하지만, 난 이미 다른 동아리의 회원이야.

2 정답 ⑤

남: 여보, 정말 근사한 저녁 식사였어요. 당신…
여: Alan, 한 소년이 길을 건너고 있어요!
남: [타이어 마찰 소리] 와, 아슬아슬했어요! 여보, 괜찮아요?
여: 네, 그리고 다행히 저 소년도 괜찮네요. 그 애가 보지도 않고 길에 들어서다니 믿을 수가 없네요.
남: 그 애는 흔한 실수를 저지르고 있었어요.

여: 그게 무슨 말이에요?
남: 부주의하게 걸으면서 스마트폰을 사용하고 있었다는 말이에요.
여: 오, 그래요. 요즘 점점 더 많은 사람들이 그러는 것을 봐요. 끔찍
　　해요!
남: 나도 그렇게 생각해요. 보도나 복도에서 내 앞에 있는 사람들이
　　스마트폰을 사용할 땐 답답해요.
여: 음, 사람들이 무심코 붐비는 거리에 들어서는 것은 답답하다는
　　말로는 부족해요. 그러면 위험해요!
남: 동의해요. 그것은 나쁜 습관이에요.

어휘 | carelessly 부주의하게 frustrating 좌절감을 주는, 답답하게 하는
sidewalk 보도 casually 아무 생각 없이, 무심코

문제해설 | 두 사람은 사람들이 보행 중 스마트폰을 사용하는 행동이 위
험하다고 이야기하고 있다.

3 정답 ⑤

남: Wendy, 너 전에 프린터를 설치해 본 적 있니?
여: 물론이지. 그런데, 좀 됐어.
남: 저기, 내가 지금 막 이 프린터를 사 왔는데, 이해가 안 돼.
여: 음… 어려운 부분은 네가 이미 다 한 것 같은데. 이제 저 전선을
　　꽂기만 하면 돼.
남: 해 봤는데, 뭔가 잘못됐어. 아마 그걸 엉뚱한 곳에 꽂았나 봐.
여: 아니, 거기가 맞아. 내가 해 볼게. [잠시 후] 그거 이상하네.
남: 아마도 고객 서비스 센터에 전화해야 할 것 같아.
여: 잠깐만. 이게 문제네. 이 전선의 끝이 파손됐어.
남: 아, 그렇네. 난 그걸 교환하러 다시 상점에 가져가야겠어.
여: 그래. 나중에 그걸 설치하는 걸 끝마치는 건 내가 도와줄게.
남: 도와줘서 고마워.

어휘 | set up 설치하다 figure out …을 이해하다[알아내다] plug in
플러그를 꽂다 cable 전선 replace 대체하다; *바꾸다, 교체하다

문제해설 | 남자는 프린터 부품을 교환하러 상점에 갈 것이다.

4 정답 ④

남: 안녕하세요! 평소처럼 모닝커피를 드시러 오신 건가요?
여: 네, 그런데 오늘은 두 잔 주세요. 친구에게 한 잔 갖다 주려고요.
남: 알겠습니다. 커피와 함께 드실 것도 하시겠어요?
여: 음… 이 블루베리 머핀이 정말 맛있어 보이네요. 그것들은 얼마
　　예요?
남: 하나에 2달러예요. 한 시간 전에 막 구웠어요.
여: 네. 그러면 그거 세 개 주세요.
남: 알겠습니다. 커피는 각각 3달러이고, 추가로 하나에 2달러인 머
　　핀 세 개를 주문하셨습니다. 그게 다인가요?
여: 네. 아, 그리고 저에게 단골 손님 카드가 있어요. [잠시 후] 와,
　　도장이 열 개가 되네요.
남: 그러면 커피 한 잔이 무료입니다.
여: 오, 정말이에요? 이거 정말 반가운 일이네요!
남: 여기 커피와 머핀이 있습니다. 좋은 하루 보내세요.

여: 감사합니다. 내일 뵈요!

어휘 | usual 평소의 absolutely 틀림없이 frequent customer 단골
손님

문제해설 | 여자는 3달러짜리 커피 두 잔을 시켰는데, 한 잔은 무료라고
했다. 또한 2달러짜리 머핀 세 개($2x3)를 주문했으므로 여자가 지불한
금액은 9달러이다.

5 정답 ①

남: 안녕하세요. 여러분 모두가 제가 말하는 것을 아주 주의 깊게 들
　　어주셨으면 합니다. 저희 구내식당의 요리사들은 여러분 모두에
　　게 맛있고 건강에 좋은 음식을 준비해 주려고 아주 열심히 일하
　　시지만, 저는 버려지는 음식물의 양이 증가하고 있다는 점을 알
　　게 되었습니다. 여러분은 모두 어리고, 여러분의 몸은 여전히 성
　　장하고 있습니다. 따라서 여러분의 몸이 필요로 하는 영양소를
　　얻기 위해서, 여러분은 많이 먹도록 해야 합니다. 게다가, 음식
　　물을 버리는 것은 환경에 나쁩니다. 음식물 쓰레기가 쓰레기 매
　　립지에 버려지면 그것은 썩어서 온실가스인 메탄을 생성합니다.
　　그러니 버려지는 음식물의 양을 줄이는 걸 돕는 데 있어 자기 역
　　할을 다 하도록 노력해 주십시오.

어휘 | cafeteria 구내식당 throw away 버리다 nutrition 영양
dump 버리다 landfill 쓰레기 매립지 rot 썩다 greenhouse gas 온실
가스

문제해설 | 남자는 버려지는 음식을 줄이도록 노력해 달라고 권고하고
있다.

6 정답 ③

남: 얘, 너 스트레스 받은 것처럼 보이는데. 무슨 일이 있니?
여: [한숨 쉬며] 이 웹디자인 소프트웨어 때문이야. 너무 복잡해.
남: 어떤 프로그램을 사용하고 있는데? 내가 좀 봐도 될까?
여: 물론이지. 난 Dreamweb이라고 불리는 이것을 사용하려고 하
　　고 있어.
남: Dreamweb이라고? 그건 정말 사용하기 어려운 프로그램이야.
　　난 Webweaver를 훨씬 더 선호해.
여: 잠깐, 너 이런 것에 대해 아니?
남: 물론이지. 난 대학에서 웹디자인을 공부했어. 너 그거 몰랐니?
여: 몰랐어, 난 네가 IT를 공부했다고 생각했어. 그럼, 내가 웹사이
　　트를 디자인하는 걸 도와줄 수 있니?
남: 물론이지. 친구 좋다는 게 뭐겠어?
여: 고마워! 네가 최고야.
남: 하지만 내가 그걸 하기 전에, 네가 어떤 스타일의 웹사이트를 생
　　각하고 있는지 알아야겠어.
여: 알았어. 커피 좀 마시면서 더 얘기해 보자.
남: 그게 좋겠다.

어휘 | stressed out 스트레스가 쌓인 complicated 복잡한 stuff 일,
것 IT 정보통신 기술(information technology)

문제해설 | 여자는 남자가 웹디자인을 전공했다는 말을 듣고, 자신의 웹사이트를 디자인하는 것을 도와달라고 부탁했다.

7 정답 ⑤

여: 우리 학교 음악 축제를 위한 포스터를 만들자.
남: 좋은 생각이야. 맨 꼭대기에 대문자로 축제 이름을 넣자.
여: 좋아! 그리고 축제 날짜를 포스터 하단 왼쪽에 넣자.
남: 그래. 밴드부 그림을 넣는 게 어떨까?
여: 좋지! 중간에 하나 넣자. 가수를 두 기타리스트 사이에 이렇게 넣어야 할까?
남: 잘 어울릴 것 같아.
여: 드러머도 추가할까?
남: 좋아. 그를 포스터의 왼쪽에 넣을까?
여: 음, 내 생각에는 가수 뒤에 그를 넣으면 더 보기 좋을 것 같아.
남: 좋은데. 거기가 딱 좋네.
여: 포스터에 티켓 가격을 넣어야 할까?
남: 당연하지. 티켓 정보를 하단 오른쪽에 넣는 게 어때?
여: 좋아. 이제 멋져 보인다!

어휘 | in capital letters 대문자로(= in capitals) date 날짜 price 가격

문제해설 | 티켓 가격을 오른쪽 하단에 넣자고 했으므로, 대화 내용과 일치하지 않는 것은 ⑤번이다.

8 정답 ③

여: 이 진열품 좀 봐. 너 새 배낭이 필요하지 않아?
남: 맞아. 내 새 노트북 컴퓨터가 이전 배낭에 딱 맞질 않아.
여: 할인 중인 것 좀 보자. 넌 얼마나 쓸 수 있어?
남: 90달러 이상은 쓰고 싶지 않아.
여: 알겠어. 그게 얼마나 커야 해?
남: 중형이나 대형이 좋을 것 같아.
여: 이 빨간색 중형 가방은 어때?
남: 싫어. 난 빨간색을 좋아하지 않아.
여: 그러면 이 파란색 중형 가방은 어때? 가격이 정말 적당해.
남: 난 파란색 좋아해. 거기에 안주머니가 몇 개 있어?
여: 딱 하나 있어. 내 생각엔 그 안에 네 노트북 컴퓨터와 나머지 물건을 위한 공간이 충분할 것 같아.
남: 사실, 난 주머니가 한 개 이상 필요해. 그래야 내가 소지품을 더 잘 정리하는 데 도움이 될 거야.
여: 그러면 어떤 가방이 너에게 제일 좋을지 확실해졌네.

어휘 | display 진열(품) backpack 배낭 laptop 휴대용[노트북] 컴퓨터 fit into …에 꼭 들어맞다 on sale 할인 중인 affordable (가격 등이) 알맞은, 감당할 수 있는 inner pocket 안주머니 organize 정리하다 belonging 《pl.》 소유물; *소지품

문제해설 | 남자는 90달러가 넘지 않고, 중형이나 대형 크기이며, 빨간색이 아니며, 안주머니가 1개보다 많은 가방을 사고 싶다고 했으므로, 남자가 구입할 배낭은 ③번이다.

9 정답 ③ 10 정답 ①

여: 창의적인 사람이 되고 싶으세요? 그렇다면 당신은 당신의 상상력을 최상의 상태로 유지하도록 노력해야 합니다. 당신은 사물을 다른 방식으로 보는 연습을 하기만 하면 됩니다. 그러기 위해서, 그저 물건 하나를 집어서 그것을 주의 깊게 살펴보세요. 그 물건이 일상에서 무슨 용도로 쓰이는가에 대해서는 생각하지 않도록 하세요. 대신, 그것의 크기, 모양, 색, 그리고 질감에 집중하세요. 이 물건이 가질 수 있는 다른 용도를 생각해 내도록 당신의 상상력을 사용하세요. 예를 들어, 찻잔은 평상시에는 단지 음료를 마시는 데 사용되지만, 그 밖에 다른 어떤 것에 사용될 수 있을까요? 당신은 동전을 보관하거나, 해변에서 작은 구멍을 파거나, 동물 인형의 모자를 만들거나, 혹은 꽃을 심는 데 그것을 사용할 수 있습니다. 이 연습을 할 때는, 가능한 한 많은 아이디어를 떠올리도록 노력하세요. 당신의 상상력이 활발하게 아이디어를 창조하게 하세요.

어휘 | creative 창의적인(n. creativity) imagination 상상력 object 물건 texture 질감 liquid 액체 dig 파다 come up with …을 생각해 내다 vivid (상상력이) 활발한 **|문제|** craft (수)공예 genius 천재 excessive 지나친, 과도한

문제해설 | 9. 여자는 창의력을 향상하기 위한 하나의 방법으로 사물의 일상적인 용도 외의 다른 용도들을 떠올리는 연습을 제시하고 있다.
① 수공예 프로젝트를 위한 아이디어들
② 예술가들이 어떻게 세상을 바라보는가
③ 창의력을 향상하는 방법
④ 역사상 창의적인 천재들
⑤ 지나친 상상의 위험성
10. 연습 도구의 예로 ① 찻잔이 언급되었다. 나머지 물건들은 찻잔의 다른 용도들을 설명하며 언급된 도구들이다.
② 동전 ③ 모자 ④ 동물 인형 ⑤ 꽃

DICTATION ANSWER pp. 12-13

1. the toughest of all / suits me best
2. that was close / while walking carelessly / beyond frustrating
3. set up a printer / plug in that cable / get it replaced
4. make it two / look absolutely delicious / get one coffee free
5. being thrown away / get the nutrition / bad for the environment
6. so complicated / studied web design / help me design a website
7. in capital letters / in the middle / Why not place
8. fit into my old one / really affordable / organize my belongings
9-10. practice seeing things / drinking liquids with / create vivid ideas

1 ①	2 ④	3 ②	4 ⑤	5 ②
6 ④	7 ③	8 ⑤	9 ③	10 ⑤

1 정답 ①

남: 엄마, 보세요! 제 운동화가 너무 낡았어요. 새것을 사야겠어요.
여: 음, 새 신발 가게에서 대규모 할인 판매를 한다고 들었어.
남: 잘됐네요! 거기로 가요. 위치가 어디예요?
여: 서점 바로 옆에 있단다.

어휘 | worn out 닳아 해진 locate 위치하다(*n.* location) **|문제|** apply 신청하다; *적용되다 around the clock 24시간 내내

문제해설 | 새로운 신발 가게의 위치를 묻는 남자의 질문에 대한 여자의 응답으로 ①번이 가장 적절하다.
② 거기서 넌 맞는 사이즈를 구할 수 있단다.
③ 할인은 주말에 적용되지 않아.
④ 그건 전 세계에 매장을 가지고 있어.
⑤ 그 가게는 24시간 영업해.

2 정답 ④

여: 너 오늘 오후에 계획이 있니?
남: 아니. 볼링 치러 가려고 했는데, Henry가 취소했어. 넌?
여: 난 미용실에 갈 거야. 머리를 좀 다듬어야 하거든.
남: 별로 신날 것 같지는 않구나.
여: 너도 머리를 좀 잘라야 할 것 같은데. 같이 가자.
남: 고맙지만, 됐어. 난 대신에 Brad Pitt가 나오는 그 신작 영화를 보러 갈까 해.
여: 그 영화가 벌써 개봉했니? 나도 그거 보고 싶은데.
남: 그럼 나랑 극장에 가지 않을래?
여: 하지만 난 벌써 미용실에 예약을 했어. 그 영화는 내일 같이 보러 가자!
남: 안 돼, 난 내일 치과에 가야 해.
여: 알았어. 내가 예약을 내일로 변경할 수 있을 것 같아.
남: 결정 잘했어. 매표소에서 4시에 만나자.
여: 좋아.

어휘 | be supposed to-v …하기로 되어 있다 beauty shop 미용실 trim 약간 자르기, 다듬기 release 개봉하다 box office (극장의) 매표소

문제해설 | 여자는 원래 오후에 미용실에 갈 예정이었으나, 미용실 예약을 다음날로 변경하고 남자와 같이 영화를 보러 가기로 했다.

3 정답 ②

남: 이 샐러드는 신선하고 맛있어 보이네요.
여: 네. 우리는 샐러드의 채소와 과일을 모두 직접 기르거든요.
남: 그렇군요. 이 리코타 치즈 샐러드는 얼마인가요?
여: 큰 샐러드는 각각 9달러, 작은 것은 각각 7달러입니다.
남: 음, 아주 비싼 것 같네요.
여: 치즈가 집에서 만든 것이라서요. 건강에 매우 좋아요.
남: 알았어요. 큰 거 하나 주세요. 그리고 감자 샐러드도 좋아 보이네요.
여: 네, 유기농이랍니다. 각각 6달러예요.
남: 흠… 감자 샐러드 세 개요. 이 소스는 얼마죠?
여: 한 병에 3달러입니다.
남: 좋아요. 한 병 살게요. 이게 다인 것 같군요. 아, 제게 10% 쿠폰이 있어요. 사용해도 되지요?
여: 물론입니다.

어휘 | grow 기르다 homemade 집에서 만든, 수제의 organic 유기농의

문제해설 | 남자는 리코타 치즈 샐러드 큰 것 하나($9), 감자 샐러드 세 개($6×3), 소스 한 병($3)을 샀고, 마지막에 10% 쿠폰을 사용했으므로, 남자가 지불할 금액은 27달러이다.

4 정답 ⑤

여: 당신 출장 준비는 다 한 거예요, George?
남: 음, 짐은 거의 다 쌌어요. 그런데 뭔가 잊은 것 같아요.
여: 생각해 봐요. [잠시 후] 당신 여권이랑 티켓은 챙겼나요?
남: 네, 난 그것들을 다른 가방에 넣었어요. 아, 이제 기억나요. 당신 지금 컴퓨터를 하고 있나요?
여: 네, 여보. 난 Jenny한테 이메일을 보내는 중이에요.
남: 내 출장 일정을 대신 출력해 줄 수 있나요?
여: 물론이죠. 그 일정을 어디에서 찾으면 되죠?
남: 내가 그걸 바탕화면에 저장해 뒀어요.
여: 알겠어요. 아, 이번에는 당신 노트북을 챙기는 걸 잊지 말아요.
남: 그건 이미 챙겼어요. 그럼 이제 갈 준비가 됐네요.

어휘 | business trip 출장 pack (짐을) 싸다 passport 여권 separate 별도의 desktop 탁상용 컴퓨터; *바탕화면(컴퓨터 작동 후의 화면) laptop 노트북

문제해설 | 남자는 여자에게 자신의 출장 일정을 출력해 달라고 부탁했다.

5 정답 ②

남: 안녕하세요. 어떻게 도와 드릴까요?
여: 제 차를 멈출 때마다 삐걱거리는 소리가 들려요.
남: 그거 심각할 수도 있겠군요. 오래된 차인가요?
여: 아니요. 산지 1년이 조금 넘었어요.
남: 무엇이 그런 소리를 내는 건지 확인하러 브레이크를 살펴봐야겠습니다.
여: 오늘 오후에 하실 시간이 있나요?
남: 물론이죠. 30분쯤 후에 시작할 수 있어요. 기다리시겠어요?
여: 물론이에요. 전 오후 내내 한가해요.
남: 알겠습니다. 이 서류 좀 작성해 주시고 키는 저에게 주세요.

여: 제가 빌릴 수 있는 펜이 있나요?
남: 여기 있습니다. 그리고 대기실에서 커피를 편하게 드세요.

어휘 | grinding 삐걱거리는 inspect 조사하다 brake 브레이크, 제동장치 cause …의 원인이 되다, 일으키다 fill out a form 용지에 써넣다, 서식에 기입하다 waiting area 대기실

문제해설 | 여자는 자동차에서 이상한 소리가 난다고 하고, 남자는 브레이크를 살펴보겠다고 하므로 자동차 수리공과 차 주인 간의 대화임을 알수 있다.

6 정답 ④

남: 도와 드릴까요?
여: 안녕하세요. 저는 Diana Dunstet이에요. 저의 지역 자원봉사 장학금 신청이 거부되었다는 이메일을 받았는데, 이유가 설명되어 있지 않아서요.
남: 음… 제때에 신청하셨나요?
여: 네. 필요한 성적 평균이 적어도 B는 되어야 한다는 것도 아는데, 제 성적은 A예요!
남: 네, 여기 그렇게 되어 있네요. 또 지역 봉사 활동을 적어도 100시간 해야 하는데, 그렇게 했군요.
여: 맞아요! 저는 동물 보호소에서 토요일마다 일을 도왔어요. 그밖에 다른 것이 있나요?
남: 지역 주민으로 1년 이상 거주 중이어야 해요.
여: 아, 이런! (장학금) 프로그램의 요건을 읽으면서 제가 그걸 놓친게 틀림없어요.
남: 음, 좋은 소식은 다음 학기에는 자격이 된다는 거예요.
여: 다행이네요! 꼭 그때 다시 신청할 거예요. 정보 감사합니다.

어휘 | scholarship 장학금 application 지원, 신청 reject 거부하다 on time 정각에 required 필수의, 요구되는 shelter 보호소, 쉼터 resident 거주민 requirement 필요조건, 요건 eligible (…할) 자격이 있는 relief 안도, 안심 definitely 틀림없이

문제해설 | 장학금을 받으려면 지역에서의 거주 기간이 1년 이상이 되어야 하는데, 여자는 그 요건을 충족시키지 못했다.

7 정답 ③

남: 이번 봄에, 채널 5에서는 회당 한 시간씩 총 8부작의 Brenda Stone의 새로운 쇼, 〈Tough Love〉를 방영합니다. 그것은 2월 15일 일요일 저녁 8시에 시작합니다. 이 새로운 시리즈는 왜 자신이 아직 미혼인지를 이해할 수 없는 세상의 모든 정말 멋진 남성들을 위한 것입니다. 쇼에서는, 뉴욕의 결혼 중매인인 Brenda Stone이 미혼 남성들에게 여성들이 무엇을 생각하고 느끼는지에 관해 가르쳐 줍니다. 그녀는 또한 그들에게 데이트를 할 때, 왜 그들이 여자들을 감동시키지 못하는지에 대해 솔직하게 말해 줍니다. Brenda의 솔직한 조언은 그녀 자신을 미국에서 가장 성공한 결혼 중매인으로 만들어 주었습니다. 그녀는 남성들이 듣고 싶어 하는 것이 아니라, 사랑을 찾기 위해 그들이 들어야만 하는 것을 남성들에게 말해 줄 용기가 있습니다.

어휘 | episode 1회 방송분 series 시리즈, 연속물 matchmaker 결혼 중매인 truthfully 솔직하게 impress 감동시키다 go on a date 데이트를 하다 courage 용기

문제해설 | ③ 새 방송 프로그램에서는 미혼 남성들에게 여성들의 생각과 감정을 가르쳐 준다고 했다.

8 정답 ⑤

[휴대전화가 울린다.]
남: 안녕, 여보. 공항에 무사히 도착했어요?
여: 네. 당신을 일주일이나 혼자 있게 해서 미안해요.
남: 괜찮아요. 출장이니까, 일에만 집중해요.
여: 고마워요. 그런데 너무 급하게 서두르느라 몇 가지 집안일을 끝내지 못했어요.
남: 그게 뭔지 말해주면, 내가 그것들을 처리할게요.
여: 좋아요. 먼저, 설거지를 하는 걸 잊은 것 같아요.
남: 그렇네요. 싱크대에 접시들이 많아요.
여: 그리고 쓰레기를 버려줘요. 쓰레기통이 이미 꽉 찼어요.
남: 아, 맞아요. 내가 더 일찍 버리려고 했는데.
여: 할 수 있으면 탁자도 정돈해 줘요. 너무 지저분해요.
남: 알았어요.
여: 또 베란다 문도 닫아줘요. 오늘 밤에 비가 온다고 했거든요.
남: 걱정하지 말아요. 전부 다 처리할 수 있어요. 그나저나, 베란다에서 빨래들을 걷어야 하나요?
여: 아뇨, 그건 제가 벌써 했으니 당신은 걱정할 필요 없어요.

어휘 | in a rush 급하게, 서둘러 household chores 가사일 handle 다루다, 처리하다 straighten up 정돈하다, 치우다 messy 지저분한 veranda 베란다 bring in …을 들여오다 laundry 세탁물

문제해설 | 여자가 이미 빨래를 걷었다고 했으므로, 대화의 내용과 일치하지 않는 것은 ⑤번이다.

9 정답 ③   10 정답 ⑤

여: 여러분 안녕하세요. Northeast 마케팅 협회의 연례 회의에 오신 것을 환영합니다. 연구 결과 온라인 쇼핑이 고객들이 식료품에 쓰는 금액을 감소시키고 있습니다. 오늘 저는 더 많은 고객들이 여러분의 매장을 방문하게 하는 데 도움이 될 만한 제안을 몇 가지 드리고자 합니다. 모든 매장은 소셜미디어를 이용해야 합니다. 고객들에게 매장 전시 사진을 공유하고 디지털 쿠폰을 제공하세요. 무료 요리 수업 또한 매우 인기 있습니다. 여러분이 매주 또는 매월 요리 또는 제빵 수업을 제공하시는 것을 제안합니다. 고객들은 새로운 조리법을 배우기 위해 여러분의 매장으로 올 것이고, 그들 중 대부분은 그 요리들을 집에서 만들기 위해 여러분의 매장에서 재료를 구매할 것입니다. 또 다른 좋은 전략은 여러분의 매장 곳곳에서 다양한 무료 샘플을 제공하는 것입니다. 제품의 맛을 보면 고객들은 그것을 구매할 가능성이 더 커집니다. 신선하게 요리된 음식의 무료 샘플은 온라인 쇼핑 경험이 아니기 때문에 그것은 또한 고객들에게 여러분의 매장을 방문할 동기를 줍니다.

어휘 | association 협회 annual 연례의 customer 고객, 손님
grocery 《pl.》 식료품류 suggestion 제안(v. suggest) make use
of …을 이용하다 share 공유하다 display 전시, 진열 provide 제
공하다 recipe 조리법 purchase 구매하다 ingredient 재료 dish
요리 strategy 전략 taste 맛보다 incentive 자극, 동기 |문제|
advantage 장점 benefit 이점

문제해설 | 9. 여자는 식료품을 구매하러 매장에 오는 고객을 늘리기 위
해 사용할 수 있는 마케팅 전략에 대해 이야기하고 있다.
① 온라인 쇼핑의 장점
② 무료 샘플 제공의 이점
③ 슈퍼마켓을 위한 마케팅 전략
④ 효과적인 요리 수업을 준비하는 방법
⑤ 고객들이 식료품에 돈을 덜 쓰는 이유
10. 마케팅 전략으로 ⑤ 온라인으로 제품 후기를 보여주기에 대해서는
언급되지 않았다.
① 소셜미디어 이용하기
② 디지털 쿠폰 제공하기
③ 무료 요리 수업 제공하기
④ 무료 샘플 제공하기

DICTATION ANSWER   pp. 16-17

1. worn out / a big sale
2. go bowling / already been released / change my
   appointment
3. fresh and tasty / the cheese is homemade /
   discount coupon
4. pack your passport / print out / don't forget to
5. stop my car / what is causing / fill out this form
6. apply on time / have been a local resident / be
   eligible
7. figure out / what women think and feel / most
   successful matchmaker
8. left you alone / wash the dishes / bring in the
   laundry
9-10. offer some suggestions / a variety of / an
   incentive to visit

04강 실전 모의고사   pp. 18-19

1 ④	2 ①	3 ③	4 ⑤	5 ④
6 ③	7 ④	8 ⑤	9 ⑤	10 ⑤

1 정답 ④

남: 서둘러, Emily. 우리 결혼식에 늦겠어.

여: 알아, 근데 청첩장을 못 찾겠어. 거기에 약도가 있거든.
남: 네 휴대전화로 사진을 찍지 않았니?
여: <u>아, 맞다. 그걸 잊고 있었어!</u>

어휘 | invitation 초대(장)

문제해설 | 남자가 여자에게 휴대전화로 결혼식장의 약도 사진을 찍었는
지 물었으므로, 이에 대한 여자의 응답으로 ④번이 가장 적절하다.
① 난 우선 청첩장을 찾아야 해.
② 난 빨리 결혼식에 가고 싶어.
③ 난 사진 찍을 시간이 없어.
⑤ 난 네 휴대전화가 어디 있는지 몰라.

2 정답 ①

여: 뭘 보고 있니, Tom?
남: 전 세계 사람들이 서로 인사하는 법에 대한 다큐멘터리야.
여: 재미있겠다.
남: 맞아. 너 악수가 고대 그리스인들에 의해 시작되었다는 걸 알고
   있었어?
여: 아니. 그게 정말이야?
남: 응. 그들은 친목, 환대, 그리고 신뢰에 대한 환영의 표시로 그것
   을 사용했어.
여: 그런데 난 그게 고대 이집트의 파라오들에 의해 시작되었다고
   들었어.
남: 그건 또 다른 학설이야. 어쨌든, 대부분의 전문가들은 현대식 악
   수가 중세 유럽에서 시작되었다는 데 동의해.
여: 와, 정말 오래되었네.
남: 응. 왕들과 기사들이 감춰둔 무기를 소지하고 있지 않다는 증거
   로 서로 악수를 하곤 했어.
여: 오! 오늘날엔 그게 좀 더 격의 없는 제스처인 것 같아.
남: 맞아. 대부분의 사람들이 무기를 가지고 다니지 않지만, 그 행위
   는 여전히 두 사람 간의 평화로운 만남을 상징하지.

어휘 | greet 인사하다 ancient 고대의 friendliness 친목, 우정
hospitality 환대 theory 이론, 가설 modern 현대의 medieval 중세
의 knight 기사 extend one's hand 악수를 청하다 demonstration
증거 conceal 숨기다 weapon 무기 casual 격의 없는 symbolize
상징하다

문제해설 | 두 사람은 악수의 기원에 관해 이야기하고 있다.

3 정답 ③

여: 안녕하세요. 주문하시겠어요?
남: 네, 햄버거 하나와 감자튀김을 주세요.
여: 5달러입니다. 그것과 함께 마실 것도 추가하시겠어요?
남: 네. 콜라 한 잔 주세요.
여: 콜라는 1달러예요. 하지만, 세트로 다 추가하면, 콜라를 딱 50
   센트에 드실 수 있으세요.
남: 아, 실은 저는 무료 음료 쿠폰이 있어요.
여: 알겠습니다. 그럼 콜라가 무료입니다. 그 밖에 다른 필요하신 게

있으세요?

남: 음… 샐러드를 곁들이면 얼마인가요?

여: 곁들임용 샐러드는 2달러입니다.

남: 네, 그럼 그거 하나를 주문에 추가할게요.

여: 알겠습니다. 주문하신 것이 바로 준비될 겁니다.

어휘 | add 추가하다 side salad 곁들임용 샐러드

문제해설 | 남자가 주문한 햄버거와 감자튀김은 5달러이고, 콜라는 무료, 곁들임용 샐러드는 2달러이므로, 남자가 지불할 금액은 7달러이다.

4 정답 ⑤

남: 당신의 식물 중 하나를 죽게 한 적이 있는데 이유를 모르셨나요? 많은 사람들이 식물을 살리기에 너무 늦은 순간까지도 그것이 건강하지 않다는 것을 알아차리지 못합니다. 기본적으로 식물은 살아가기 위해 물과 햇빛이 필요합니다. 하지만 어느 것 하나도 너무 많으면 식물을 죽일 수 있습니다. 당신의 식물 잎사귀가 노랗게 변하기 시작하고 흙이 젖어 있으면, 이것은 식물에 물을 지나치게 준다는 표시입니다. 그러면 당신은 물을 주는 횟수를 줄여야 합니다. 선인장류처럼 어떤 식물은 많은 직사광선을 좋아하지만, 다른 식물은 이것을 견딜 수 없습니다. 당신의 식물이 옅어지고 색을 잃는다면, 그것은 아마도 햇빛이 덜 드는 곳으로 옮겨져야 할 겁니다.

어휘 | notice 알아차리다 basically 기본적으로 turn (…의 상태로) 변하다 soil 흙 moist 촉촉한, 젖은 overwater …에 물을 지나치게 주다 decrease 줄이다 water 물을 주다 cacti 선인장류 direct sunlight 직사광선 tolerate 견디다 pale (얼굴이) 창백한; *(색깔이) 엷은, 옅은

문제해설 | 남자는 식물의 잎사귀의 색깔과 흙의 상태를 통해 식물의 건강 상태를 읽는 법과 그에 따라 올바르게 대처하는 방법에 대해 설명하고 있다.

5 정답 ④

여: 안녕하세요. 어떻게 도와 드릴까요?

남: 며칠 더 머물려고 하는데요.

여: 알겠습니다. 체류 기간을 며칠까지 연장하고 싶으신가요?

남: 음, 학회는 5일에 끝나지만, 전 7일까지 머물려고요.

여: 알겠습니다. 손님의 객실 번호와 성함을 말씀해 주세요.

남: 405호이고, 제 이름은 Christopher Hill입니다.

여: 알겠습니다. 제가 예약 상황을 확인해 보겠습니다. [잠시 후] 그렇게 하셔도 되겠네요.

남: 잘됐군요. 아, 그런데, 제 방의 인터넷 연결이 안 되어서요, 내일 회의 전에 이메일을 확인해야 해요.

여: 아, 불편을 끼쳐 죄송합니다. 지금 바로 그걸 고칠 사람을 보내겠습니다. 그 밖에 제가 해 드릴 일이 더 있나요?

남: 아, 네. 깜박할 뻔했네요. 제 세탁물은 다 됐나요?

여: 물론이죠, 제가 바로 가져다 드리겠습니다.

남: 감사합니다.

어휘 | stay 머무르다; 체류 extend 연장하다 conference 회의, 학회 by the way 그런데 inconvenience 불편

문제해설 | 남자는 호텔 투숙 기간을 연장하려는 투숙객이고, 여자는 예약 상황을 확인하고 불편 사항을 점검하는 것으로 보아 호텔 직원임을 알 수 있다.

6 정답 ③

남: Chloe, 한참 찾았어요. 여기서 뭐하고 있어요?

여: 뭘 좀 살까 생각 중이에요.

남: 무선 이어폰이요? 이미 한 쌍이 있잖아요.

여: 아니오, 블루투스 스피커요.

남: 오, 좋아요. 집에서 함께 음악을 들을 수 있겠네요.

여: 맞아요. 판매원이 오기를 기다리고 있어요. 스피커에 대해 물어볼 것이 좀 있거든요.

남: 알겠어요. 그럼, 난 잠깐 운동복 매장을 둘러볼게요.

여: 알겠어요. 하지만 우린 세탁기를 고를 시간이 충분하지 않을까 봐 걱정이에요.

남: 그럼 내가 먼저 가전 코너를 확인할게요. 쇼핑 다 끝나면 내게 전화해요.

여: 알겠어요. 오래 걸리진 않을 거예요.

어휘 | wireless 무선의 earbud 귀 안에 넣는 이어폰 salesperson 판매원 sportswear 운동복 department 부서; *(백화점의) 매장 for a while 잠시 동안 washing machine 세탁기 home appliance 가정용 전기 제품

문제해설 | 여자가 세탁기 살 시간이 부족할 것 같다고 하자 남자는 가전 코너에 가서 확인하겠다고 했다.

7 정답 ④

[전화벨이 울린다.]

남: True Fashion Clothing입니다. 어떻게 도와 드릴까요?

여: 제가 지난주에 웹사이트에서 티셔츠를 주문했는데, 아직도 그것을 못 받았어요.

남: 오. 정확한 주소를 기재하신 게 확실한가요?

여: 네. 확실해요. 그리고 그때 웹사이트에 티셔츠 재고가 없다는 말은 전혀 없었고요.

남: 주문 확인 번호를 가지고 계신가요?

여: 네, K59-001이에요.

남: 알겠습니다. [잠시 후] 컴퓨터 시스템에는 주문이 처리되었다고 나오는데요.

여: 택배 회사가 그것을 창고에서 가져갔나요?

남: 네, 그런데 요즘 주문이 폭주해서 배송이 지연되는 것 같아요.

여: 음… 그럼 언제 그걸 받을 수 있을까요?

남: 금요일까지는 도착할 거예요. 늦어져서 정말 죄송합니다.

어휘 | out of stock 재고가 없는 confirmation 확인 process 처리하다 warehouse 창고 shipment 배송 pour 쏟아져 들어오다

문제해설 | 여자는 주문량 폭주로 인해 배송이 지연되어 상품을 받지 못한 상태이다.

8 정답 ⑤

여: 여러분은 가지를 좋아하세요? 이것은 세계적으로 인기 있는 채소입니다. 이 식물은 원래 인도에서 왔으며 아프리카를 통해 유럽으로 전파되었습니다. 그러나, 많은 사람들이 알지 못하는 것은 15세기 이전에 이 식물은 주로 장식용이었다는 것입니다. 가지가 독성이 있다고 믿었기 때문에 사람들은 그것을 먹기를 두려워했습니다. 가지라는 이름은 1700년대 유럽에서 재배되던 어떤 식물들의 열매로부터 유래되었는데, 그것은 노란색이거나 흰색이었고 거위의 알과 닮았습니다. 비록 어떤 특정한 비타민이나 미네랄이 풍부하지는 않지만, 가지는 지방이 거의 없습니다. 그것은 또한 요리하기가 쉽고 두툼한 질감을 가지고 있어서, 주요리나 파스타와 같은 요리의 첨가물로서 훌륭합니다. 오늘 저녁으로 가지를 드시는 것은 어떠신가요?

어휘 | eggplant 가지 originally 원래 ornamental 장식용의 poisonous 독이 있는 originate 유래하다 resemble (…와) 닮다 goose 거위 fat 지방 texture 질감 addition 추가된 것, 부가물

문제해설 | ⑤ 가지에는 특정 비타민과 미네랄이 풍부하지 않다고 했다.

9 정답 ⑤   10 정답 ⑤

남: 안녕하세요, 여러분. Georgia 고등학교 연례 축제에 와 주셔서 감사합니다. 많은 분들이 학교 밴드의 공연으로 축제가 시작되길 기대하고 있는 것으로 알고 있습니다. 유감스럽게도, 그 밴드가 현재 심한 교통 체증으로 꼼짝 못 하고 있습니다. 그래서 저희는 그들의 공연을 오후 2시로 미뤘습니다. 대신, 축제는 학교 댄스 동아리의 멋진 브레이크 댄스 공연으로 막을 열겠습니다. 그 후에, 여러분이 놓치고 싶지 않을 연극 동아리의 단막극이 있을 예정입니다. 오후 1시에 여러분은 퀴즈 대회에 참여할 수 있는데, 분명 굉장히 재미있을 겁니다. 우승자는 Shrimp City 상품권도 받게 됩니다. 1시간 후에는 밴드가 공연할 준비가 될 것입니다. 또한 학교 여기저기에 마련된 부스들을 방문하는 것도 잊지 마세요. 여러분 모두가 축제를 즐기길 바랍니다. 그리고 모금한 모든 수익금은 우리 시의 노숙자들을 돕는 데 쓰인다는 것을 기억해주세요!

어휘 | performance 공연(v. perform) stuck in traffic 교통이 정체 된 push back (시간을) 미루다 gift certificate 상품권 arrange 마련하다 raise (돈을) 모으다 the homeless 노숙자들 |문제| cancellation 취소 postpone (일정을) 미루다, 연기하다 bazaar 바자회

문제해설 | 9. 남자는 공연을 하기로 한 밴드가 교통 체증으로 늦어지면서 축제 일정이 변경되었다며 이를 공지하고 있다.
① 행사 취소
② 학교 축제가 연기되는 이유
③ 학교 동아리와 활동의 종류
④ 지역 밴드 후원을 위한 모금
⑤ 일정 변경에 대한 정보
10. 축제 일정으로 ⑤ 바자회에 대해서는 언급되지 않았다.
① 밴드 공연 ② 브레이크 댄스 공연 ③ 단막극 ④ 퀴즈 대회

05강 실전 모의고사   pp. 22-23

| 1 ④ | 2 ② | 3 ③ | 4 ⑤ | 5 ② |
| 6 ⑤ | 7 ⑤ | 8 ③ | 9 ④ | 10 ④ |

1 정답 ④

남: 새해가 다가오고 있어!
여: 응, 새해를 맞이해서 정말 신이 나.
남: 새해 결심은 세웠니?
여: 응, 난 드럼 치는 법을 배울 계획이야.

어휘 | greet 맞다, 환영하다 resolution 결심, 계획 |문제| observe 관찰하다; *(의식·관습 등을) 지키다 lunar 달의; *음력의

문제해설 | 새해를 맞이하여 새해 결심을 묻는 남자의 말에 대한 여자의 응답으로 ④번이 가장 적절하다.
① 너도 새해 복 많이 받아!
② 난 음력 설을 쇠는걸.
③ 아니, 난 어떤 문제도 풀지 못했어.
⑤ 응, 난 새해 전날에 가족과 만나서 저녁 식사를 해.

2 정답 ②

여: Harry, 너 Claire의 생일 파티에 초대받았니?

남: 응. 난 그녀에게 줄 향초를 샀어. 넌 파티에 뭘 가져갈 거야?
여: 사실, 난 아직 결정 못했어.
남: 내가 추천해 줄까?

어휘 | invitation 초대 aroma 향기, 방향 |문제| suggestion 제안, 추천 throw a party 파티를 열다

문제해설 | 여자가 생일 파티에 가져갈 것을 결정하지 못했다고 했으므로, 이에 대한 남자의 응답으로 ②번이 가장 적절하다.
① 그게 방에서 정말 좋은 냄새가 나게 할 거야.
③ 난 생일 선물로 기타를 받았어.
④ 파티를 함께 준비하는 게 어때?
⑤ 우리가 어디서 파티를 열어야 할지 못 정하겠어.

3 정답 ③

남: 공원에서 걷기에 아주 좋은 날이야. 오, 저 새의 화려한 색 좀 봐.
여: 와, 정말 아름답다. 오늘 여기 새들이 정말 많고, 아주 큰 소리로 노래하고 있네.
남: 새들이 노래하는 걸 들으니 참 좋다. 근데 넌 새가 왜 노래하는지 아니?
여: 기분을 표현하기 위한 건가?
남: 아니. 사실 수컷 새들은 주로 암컷을 유인하기 위해 노래를 불러. 그건 중요한 짝짓기 의식이야.
여: 암컷은 어느 수컷을 고를지 어떻게 결정해?
남: 노래를 가장 많이 하는 새를 고르지.
여: 수컷이 노래하는 것에 감동해서인 거야?
남: 아니. 사실 노래는 수컷이 먹이를 많이 가지고 있고 좋은 짝이 될 거라는 걸 보여주거든.
여: 이해가 안 돼. 노래가 어떻게 먹이랑 연관이 돼?
남: 음, 새가 노래를 많이 한다면, 그건 먹이를 찾는 데 많은 시간을 쓰지 않아도 된다는 의미잖아.
여: 아, 그렇구나. 정말 재미있네.

어휘 | male 남자의, 수컷의(↔ female) attract 유인하다 mating ritual 짝짓기 의식 mate 짝; 짝짓기하다 connected to …와 관련 있는 search for …을 찾다

문제해설 | 두 사람은 새가 노래하는 이유에 관해 이야기하고 있다.

4 정답 ⑤

여: 아빠, 이렇게 멋진 저녁을 사 주셔서 감사해요!
남: 넌 그걸 누릴 자격이 있어! 그리고 네가 열어 볼 다른 선물이 또 있단다.
여: 다른 선물이요? 믿을 수가 없어요!
남: 여기 있다! 졸업을 축하한다!
여: 감사해요! 이 봉투에 뭐가 들어있는지 궁금해요. [잠시 후] 와, 뮤지컬 표네요!
남: 음, 네가 뮤지컬을 좋아하는 걸 알고 있어. 그리고 그게 요즘 가장 인기 있는 거라고 들었어.

여: 맞아요. 이거 보고 싶었는데, 너무 비싸서 볼 수가 없었어요.
남: 잘됐네. 가장 친한 친구와 함께 가는 게 어떠니? 표가 두 장이야.
여: 더 좋은 생각이 있어요. 우리 그걸 함께 보는 게 어때요? 그게 저에게는 더 의미가 있을 것 같아요.
남: 정말 사려 깊구나! 고맙다, 얘야.
여: 천만에요. 아빠가 최고예요!

어휘 | fabulous 굉장한, 멋진 deserve (…을) 누릴 자격이 있다 graduate 졸업하다 wonder 궁금하다 envelope 봉투 meaningful 의미 있는 considerate 사려 깊은

문제해설 | 여자가 남자에게 함께 뮤지컬을 보러 가자고 했으므로, 남자는 여자를 위해 뮤지컬을 보러 함께 갈 것이다.

5 정답 ②

남: 안녕하세요? 무엇을 도와 드릴까요?
여: 네, 전 여기 새 회원인데 운동 강좌를 좀 신청하고 싶어요.
남: 좋은 생각입니다. 현재 요가 강좌와 에어로빅 강좌가 있어요.
여: 요가가 좋겠어요. 그 강좌는 얼마나 자주 있나요?
남: 주 3일 수업하는 반이 하나 있고, 주 5일 수업하는 또 다른 반이 있어요.
여: 비용은 얼마인가요?
남: 주 5일반은 한 달에 120달러이고, 주 3일반은 20달러가 더 싸요.
여: 좋아요. 전 주 3일 수업하는 선택할게요.
남: 그리고 석 달 치를 다 등록하시면, 10퍼센트 할인을 받을 수 있습니다.
여: 좋은 조건인 것 같네요. 바로 그렇게 할게요.

어휘 | sign up for …을 신청하다 option 선택 사항 deal 거래

문제해설 | 여자는 주 3일 수업 석 달 치를 등록하겠다고 했다. 주 3일 수업은 주 5일 수업보다 20달러가 저렴한데($100), 석 달 치를 한꺼번에 등록하면 10퍼센트 할인을 받으므로, 여자는 270달러를 지불하면 된다.

6 정답 ⑤

여: 우리는 이 근처를 한 시간 넘게 돌고 있어.
남: 이해가 안 돼. 캠프장이 분명히 이 근처 어딘가에 있는데.
여: 음. 내비게이션 시스템을 켜는 건 어때?
남: 안타깝게도, 그건 고장 났어. 아, 캠프장은 이 길 아래인 것 같아.
여: 너 농담하니? 우리 아까 저 길을 따라 갔었잖아. 내 생각엔 우린 누군가에게 도움을 요청해야 할 것 같아.
남: 잠깐만. 분명히 찾을 수 있을 것 같은데…
여: 설상가상으로, 우린 기름이 거의 다 떨어졌어.
남: 저런! 주유소에 잠시 들러서 차에 기름을 가득 넣자.
여: 정말 그래야만 해. 그리고 그곳에서 길을 물어볼 수 있겠다.
남: 좋은 생각이야! 내가 길을 묻는 동안 넌 물 한 병을 사다 줄래?

여: 물론이지.

어휘 | campsite 야영지, 캠프장 definitely 확실히 to make things worse 설상가상으로 out of gas 휘발유가 다 떨어진 stop off …에 잠시 들르다 fill up …을 가득 채우다 direction 방향

문제해설 | 남자는 여자에게 자신이 주유소 직원에게 길을 묻는 동안 물 한 병을 사다 줄 것을 부탁했다.

7 정답 ⑤

남: 실례합니다, 부인. 뭘 하고 계시죠?
여: 오, 이런! 깜짝 놀랐어요. 주차장에 다른 사람이 있는지 몰랐네요.
남: 저는 여기에서 야간 근무 시간에 차들을 지켜봐요. 그런데, 뭘 하고 계셨어요?
여: 차에 열쇠를 꽂아 놓고 잠가버렸어요. 창문으로 손을 넣어 문을 열려고 하고 있었어요.
남: 그렇군요. 이게 당신 차인가요?
여: 음, 아뇨. 이건 회사차예요. 저는 Business Limousine Service라는 회사에서 일해요.
남: 알겠습니다. 제가 도와드릴 수 있는데, 그 전에 신분증을 볼 수 있을까요?
여: 네. 여기 있어요. 저는 마케팅팀에 소속되어 있어요.
남: [잠시 후] 네. 잠시만 여기서 기다리세요. 사무실에서 보조 열쇠를 가지고 올게요.
여: 도와주셔서 감사해요.

어휘 | scare 겁주다, 놀라게 하다 garage 주차장, 차고 keep an eye on …을 계속 지켜보다 night shift 야간 근무 unlock 열다 belong to …에 속하다 extra 여분의, 추가의

문제해설 | 남자가 주차장에서 차들을 지켜보는 일을 하고, 열쇠를 꽂아 둔 채 차 문을 잠근 여직원을 위해 보조 열쇠를 가지고 온다고 하는 것으로 보아 경비원과 직원 간의 대화임을 알 수 있다.

8 정답 ③

여: 안녕하세요, 손님. 어떻게 도와 드릴까요?
남: 내일 저녁 Chicago행 열차를 타야 하는데요. 시간표를 볼 수 있을까요?
여: 물론이죠, 손님. 여기 주말 시간표가 있습니다.
남: 고맙습니다. 약속이 8시라서, 한 시간쯤 일찍 그곳에 도착하고 싶어요.
여: 알겠습니다. 이 급행열차를 타시면 정시에 그곳에 도착하실 거예요.
남: 네, 그런데 15달러는 편도 승차권으로는 너무 비싸네요.
여: 그렇다면, 완행열차를 타시는 게 어떠세요? 이 열차라면 손님 일정에 맞을 거예요.
남: 네, 저도 그렇게 생각해요. 그런데 왜 급행열차 213호는 다른 열차들보다 더 저렴하죠?
여: 그 열차는 저희의 가장 혼잡한 시간대 전에 운행해서 가격이 더

저렴합니다.
남: 그렇군요. 그런데 그걸 타고 가면 그곳에 너무 일찍 도착하네요. 저는 이 완행열차로 할게요.
여: 알겠습니다, 손님. 여기 표가 있습니다.

어휘 | appointment 약속 express train 급행열차 one-way 편도의 local train 보통[완행]열차 fit 맞다, 적절하다 peak 절정; *최고조의 rush-hour (출퇴근) 혼잡 시간대의 period 기간, 시기

문제해설 | 남자는 약속 시각(8시) 한 시간 전쯤(7시)에 도착하기를 원하고, 15달러의 급행열차 티켓은 너무 비싸서 완행열차를 타고 가겠다고 했으므로, ③번 열차표를 구매할 것이다.

9 정답 ④ 10 정답 ④

여: 세계 어디를 가든지, 여러분은 다양한 질병을 위한 민간요법을 발견하게 될 것입니다. 그것들이 모두 의학적으로 증명되지는 않았지만, 이런 요법은 온갖 종류의 문제를 치료하는 데 오랫동안 사용되었습니다. 예를 들어, 닭고기 수프는 미국에서 보편적인 감기 치료 요법입니다. 한 연구에서 그것이 실제로 호흡기 질환의 증상을 완화하는 데 효과적이라는 것이 증명되었습니다. 그러나, 일본에서 감기는 생강차로 치료됩니다. 이것은 혈액의 순환을 활발하게 해서, 몸이 더 빨리 회복되도록 도와줍니다. 중국에서 두통이 생기면, 누군가가 머리, 얼굴, 그리고 목을 따뜻한 막 삶은 달걀로 문지르는 전통적인 달걀 문지르기를 추천할 겁니다. 독일에서, 화상은 때때로 사과 식초로 치료됩니다. 식초는 또한 러시아와 우크라이나에서 열병 증상을 완화하기 위해 보편적으로 쓰입니다. 이 방법은 면으로 된 시트를 식초와 물을 섞은 것에 적셔서, 그것을 아픈 사람의 몸을 구석구석 닦는 데 사용하는 것을 포함합니다.

어휘 | remedy 치료(약), 요법 illness 병(a. ill) medically 의학적으로 prove 증명하다 symptom 증상 respiratory 호흡기의 ginger tea 생강차 stimulate 자극하다; *활발하게 하다 circulation 순환 rub 문지르기; 문지르다 sunburn 화상 apple cider vinegar 사과 식초 relieve 완화시키다 fever 열, 열병 soak 적시다 cotton 면 bed sheet 시트, (침대에) 까는 천 mixture 혼합물 wipe down …을 구석구석 닦다 |문제| misconception 오해 concern 우려, 걱정

문제해설 | 9. 여자는 미국, 일본, 중국, 독일 등에서 널리 쓰이는 민간요법에 대해 이야기하고 있다.
① 민간요법에 대한 오해들
② 민간요법이 널리 쓰이는 이유들
③ 민간요법에 대한 늘어난 염려들
④ 다양한 국가에서 쓰이는 민간요법
⑤ 민간요법이 현대 의학에 미치는 영향
10. 사과 식초는 독일에서 민간요법으로 쓰인다고 했지만, ④ 사과 주스는 언급되지 않았다.
① 닭고기 수프 ② 생강차 ③ 달걀 ⑤ 식초

1. is coming up / a New Year's resolution
2. get the invitation / I haven't decided yet
3. why they sing / to attract females / connected to food
4. You deserve it / tickets to a musical / more meaningful to me
5. do those classes meet / costs $120 per month / a good deal
6. turn on your navigation / To make things worse / fill the car up with
7. keep an eye on / locked my keys in the car / get the extra key
8. about an hour earlier / fits your schedule / cheaper than the others
9-10. a common cold remedy / treated with ginger tea / to relieve fever symptoms

06강 실전 모의고사   pp. 26-27

| 1 ① | 2 ⑤ | 3 ① | 4 ④ | 5 ⑤ |
| 6 ① | 7 ③ | 8 ⑤ | 9 ① | 10 ③ |

1 정답 ①

남: 소풍 갈 준비 되었어?
여: 되었는데, 공기 중에 미세먼지가 너무 많아.
남: 그러네. 그걸 들이마시면 안 되지만, 우리 계획을 취소하고 싶진 않아.
여: <u>그러면 우리는 마스크를 쓰는 게 좋겠어.</u>

어휘 | fine dust 미세먼지 breathe in …을 들이마시다 cancel 취소하다

문제해설 | 소풍 갈 계획을 취소하지 않으면서 미세먼지를 들이마시지 않게 하자는 남자의 말에 대한 여자의 응답으로 ①번이 가장 적절하다.
② 비가 금방 그쳤으면 좋겠다.
③ 나도 동의해. 집에 있자.
④ 우리는 먹을 게 너무 많아.
⑤ 우리는 그것을 걱정하지 않아도 돼.

2 정답 ⑤

남: Sally, 너 뭐 하고 있니?
여: 부모님 결혼기념일에 딱 맞는 선물을 찾고 있어.
남: 그냥 작년처럼 부모님을 위한 파티를 여는 건 어때?
여: 아니야, 그건 너무 뻔하잖아. 올해는 뭔가 특별한 걸 하고 싶어.
남: 그럼 부모님을 위한 반지를 만드는 건 어때? 내 여동생이 남자친구를 위해 그걸 하고 있거든.
여: 오, 좋은 생각이야. 그런데 내가 그걸 할 수 있을지 모르겠어.
남: 걱정하지 마. 몇몇 가게에서 그런 종류의 수업을 제공한다고 들었어. 인터넷에서 찾아보면 돼.
여: 난 온라인에서 검색하는 데 서툴러. 너 혹시 좋은 곳 알아?
남: 음, 난 모르지만, 내 여동생은 분명 알 거야. 그 애에게 전화해서 물어볼게.
여: 고마워. 부모님은 내 선물에 감동하실 거야.
남: 확실히 그럴 거야. 손수 만든 선물에는 특별한 게 있으니까.

어휘 | anniversary 기념일 throw a party 파티를 열다 predictable 예상할 수 있는 look up 찾아보다 happen to-v 우연히[혹시] …하다 impressed 감동한 handmade 손으로 만든

문제해설 | 남자는 여동생에게 전화해서 반지를 직접 만드는 수업을 제공하는 가게를 아는지 물어볼 것이다.

3 정답 ①

남: 안녕하세요. 건전지 있나요? 못 찾겠네요.
여: 아, 우리는 건전지를 모두 계산대 뒤에 둬요. 어떤 종류가 필요하세요?
남: 그냥 리모컨에 넣을 표준 AAA 건전지요.
여: 네. 그것들은 두 개로 묶인 팩으로 나와요. 팩 하나에 2달러 50센트예요.
남: 음, 사실 제 리모컨은 건전지가 세 개 필요해요.
여: 10개짜리 팩도 있어요. 그건 하나에 10달러예요.
남: 그렇게 많은 건전지는 필요하지 않아요. 그냥 작은 팩 두 개를 주세요.
여: 네, 손님. 회원 카드가 있으세요? 회원 카드가 있다면 10% 할인을 받으실 수 있어요.
남: 네, 있긴 한데 집에 놓고 왔네요.
여: 괜찮아요. 전화번호만 말씀해 주세요.
남: 알겠습니다.

어휘 | counter 계산대 standard 표준의 remote control 리모컨

문제해설 | 남자는 2달러 50센트인 작은 건전지 팩을 두 개($2.5×2) 사려고 하는데, 10% 할인이 되므로, 4달러 50센트를 지불하면 된다.

4 정답 ④

여: 안녕하세요, 여러분. 저희의 신형 노트북 출시와 관련하여 안내 말씀을 드리고자 합니다. 모두 아실 줄 알지만, 이것은 정말 혁신적인 제품이며, 저는 그것을 개발하는 데 들인 모든 노력이 정말 자랑스럽습니다. 유감스럽게도, 사소한 몇몇 기술적인 결함 때문에 제품 출시를 한 달 늦추어야 합니다. 예정된 출시 날짜는 더 이상 10월 10일이 아니고, 11월 10일입니다. 제품이 최고의 품질기준을 충족시키기 위해서 이 추가 시간이 필요합니다. 저는 이 작은 문제들이 빨리 해결되고, 저희의 신형 노트북이 큰 성공을 거둘 거라고 믿습니다. 시간을 내 들어주셔서 감사합니다.

어휘 | regarding (…에) 관하여 release 출시 revolutionary 혁명적인 go into (돈·시간·노력 등이) 투입되다, 쓰이다 develop 개발하다 minor 사소한, 작은 delay 늦추다 issue 문제 resolve 해결하다

문제해설 | 여자는 기술적인 결함으로 인해 신형 노트북의 출시가 한 달 지연된다고 이야기하고 있다.

5 정답 ⑤

남: 안녕하세요, Smith 교수님. 말씀 좀 나눌 수 있을까요?
여: 그럼, Justin. 자리에 앉으렴.
남: 감사합니다. 생물 강좌 과목의 성적을 봤어요.
여: 그래, 내가 오늘 아침에 성적을 올렸지.
남: 솔직히, 아주 실망했어요.
여: 넌 네가 더 좋은 성적을 받을 줄 알았구나?
남: 네. 전 시험을 잘 봤고, 보고서도 좋은 점수를 받았어요.
여: 그래, 하지만 성적은 그 외의 것에도 근거해 매겨졌단다.
남: 네, 그런데 전 출석도 완벽했고, 태도도 좋았어요.
여: 실은, 네 조원들에게 부정적인 평가를 받았다. 그들은 네가 충분히 적극적이지 않았다고 했어. 그것이 네 성적에 영향을 끼쳤단다.
남: 조별 활동이 성적에 포함되는지 몰랐어요.
여: 학생들은 조별 활동에서 적극적인 역할을 해야만 좋은 성적을 받을 수 있어.
남: 네. 알겠습니다.

어휘 | biology 생물학 post 게시하다, 올리다 be based on …에 기초하다[근거하다] attendance 출석 attitude 태도 negative 부정적인 active 적극적인 influence (…에) 영향을 미치다 count toward …에 포함되다[가산되다]

문제해설 | 남자는 조별 활동에서 소극적이어서 남자가 생각한 것보다 낮은 성적을 받았다.

6 정답 ①

여: 안녕하세요, 선생님. 도와 드릴까요?
남: 네, 제 허리를 삔 것 같아요. 척추에 찌르는 듯한 통증이 있어요.
여: 무슨 일이 있었나요? 넘어지셨나요?
남: 아니요, 무거운 가구를 좀 옮기다가 다쳤어요. 제가 새 아파트로 막 이사했거든요.
여: 음, 등에 이 파스를 붙이세요. 그게 근육을 진정시켜줄 거예요. 그리고 이 약도 드셔야 합니다.
남: 그것을 얼마나 자주 복용해야 하나요?
여: 매 식후 30분에 한 알을 드셔야 해요.
남: 정말 감사합니다. 이것들이 효과가 있으면 좋겠네요.
여: 그것들이 분명 당분간 환자분의 상태가 나아지게 도와줄 거예요. 하지만 통증이 계속되면 병원에 가시는 게 나아요.
남: 네, 감사합니다.

어휘 | back 등, 허리 pain 고통 spine 척추 injure 부상을 입히다[입다] pain relief patch 파스 soothe 진정시키다 muscle 근육 tablet 알약 for now 우선은, 현재로는, 당분간은 persist 계속되다

문제해설 | 허리를 삔 남자에게 여자가 파스와 약을 주고, 통증이 계속되면 병원에 가라고 조언하는 것으로 보아 약사와 손님 간의 대화임을 알 수 있다.

7 정답 ③

남: 안녕하세요. 저는 여러분에게 저희 반이 참여했던 '열대 우림을 위해 일어나라.'라는 최근의 행사에 대해 말씀드리고 싶습니다. 그 행사는 저희 지리학 선생님의 생각이었습니다. 선생님은 멸종 위기에 처한 생태계에 대한 수업이 우리에게 정말로 어떤 의미를 주기를 원하셨습니다. 그래서, 선생님은 각각의 학생들에게 열대 우림에서 발견되는 희귀한 동식물의 종(種)을 조사하도록 하셨습니다. 그리고 나서, 우리 각자는 반 학생들에게 간단한 발표를 했습니다. 그 다음에, 우리는 세계의 열대 우림의 멸종 위기에 처한 생태계에 관해 몇 편의 다큐멘터리를 봤습니다. 그러고 나서, 우리는 사람들에게 열대 우림이 입고 있는 피해를 알려주는 포스터들을 디자인했습니다. 우리는 그것들을 스캔해서 모든 사람들이 볼 수 있도록 우리 학교 웹사이트에 올렸습니다. 그것은 정말 멋진 행사였고, 우리는 많은 것을 배웠습니다.

어휘 | take part in …에 참여[참가]하다 rainforest 열대 우림 geography 지리학 endangered 멸종 위기에 처한 ecosystem 생태계 rare 희귀한 species 종(種) inform A of B A에게 B를 알리다

문제해설 | ③ 학생들은 다큐멘터리를 제작한 것이 아니라 시청했다.

8 정답 ⑤

[전화벨이 울린다.]
여: 여보세요?
남: 안녕하세요, Susan. 저 Mark예요. 가벼운 차 사고가 나서 스튜디오에 늦을 것 같아요.
여: 오, 이런! 괜찮으세요?
남: 네, 전 괜찮아요. 단지 촬영 준비가 모두 되었는지 확인하고 싶어서요.
여: 네. 음, 제가 방금 방 한가운데에 정사각형 탁자랑 그 주위에 의자 4개를 놓아두었어요.
남: 잘했어요. 창문 앞에 체크무늬 커튼을 묶었나요?
여: 네. 벽에 그 프라이팬들도 걸었어요.
남: 좋아요. 누군가가 천장에 샹들리에를 걸었나요?
여: 네. 모두 처리했어요. 그리고 둥근 사진 액자는 왼쪽 벽에 걸려 있고요.
남: 훌륭해요. 다 된 것 같네요. 전 아마 한 시간쯤 뒤에 스튜디오에 도착할 거예요.
여: 알겠어요. 곧 봬요.

어휘 | minor 가벼운, 심각하지 않은 confirm 확인하다 filming 촬영 checkered 체크무늬의 tie back 끈으로 고정시키다 chandelier 샹들리에 ceiling 천장 take care of …을 처리하다[해결하다]

문제해설 | 왼쪽 벽에는 둥근 사진 액자가 걸려 있다고 했으므로, 대화의 내용과 일치하지 않는 것은 ⑤번이다.

9 정답 ①

여: 안녕, Marcus. 영어 수업 과제물 끝냈어?
남: 아직. 하고 있는데, 내 글이 너무 짧아.
여: Alden 선생님께서 수업 중에 제안하신 대로 주제를 써서 시작했니?
남: 그렇게 했어. 내 주제는 아주 좋은 것 같아.
여: 단락을 몇 개 썼어?
남: 세 개. 서론, 본론, 결론으로 말이야.
여: 너는 본론을 두 단락 더 써야 할 것 같은데. 그러면 네 글을 더 길고 효과적으로 만들 수 있을 거야.
남: 본론을 세 단락으로? 어떻게 그렇게 할 수 있지?
여: 네 주제를 뒷받침하는 세 개의 화제를 골라야 해.
남: 그리고 각 화제마다 본문 한 단락을 쓰는 거야?
여: 맞아. 각 화제마다 한 단락을 써 봐. 주제 안의 네 의견을 각각의 화제가 어떻게 뒷받침하는지 설명해.
남: 그거 좋은 방법이다. 그렇게 해 볼게.

어휘 | essay 글, 과제물 thesis 논지, 주제 paragraph 단락 introduction 소개; *서론 body 몸; 중심부; *본문 conclusion 결론 support 지지하다; *뒷받침하다 method 방법

문제해설 | 과제로 작성한 글이 너무 짧아 고민인 남자에게 여자는 주제를 뒷받침하는 본문 단락을 더 늘리라고 조언하고 있다.

10 정답 ③

남: 자, 우리의 유럽 여행에 대한 내 계획에 대해 어떻게 생각해?
여: 파리, 로마, 그리고 빈은 탁월한 선택이라는 데 동의해.
남: 좋아! 그 계획에서 바꾸고 싶은 게 있니?
여: 음, 난 그 목록에 런던을 추가하고 싶어. 난 그곳에 정말 가고 싶거든.
남: 하지만 그럼 우리 여행이 더 길어지고 비용도 늘어나게 될 걸.
여: 알아, 하지만 난 거기에 정말 방문하고 싶은 친구들이 몇 명 있어. 우리는 그들의 집에 머물 수 있어.
남: 아, 정말? 그럼 확실히 돈을 좀 절약할 수 있겠다.
여: 식비도 줄일 수 있을 것 같아.
남: 알겠어. 그게 네가 정말로 원하는 거라면, 난 좋아.
여: 좋아. 내 친구들에게 우리가 집에 방문해도 되는지 물어볼게.

어휘 | cut down (비용을) 줄이다

문제해설 | 여자는 런던에 사는 친구 집에 머물면 숙박료와 식비를 줄일 수 있다고 남자를 설득했고, 남자가 이를 받아들였으므로, 이에 대한 여자의 응답으로 ③번이 가장 적절하다.
① 넌 나에게 훨씬 더 일찍 말했어야 했어.
② 그게 바로 우리가 함께 유럽을 여행해야 하는 이유야.
④ 글쎄, 난 정말 로마나 파리에는 아무 관심이 없어.
⑤ 그들에게 우리의 문제를 말한다면, 우리가 그들과 함께 지내도록 해 줄 거야.

1. ready for / so much fine dust
2. throw a party / look it up online / call and ask her
3. Those come in / two of the smaller packs / left it at home
4. make an announcement / The scheduled release date / will be resolved quickly
5. posted the grades / were based on / take active roles
6. my back went out / soothe your muscles / help you feel better
7. made a short presentation / designed posters / uploaded them
8. everything is ready / hung those pans up / taken care of
9. finish your essay / make your essay longer / supports the opinion
10. want to add / save us some money / okay with it

07강 실전 모의고사　　　pp. 30-31

| 1 ③ | 2 ③ | 3 ⑤ | 4 ④ | 5 ③ |
| 6 ⑤ | 7 ② | 8 ④ | 9 ① | 10 ③ |

1 정답 ③

남: 이 스웨터를 입어봐도 될까요?
여: 그럼요. 그건 요즘 가장 잘 팔리는 품목이에요. 검은색도 있어요.
남: 저는 이 파란색이 좋아요. 더 큰 사이즈가 있나요? 저한테는 작아 보여서요.
여: 아, 네. 손님 사이즈로 재고가 있는지 확인해 볼게요.

어휘 | try on 입어보다 item 물품, 품목 |문제| business hour 영업시간 be in stock 재고가 있다

문제해설 | 남자가 더 큰 사이즈의 파란색 스웨터가 있는지 묻고 있으므로, 이에 대한 여자의 응답으로 ③번이 가장 적절하다.
① 죄송하지만, 저희 영업시간이 끝났어요.
② 음, 검은색이 더 잘 어울리시는 것 같아요.
④ 네, 더 작은 사이즈를 가지고 금방 올게요.
⑤ 네, 오늘은 할인을 좀 받으실 수 있어요.

2 정답 ③

여: 안녕 Tony, 오늘 아침 요가 수업에서 너 안 보이더라.

남: 맞아, 나 못 일어났어. 나도 너의 에너지를 가졌으면 좋겠다.

여: 우린 똑같은 에너지를 갖고 있다고 생각하는데.

남: 정말? 그러면 넌 왜 항상 그렇게 많은 일을 해내는 거야?

여: 우리가 그저 다른 선택을 하기 때문인 것 같아.

남: 난 그렇게 생각하지 않아. 나는 요가에 가고 싶었어. 그렇게 못 했고.

여: 왜 잠에서 깨지 못한 거야?

남: 온라인 게임을 하느라 늦게까지 깨어 있었어.

여: 그러면, 요가와 컴퓨터 게임 중 어떤 것이 너에게 더 중요하니?

남: 음, 요가. 내 건강이 우선이니까.

여: 맞아. 그러면 넌 일찍 자는 걸 선택했어야 해. 네가 해야 할 것이 많을 때, 가장 중요한 것을 먼저 하도록 해.

남: 알겠어. 내가 중요한 것에 집중하면 더 많은 것을 해낼 수 있을 거야.

어휘 | wake up (잠에서) 깨다, 일어나다 amount 양 get ... done …을 끝내다, 마치다 priority 우선 사항 accomplish 완수하다, 해내다

문제해설 | 밤 늦게까지 게임을 하느라 다음 날 요가 수업에 가지 못한 남자에게 여자는 우선 순위에 따라 선택하고 처리하면 많은 일을 할 수 있다고 조언한다.

3 정답 ⑤

[전화벨이 울린다.]

여: 여보세요?

남: 안녕, Marcy. 물리 수업을 같이 듣는 Calvin이야. 오늘 저녁 에 있을 스터디 모임에 대해 알려주려고 전화했어.

여: 아, 고마워. 완전히 잊고 있었어. 우리 몇 시에 만나지?

남: 공립 도서관에서 7시에 만날 거야.

여: 정말? 미안하지만, 난 거기 제시간에 못 갈 거야.

남: 왜? 무슨 일이야?

여: 내가 지금 할머니 댁에 있어. 거기에 도착하는 데 시간이 좀 걸릴 거야.

남: 오, 정말? 그럼 네가 준비한 오늘 저녁 학습 자료는?

여: 걱정하지 마. 그걸 내 USB 메모리 스틱에 저장해두었어.

남: 정말 다행이다! 그걸 내게 이메일로 보내면, 널 위해서 미리 전부 출력해둘게.

여: 고마워. 지금 바로 보낼게. 다른 애들에게 내가 늦는다고 말해줘.

남: 알았어. 이따 봐.

어휘 | physics 물리학 remind 상기시키다 totally 완전히 in time 제시간에 material 자료 relief 안도, 안심 in advance 미리

문제해설 | 남자는 여자가 준비한 학습 자료를 출력할 것이다.

4 정답 ④

남: 여러분께서 아시다시피, 우리 학교 축제가 6월에 열립니다. 올해 축제는 6월 10일부터 14일까지 열릴 예정입니다. 저희는 축제가 어느 때보다 멋질 거라고 생각합니다. 매년 축제의 백미는 마지막 날에 있는 야외 노래자랑입니다. 모든 학생들의 참가를 환영하며, 저희가 계속해서 자원봉사자가 필요하다는 것을 여러분께 상기시키고 싶습니다. 저희는 무대를 설치하고 방문객들을 안내하는 걸 도와줄 사람들이 필요합니다. 여러분의 도움으로 저희는 모든 학생들을 위해 행사를 성공적으로 만들 수 있습니다. 축제에 도움이 되고 싶으시다면, 자원봉사자 신청 모임에 오십시오. 그 모임은 학교 도서관에서 5월 5일 화요일 저녁 7시에 열립니다. 모든 자원봉사자들은 인기 스포츠 브랜드에서 후원하는 티셔츠를 무료로 받습니다. 올해 축제가 또 성공하도록 저희를 도와주십시오!

어휘 | highlight 가장 좋은 부분 outdoor 야외의 participate in …에 참가하다 set up 설치하다 sponsor 후원하다 hit 성공

문제해설 | 남자는 학교 축제의 진행을 도와줄 자원봉사자를 모집하고 있다.

5 정답 ③

[전화벨이 울린다.]

여: 안녕, Ira.

남: 안녕, Victoria. 네게 부탁 좀 하려고 전화했어. 너 독일에 가본 적 있니?

여: 한 번 가본 적 있어. 왜?

남: 인터넷에서 좋은 조건의 베를린 여행 상품을 찾았어.

여: 정말? 좋겠다. 언젠가 다시 가고 싶어.

남: 나랑 같이 갈래?

여: 와! 너랑 같이 베를린에 정말 가고 싶어. 비용이 얼마야?

남: 1인당 1,350달러이고, 호텔과 왕복 항공권이 포함되어 있어.

여: 나쁘지 않네. 여행 날짜는 언제야?

남: 9월 두 번째 주야. 갈 수 있어?

여: 아, 안 돼. 일 때문에 너랑 갈 수 없겠어.

남: 휴가를 낼 수 없니? 난 이 기회를 놓치고 싶지 않은데.

여: 미안해, Ira. 9월은 우리 회사가 정말 바쁜 시기야.

어휘 | deal 거래 round-trip 왕복 여행의 take time off 휴가를 내다 extremely 극도로 firm 회사

문제해설 | 여자는 9월이 회사 일로 매우 바쁜 시기여서 남자가 제안한 여행을 가지 못한다고 했다.

6 정답 ⑤

남: 우리 투어의 다음 장소는 Lockwood 도서관입니다.

여: 우와! 정말 오래되어 보여요.

남: 그렇습니다. 사실 그건 캠퍼스에서 가장 오래된 건물입니다.

여: 학생들이 거기에서 아직도 공부를 하나요?

남: 물론이죠. 사실 저도 역사 과제 때문에 조사를 하느라 어젯밤 거기에 있었어요.

여: 이 대학에서는 과제를 많이 해야 하나요?

남: 음, 학생이 고등학교에서 하는 것보다 훨씬 많아요.

여: 저는 과제량을 다 처리할 수 없을까 봐 걱정 돼요.

남: 대학 생활에 적응하는 것은 쉽지 않습니다. 하지만 열심히 노력

하면 처리할 수 있을 거예요.

여: 당신은 어려웠나요?

남: 솔직히 첫 학기는 아주 힘들었어요. 하지만 그 다음에 변화에 익숙해졌습니다. 이제는 여기서 공부하는 것이 좋아요.

여: 잘됐네요.

남: 네. 이제 다음 흥미로운 장소로 이동할까요? 모두들 저를 따라오세요.

어휘 | do research 조사를 하다, 연구하다 paper 종이; *논문, 과제 handle 다루다, 처리하다 workload 업무량, 작업량 adjust to …에 적응하다 challenging 능력을 시험하는, 어려운 get used to …에 익숙해지다

문제해설 | 남자가 한 무리의 사람들을 인솔하여 대학교 안의 건물에 대해 설명을 하고, 여자는 남자의 설명을 들으며 대학 생활에 대해 궁금한 점을 묻는 것으로 보아 대학생과 대학 캠퍼스 투어 참가자 간의 대화임을 알 수 있다.

7 정답 ②

여: 오늘 밤의 초대 손님은 Gina Lee라는 이름의 재능 있는 젊은 여배우입니다. 작년에, Lee 양은 로맨틱 코미디 〈Two Days〉에서의 연기로 여우주연상을 받았습니다. 그 이후로, 그녀는 두 편의 영화에 더 출연했습니다. 최신작은 그녀가 이전에 출연했었던 코미디 영화들로부터 큰 변화가 있습니다. 그것은 〈Midnight〉인데요, 거기서 그녀는 흡혈귀를 연기합니다. 〈Midnight〉은 공식적으로 다음 주에 개봉될 예정이지만, 이미 여러 영화제에서 상을 탔습니다. 영화에 출연하는 것 외에도, Lee 양은 또한 다양한 TV 시트콤에 출연해 왔고, 현재는 그녀 자신의 노래들을 담은 앨범을 녹음 중입니다. Gina Lee 양을 따뜻하게 맞아 주십시오!

어휘 | talented 재능이 있는 award 상 appear (…에) 출연하다 recent 최근의 previously 이전에 vampire 흡혈귀 officially 공식적으로 currently 현재 give a warm welcome 따뜻하게 맞이하다

문제해설 | ② 영화 〈Two Days〉 이후에 두 편의 영화에 더 출연했다고 했다.

8 정답 ④

여: 그리고 여기가 내 방이야.

남: 와! 정말 좋아 보인다! 하트 모양이 있는 담요 좀 봐! 네 취향은 아닌 것 같은데.

여: 음, 내 취향이 아니야. 우리 엄마가 그냥 사 주신 거야.

남: 그렇구나. 오, 이건 내가 지난번 네 생일에 사 준 곰 인형이니?

여: 맞아. 그건 항상 내 침대 위에 있어. 난 그걸 정말 좋아해.

남: 그 얘기를 들으니 기쁘다. 아, 책상 위 책꽂이에 책이 많네.

여: 응, 난 책을 읽는 걸 좋아해. 그리고 지리학에도 정말 관심이 많아.

남: 그래서 벽에 이 세계 지도를 붙여놨구나.

여: 응, 난 언젠가 세계 여행을 가려고 생각 중이거든. 전 세계 사람

들에게 기타를 연주해 주고 싶어.

남: 그거 멋진데! 그럼, 책상 옆에 이 기타가 네 거야? 날 위해 한 곡 연주해 줄 수 있니?

여: 물론이지.

어휘 | blanket 담요 bookshelf 책장, 책꽂이 be into …에 관심이 많다 geography 지리학 awesome 굉장한

문제해설 | 벽에는 시간표가 아닌 세계 지도가 붙어 있다고 했으므로, 대화의 내용과 일치하지 않는 것은 ④번이다.

9 정답 ① 10 정답 ③

남: 여러분은 첫인상이 중요하다고 생각하세요? 자, 전문가들에 따르면, 누군가가 여러분을 평가하는 데 힐끗 보는 것만으로도 충분하다고 합니다. 이 짧은 시간에 누군가는 여러분의 외모와 옷차림에 근거하여 당신에 대한 오래 지속될 견해를 형성할 수 있습니다. 이에 첫 만남이 굉장히 중요합니다. 그러니 누군가를 만날 때, 반드시 여러분 자신을 적절하게 보여주도록 하십시오. 여러분의 옷과 스타일이 각기 다른 환경과 행사에 얼마나 적절한지 고려하십시오. 예를 들어, 구직 면접이나 첫 데이트에는 산뜻하고 멋진 옷을 입으십시오. 전체적인 스타일 이외에도, 친근한 미소는 상대방을 편안하게 해 줄 겁니다. 대화를 할 때는, 여러분이 긴장감으로 고군분투하고 있더라도 자신감 있고 긍정적인 태도를 보이는 걸 기억하세요. 대화를 이어나가기 위해 사람들에게 그들에 대한 질문을 하는 것도 잊지 마세요.

어휘 | first impression 첫인상 expert 전문가 glance 흘낏 봄 evaluate 평가하다 lasting 지속적인, 영구적인 appearance 외모 encounter 만남 present 보여주다, 제시하다 appropriate 적절한 overall 전체적인 put … at ease …를 편안하게 하다 project 보여주다, 나타내다 confident 자신감 있는 positive 긍정적인 struggle with …와 싸우다 nervousness 긴장 **|문제|** represent 대표하다, 대변하다

문제해설 | 9. 남자는 상황에 맞는 옷차림 갖추기, 친근한 미소 짓기, 자신감 있고 긍정적인 태도 보이기, 상대방에 대해 질문하기 등을 통해 첫인상을 좋게 하기 위한 방법을 알려주고 있다.
① 좋은 첫인상을 만드는 방법
② 첫인상을 믿는 것의 문제점들
③ 당신의 옷 스타일이 왜 당신을 대변하는가
④ 사람들이 외모에 신경 쓰는 이유들
⑤ 누군가와 처음 만나기 전에 긴장을 푸는 방법
10. 남자는 첫인상을 좋게 만드는 요소로 ③ 유머 감각은 언급하지 않았다.
① 외모 ② 옷 ④ 미소 ⑤ 긍정적인 태도

1. Can I try on / looks small on me
2. wish I had / get so much done / focus on

08강 실전 모의고사   pp. 34-35

| 1 ④ | 2 ③ | 3 ② | 4 ③ | 5 ④ |
| 6 ③ | 7 ④ | 8 ① | 9 ④ | 10 ③ |

1 정답 ④

남: 오늘 장 교수님을 만나야겠어. 교수님께 여쭤볼 질문이 있거든.
여: 교수님이 입원 중이신 것 모르니? 교통사고를 당하셨잖아.
남: 정말? 난 몰랐어. 언제 돌아오실까?
여: 넌 다음 주 월요일까지 기다려야 해.

어휘 | in (the) hospital 입원 중인 **|문제|** injury 부상 apologize 사과하다

문제해설 | 남자는 병원에 입원한 교수님이 언제 학교로 복귀하실지 궁금해하는 상황이므로, 남자의 질문에 대한 여자의 응답으로 ④번이 가장 적절하다.
① 약 한 달 전에.
② 심각한 부상은 아니야.
③ 당연히 교수님을 방문할 수 있지.
⑤ 네가 사과드릴 때까지 오시지 않을 거야.

2 정답 ③

여: 정말 신난다. 전시회가 이번 주말이라는 게 믿기지 않아.
남: 나도 그래. 이제 모든 게 준비되었는지 마지막으로 확인해야 해.
여: 그래. 벽에 현수막은 걸었어?
남: '제7회 교내 미술 전시회'라고 적힌 것 말이지? 응, 이미 했어.
여: 잘했어. 조각상은 어떻게 했어?
남: 그건 전시관 중앙에 두었어.
여: 좋아. 그런데 왜 이 그림들은 아직 바닥에 있는 거야?
남: 오! 벽에 거는 걸 깜박했어. 내일 아침에 걸게.
여: 알겠어. 내가 도와줄게. 그리고 내가 여기 탁자 위에 팸플릿들을

모두 쌓아 놓았어.
남: 오, 근사해 보여! 난 이제 문 옆에 이 화분을 놓을 거야.
여: 완벽해. 내 생각엔 우리가 전시회 준비를 거의 다 한 것 같아.

어휘 | exhibition 전시회 banner 현수막 sculpture 조각품 gallery 미술관, 전시관 hang 걸다 stack up 쌓아 올리다 pamphlet 팸플릿, 소책자

문제해설 | 바닥에 그림들이 놓여 있고, 남자는 내일 아침에 그것들을 벽에 건다고 했으므로, 대화의 내용과 일치하지 않는 것은 ③번이다.

3 정답 ②

여: 아, 이럴 수가!
남: 뭐가 잘못됐어?
여: 내가 어제 책을 잘못 샀다는 걸 방금 알았어.
남: 뭘 샀는데?
여: 난 「Chemistry Masters」라는 책을 샀는데, 「Chemistry Matters」를 샀어야 했어.
남: 응. 나도 똑같은 실수를 했었어. 제목이 정말 비슷하잖아.
여: 음, 난 어떻게 해야 하지? 이 책은 비쌌거든.
남: 대학 서점에서는 분명 네가 그걸 교환하게 해 줄 거야. 사실, 나 지금 거기 가는 중이야. 나랑 같이 갈래?
여: 난 못 가. 잠시 후에 학생회 회의가 있거든. 오늘 오후에 그 책을 교환하는 게 좋을 것 같아.
남: 그럼, 내가 너 대신 해줄게. 영수증 갖고 있니?
여: 응, 여기 있어. 정말 고마워.
남: 괜찮아. 회의가 끝나면 나한테 전화나 해.

어휘 | chemistry 화학 exchange 교환하다 student council 학생회 receipt 영수증

문제해설 | 남자는 여자가 잘못 구입한 책을 학교 서점에 가는 길에 대신 교환해 주겠다고 했다.

4 정답 ③

여: 안녕하세요. 책을 제본해 주시나요?
남: 네. 책이 총 몇 페이지인가요?
여: 음, 지금은 112페이지인데, 그중 100페이지만 제본하려고요.
남: 컬러로 해 드릴까요, 아니면 흑백으로 해 드릴까요?
여: 컬러는 얼마예요?
남: 페이지당 30센트요.
여: 정말요? 흑백은요?
남: 페이지당 10센트밖에 안 해요. 원하신다면, 일부 페이지들은 컬러로 선택하고, 나머지는 흑백으로 하실 수 있어요.
여: 좋은 생각인 것 같네요. 어디 보자… 전 이 10페이지만 꼭 컬러로 필요해요.
남: 좋아요. 그럼 90페이지는 흑백으로, 10페이지는 컬러로, 맞죠?
여: 맞아요.
남: 좋습니다. 오후 2시까지 될 겁니다.

어휘 | bind 묶다; *(책을) 제본하다 select 선택하다

문제해설 | 여자는 총 100페이지 중 10페이지는 컬러(¢30×10)로, 나머지 90페이지는 흑백(¢10×90)으로 복사한 후 제본하기로 했으므로, 여자가 지불할 금액은 12달러이다.

5 정답 ④

[전화벨이 울린다.]
여: 여보세요?
남: 안녕, Tracy. 나 John이야.
여: 안녕, John. 무슨 일이야?
남: 있지, 부탁 좀 하려고.
여: 좋아. 뭔데?
남: 네가 다음 주에 엄마와 아빠를 공항에 모셔다드려도 괜찮겠니?
여: 네가 모셔다드리는 줄 알았는데. 아직도 그 중요한 발표를 끝내느라 바쁜 거야?
남: 아니, 실은 그 발표는 어제 했어. 그게 매우 잘 풀려서 내 상사가 날 특별 학회가 열리는 하와이로 보내려고 하셔.
여: 축하해! 정말 잘 됐다!
남: 응, 그런데 학회가 다음 주야. 엄마와 아빠가 떠나기 전날 그곳에 가야 해.
여: 알겠어. 음, 그러면 내가 엄마와 아빠를 공항에 모셔다드릴게.
남: 고마워, Tracy.

어휘 | ask a favor 부탁하다 go well 잘 되다 conference 학회

문제해설 | 남자는 하와이에서 열리는 학회에 참석해야 해서 부모님을 배웅할 수 없다고 했다.

6 정답 ③

남: 자, 이곳은 어떠세요?
여: 음. 좀 작긴 하지만, 괜찮은 것 같아요.
남: 집주인이 저한테 여기에 냉장고를 놔두고 갈 거라고 했어요.
여: 아, 그거 좋네요.
남: 네. 그리고 원하시면 오래된 가구는 버리시고, 대신 새것들을 사셔도 돼요.
여: 아마도 그렇게 해야겠네요. 전망은 어떤가요?
남: 오셔서 창밖을 한번 보세요. 저쪽의 산들을 보실 수 있고, 이 주변의 공기는 정말 좋답니다.
여: 오, 정말 좋네요! [잠시 후] 침실은 어때요?
남: 페인트칠을 새로 해야 하지만, 보시다시피, 충분히 괜찮아요.
여: 네, 그렇군요. 음, 집세도 충분히 적당하고요. 이곳으로 할게요.
남: 좋습니다. 후회하지 않으실 거예요.

어휘 | owner 주인 refrigerator 냉장고 get rid of …을 없애다 view 경관, 전망 coat 외투; *(페인트) 칠 rent 집세 reasonable 적정한, 비싸지 않은 regret 후회하다

문제해설 | 남자는 여자에게 집을 보여주고 있고, 여자는 집안을 둘러보고 있는 것으로 보아, 남자는 부동산 중개인이고 여자는 고객이다.

7 정답 ④

여: 저기요, 학생들에게 다음 달에 예정된 소풍에 대해서 알렸어요?
남: 그럼요. Balboa 공원에 간다고 모두 들떠 있는 걸요.
여: 잘됐네요. 제 학생들도 매우 들떠 있어요. 그런데, 공원에서 장기 자랑을 한다는 게 사실이에요?
남: 네. 우리 반 학생들 중 몇 명은 그걸 위해 벌써 연습하기 시작했어요.
여: 멋지네요. 대략 300명의 학생들이 갈 것 같아요.
남: 저도 그렇게 들었어요. 학생들이 모두 조심하길 바라야죠. 사고가 나면 안 되잖아요.
여: 맞아요. 하지만, 무슨 문제가 있을 것 같지는 않아요. 그런데, 우리 점심은 어디에서 먹을 거죠?
남: 호수 근처에서 먹을 거예요.
여: 그렇군요. 그러면 모든 학생들에게 각자 자기 점심을 가져오라고 해야겠네요.
남: 네, 호수 근처에는 점심을 살 만한 곳이 없어요.
여: 음, 신나는 날이 될 거예요.
남: 네, 분명 그럴 거예요.

어휘 | notify A of B A에게 B를 알리다[통지하다] outing 여행, 야유회 scheduled 예정된 talent show 장기 자랑

문제해설 | Balboa 공원으로 약 300명의 학생들이 소풍을 가며, 소풍 프로그램으로 장기 자랑 행사를 하고, 점심은 호수 근처에서 먹는다고 했다. 안전 대책에 대해서는 언급되지 않았다.

8 정답 ①

여: 안녕, Elton. 뭐 하고 있니?
남: 새 무선 스피커를 사기에 가장 좋은 곳을 찾고 있어.
여: 그렇구나. Tech Town은 늘 그렇듯이 가격이 너무 비싼 것 같네.
남: 맞아, 하지만 난 단지 기본 가격만 보기보다는 배송료와 보증서가 있는지 유의해 보고 있어.
여: 아, 넌 보증서가 없는 스피커는 사고 싶지 않구나.
남: 당연히 아니지! 그리고 Tech Town은 상품을 무료로 배송해줘.
여: 좋아. 하지만 이곳들을 좀 봐. 보증서도 있고, 무료 배송이야.
남: 그래? 아, 그리고 가격도 훨씬 더 싸네.
여: 그럼, 더 저렴한 가격인 사이트를 이용해.
남: 알았어.

어휘 | overpriced 너무 비싼 as usual 늘 그렇듯이 pay attention to …에 주의하다 shipping charge 배송료 warranty 보증(서) base price 기본 가격 ship 운송하다

문제해설 | 남자는 보증서를 제공하고, 무료 배송을 해 주는 웹사이트 중 가격이 가장 싼 곳에서 스피커를 구입하기로 했으므로, 남자가 스피커를 구입할 곳은 ①번이다.

9 정답 ④

여: 안녕하세요, 학생 여러분, 기말고사가 이번 달 22일에 213호실에서 치러질 겁니다. 시험은 50개의 객관식 문제로 구성됩니다. (시험) 내용은 교과서의 10과부터 20과까지 다루게 됩니다. 저는 30일까지 시험 채점을 끝낼 것입니다. 그러니 그날 여러분의 성적을 확인하러 저에게 와도 됩니다. 시험에서 떨어지면 여러분이 재시험을 볼 기회는 없을 것이므로, 꼭 열심히 공부하세요. 그것은 이번 학기 성적의 40%를 차지하고, 만일 여러분이 이번 수업에 낙제하면 이 수업을 다시 수강해야 할 겁니다. 질문이 있으면 시험 전에 언제든지 저에게 와서 물어도 됩니다.

어휘 | multiple-choice question 객관식 문제 in terms of …에 관하여 content 내용 cover 다루다, 포함시키다 grade 성적을 매기다; 성적 retake (시험을) 다시 보다

문제해설 | ④ 낙제하면 재시험을 볼 기회가 없다고 했다.

10 정답 ③

남: 어느 날 길을 걷다가, Grace는 고등학교를 함께 다녔던 한 여자를 보았다. 그들은 한때 친구 사이였는데, 졸업 이후로 서로를 보지 못했었다. Grace는 그녀의 옛 동창을 바로 알아보고 인사를 했다. 그 여자는 친절하게 미소를 지었지만, Grace가 누구인지 몰랐다. Grace는 자신이 수년 동안 너무 많이 변해서 그 친구가 자신을 알아보지 못하는 거라고 생각했다. 하지만 Grace가 그 여자에게 자신이 누구인지를 말한 후에, Grace는 자신이 실수를 했다는 것을 깨달았다. 그 여자는 그녀의 옛 친구가 아니었던 것이다. 이런 상황에서, Grace가 그 여자에게 할 말로 가장 적절한 것은 무엇인가?
Grace: 당신은 제 옛 친구와 정말 닮았군요.

어휘 | graduation 졸업 immediately 즉시, 바로 recognize 인지하다, 알아보다 politely 공손하게 assume 생각하다, 추정하다 turn out …인 것으로 드러나다 **|문제|** mistake A for B A를 B로 착각하다

문제해설 | 길에서 우연히 고등학교 동창을 닮은 여자에게 아는 척을 했지만, 결국 낯선 사람을 친구로 착각한 상황이므로, Grace가 할 말로 ③번이 가장 적절하다.
① 넌 고등학교 이후로 많이 변했구나.
② 당신은 저를 다른 사람으로 착각하셨어요.
④ 당신이 저를 알아보지 못해서 실망이에요.
⑤ 고등학교 때 그 여자를 기억하세요?

09강 실전 모의고사 pp. 38-39

| 1 ⑤ | 2 ⑤ | 3 ④ | 4 ① | 5 ⑤ |
| 6 ⑤ | 7 ③ | 8 ③ | 9 ③ | 10 ④ |

1 정답 ⑤

여: 안녕, David. 너 Jenny에 관한 소식 들었어?
남: 그 애가 이번 학기에 반에서 최고 점수를 받은 소식 말이야?
여: 맞아. 그 애는 어떻게 그렇게 잘할 수 있었을까?
남: 그 애는 항상 선생님들의 수업에 집중하잖아.

어휘 | semester 학기 **|문제|** deserve (…을) 받을 자격이 있다 do one's best 최선을 다하다

문제해설 | 반에서 최고 점수를 받은 친구의 비결에 대해 궁금해하는 여자의 질문에 대한 남자의 응답으로 ⑤번이 가장 적절하다.
① 그 애는 그 상을 받을 자격이 있어.
② 안경 쓴 키 큰 여자애 말하는 거야?
③ 이걸 너에게 어떻게 말해야 할지 몰랐어.
④ 힘내! 어쨌든 넌 최선을 다했잖아.

2 정답 ⑤

여: 안녕하세요 Tom, 이번 학기에 선생님 학생들은 어떻게 하고 있어요?
남: 많은 학생들이 시험 성적이 낮아요.
여: 저도 교직 생활 첫 해 동안 같은 문제를 겪었어요.
남: 정말요? 선생님은 교수법을 바꾸셨나요?
여: 제가 가르치는 방식을 바꾸지는 않았어요. 제가 학생들을 대하는 방식을 바꿨죠.
남: 더 엄격해지셨나요?
여: 아니오, 저는 학생들에 대한 기준을 높였어요. 그들이 제 시험에서 잘할 거라고 기대한다는 것을 아이들이 알게 했죠.

남: 학생들이 스트레스를 받지 않던가요?
여: 전혀요. 선생님이 학생들의 능력을 믿는다는 것을 학생들이 알
　게 하면, 그들도 자기 자신을 믿게 될 거예요.
남: 그러면 더 높은 기준을 세워서 우리 학생들에게 더 많은 자신감
　을 줄 수 있군요.
여: 맞아요. 그리고 시험에서 더 잘 할 거예요.
남: 고마워요. 그렇게 한번 해 볼게요.

어휘 | method 방법 treat 대하다, 다루다 strict 엄격한 standard 기
준, 수준 expect A to-v A가 …하기를 기대하다 feel stressed 스트레
스를 받다 ability 능력, 재능 confidence 자신감

문제해설 | 자기 반 학생들의 시험 성적이 낮아서 고민인 남자에게 여자
는 학생들의 능력을 믿고 더 높은 기준을 달성할 수 있다고 지지해줌으
로써 학생들에게 자신감을 줄 수 있다고 이야기하고 있다.

3　정답 ④

남: 와, 우리 파티가 대성공이에요!
여: 그래요. 난 이렇게 많은 사람들이 올 거라고 예상하지 못했어요.
남: 음, 이제 음식을 대접해야 할 것 같아요. 모두 자리에 앉으라고
　하죠.
여: 음, 잠깐만요. 문제가 생길 것 같아요.
남: 무슨 문제요?
여: 우린 의자가 30개밖에 없는데, 그것보다 사람들이 더 많잖아요.
남: 걱정하지 말아요. 지하실에 접이식 의자가 많이 있어요.
여: 잘됐네요. 제가 가서 좀 가지고 올까요?
남: 아뇨, 제가 할게요. 몇 개나 필요하죠?
여: 글쎄요… 잘 모르겠어요.
남: 돌아다니면서 여기에 사람들이 몇 명이나 있는지 보고, 저한테
　알려줘요.
여: 알았어요. 잠시만 기다려요.

어휘 | serve (음식을) 제공하다, 차려 내다 take a seat 자리에 앉다
folding chair 접이식 의자 basement 지하실 hold on …을 기다리다

문제해설 | 남자는 여자가 파티에 온 손님들의 수를 세어서 알려주면 지
하실에서 의자를 가져오겠다고 했다.

4　정답 ①

여: Food World에서 구입해 주셔서 감사합니다. 모두 21달러 60
　센트입니다.
남: 21달러 60센트라고요? 죄송하지만, 제 생각엔 당신이 실수하신
　것 같아요. 너무 많이 나온 것 같은데요.
여: 영수증을 확인해 볼게요. 고객님은 3팩의 우유를 사셨죠, 맞죠?
남: 맞아요. 그것들은 각각 2달러죠.
여: 네, 맞습니다. 그리고 냉동 피자도 좀 사셨죠.
남: 두 개 샀어요. 그것들은 각각 4.5달러인 걸로 아는데요.
여: 네, 맞습니다. 아, 제 실수를 알았네요. 제가 피자 네 개 가격을
　청구했어요. 죄송합니다.
남: 괜찮아요. 그리고 제 쿠폰으로 전체 금액에서 10%를 빼 주시는

　것을 잊지 않으셨죠?
여: 어디 볼게요. 네, 할인은 정확하게 적용되었습니다.
남: 네. 그래서 정확한 전체 금액이 어떻게 되나요?
여: 제가 확인하는 동안 잠시만 기다려 주세요.
남: 네. 알겠습니다.

어휘 | make an error 실수하다 receipt 영수증 carton (우유) 한 갑
[통] frozen 냉동된 correct 정확한(*ad.* correctly) charge A for B
A에게 B를 청구하다 subtract 빼다 apply 적용하다

문제해설 | 남자는 2달러짜리 우유 3팩($2×3)과 4.5달러짜리 냉동 피
자 2개($4.5×2)를 사고 10% 할인을 받았으므로, 남자가 지불할 금액
은 13.5달러이다.

5　정답 ⑤

남: 오늘 회의를 마치기 전에, 저는 모든 분들께 우리 클럽이 다음달
　말에 10주년 기념일을 축하할 것임을 상기시켜 드리고자 합니
　다. 저는 이것이 우리 모두가 모여서 함께 했던 모든 좋은 시간
　들을 돌이켜볼 좋은 기회가 될 것이라고 믿습니다. 지금은 아직
　아무것도 계획되지 않았고 결정된 것조차 없으니, 여러분이 가
　지고 계신 어떤 아이디어라도 말씀해 주십시오. 그것이 우리의
　예산 범위 내에 있는 한, 저희는 어떤 제안들도 고려할 것입니
　다. 제게 그것들을 이메일로 보내주시거나 그냥 종이에 적어주
　셔도 됩니다. 모두 다음 주에 뵙겠습니다.

어휘 | celebrate 축하하다, 기념하다 get together 모이다 think
back on …을 회상하다 at this point 현 시점에서는 budget 예산
proposal 제안, 제의

문제해설 | 남자는 회원들에게 다음 달 말에 있을 클럽의 10주년 기념일
행사에 대한 아이디어를 제안해 달라고 요청하고 있다.

6　정답 ⑤

남: 당신의 스튜디오를 견학할 수 있게 해 주셔서 고맙습니다.
여: 별말씀을요. 저도 즐거웠어요.
남: 이제 잠시 어디 앉아서 당신의 지난 영화에 대해 이야기를 나눌
　수 있을까요?
여: 물론이죠. 여기 앉으세요.
남: 고맙습니다. 당신의 지난 작품은 대성공이었고, 많은 명성을 얻
　으셨죠.
여: 네, 정말 놀랐어요. 그 영화가 받은 평이 대단히 좋았죠.
남: 맞아요. 저희 신문도 그 영화에 대해 대단히 좋은 평을 했어요.
　그리고 대중들도 그 영화를 매우 좋아했죠.
여: 네, 그랬죠. 저는 평범한 사람들이 즐길 수 있는 영화를 만드는
　것 같아요.
남: 그럼 다음 계획은 뭐죠?
여: 몇 주 동안 짧은 휴식을 가지려고요. 그리고 나서 일을 다시 시
　작할 거예요!

어휘 | fame 명성 review 평론, 비평 average 평균의; *보통의

문제해설 | studio, film, The reviews 등으로 보아 여자는 영화감독이고, My newspaper gave it an excellent review로 보아 남자는 기자임을 알 수 있다.

7 정답 ③

여: 안녕하세요, 학생 여러분. 다음 주 월요일에 우리는 지역 재활용 센터로 현장 학습을 갈 것입니다. 거기에서, 여러분은 재활용 과정이 어떻게 진행되는지에 대한 모든 것을 배울 것입니다. 여러분은 현장 학습 후에 이 정보에 대해 시험을 보게 되니, 반드시 필기할 공책과 펜을 가져오기 바랍니다. 우리는 오전 10시에 출발해서 버스로 센터까지 이동하고, 학교에는 오후 4시쯤에 돌아올 예정입니다. 점심은 제공되지만, 원한다면 간식을 가져와도 괜찮습니다. 여러분은 또한 카메라를 가져와서 시설물들을 찍어도 됩니다. 현장 학습에 참가하는 모든 학생들은 목요일까지 부모님이 서명하신 허가서를 제출해야 합니다.

어휘 | field trip 현장 학습 take notes 필기하다 approximately 대략, 거의 be permitted to-v …하는 것을 허용하다 photograph (…의) 사진을 찍다 facility 《*pl.*》 설비, 시설 permission 허가, 허락

문제해설 | ③ 점심은 제공된다고 했다.

8 정답 ③

남: 아야! 아, 아파!
여: 무슨 일이야, Aaron?
남: 치통이 심해. 너무 아파.
여: 그럼 얼른 치과에 가야 해. 예약은 했니?
남: 안 했어. 계속 미루고 있거든.
여: 도대체 왜 그러고 있니? 너도 알다시피, 그런 종류의 통증은 저절로 사라지지 않아.
남: 알아. 하지만 난 치과에 가는 게 정말 무섭단 말이야.
여: 음, 모든 사람이 다 그래, Aaron.
남: 난 대부분의 사람들보다 더 싫어하는 것 같아. 진심이야.
여: 그렇게 싫어하는 이유가 뭐니?
남: 나도 몰라. 그걸 생각할 때마다 두려워서 막 땀이 나기 시작해.
여: <u>너는 그만 생각하고, 그냥 갈 필요가 있어.</u>

어휘 | toothache 치통 painful 아픈, 고통스러운 put off …을 미루다 on earth 도대체 dread 두려워하다 sweat 땀을 흘리다 with fear 무서워하며 |문제| reschedule 일정을 변경하다

문제해설 | 여자는 남자가 치통으로 괴로워하자 치과에 가라고 하지만, 남자는 치과에 가는 것이 생각만 해도 무섭다고 말하고 있으므로, 이에 대한 여자의 응답으로 ③번이 가장 적절하다.
① 그렇다면, 너는 치과에 가야 돼.
② 알겠어, 언제 가고 싶은지 생각해 볼게.
④ 네가 마침내 더 괜찮은 치과 의사를 찾았다니 잘됐다.
⑤ 너의 예약 일정을 변경하고 싶니?

9 정답 ③　10 정답 ④

남: 꿈은 대부분의 사람이 자는 동안 경험하는 활동입니다. 하지만 사람이 꿈을 꿀 수 있는 유일한 생명체는 아닙니다. 몇몇 과학자들은 수면 중인 동물들에게서도 꿈을 꾸는 행위를 관찰했습니다. 개인적으로, 저는 제 개가 잠들어 있을 때, 가끔 꿈을 꾸고 있는 것처럼 보인다는 것을 알게 되었습니다. 그 개는 마치 걸어 다니거나 무언가를 쫓는 듯이 다리를 움직입니다. 또한 이상한 소리도 냅니다. 때로는 너무 흥분해서 깨기도 합니다! 물론 사람들도 자는 동안 비슷한 것들을 합니다. 수면 중인 사람들의 눈은 감긴 눈꺼풀 뒤에서 움직이고, 사람들은 수면 중에 숨을 더 빨리 쉽니다. 동물들도 정확히 같은 행동을 합니다. 그들도 제가 제 개가 하는 것을 알게 된 것처럼 다리를 움직이고 소리를 냅니다. 과학자들은 동물들이 어떤 꿈을 꾸는지는 아직 모르지만, 저는 그들이 알아낼 방법을 찾길 바랍니다. 우리가 동물들이 무엇에 관해 꿈꾸는지 알 수 있게 된다면 정말 흥미로울 겁니다.

어휘 | activity 활동 creature 생명체, 창조물 capable of …을 할 수 있는 chase after …을 쫓다 eyelid 눈꺼풀 breathe 숨을 쉬다 |문제| affect 영향을 끼치다 interpretation 해석

문제해설 | 9. 남자는 자신의 경험과 과학자들의 관찰 내용을 들어, 동물들도 꿈을 꿀 수 있는 능력이 있음을 이야기하고 있다.
① 동물은 왜 꿈을 꾸는가
② 꿈은 어떻게 동물에게 영향을 미치는가
③ 동물의 꿈을 꾸는 능력
④ 동물의 꿈에 대한 해석
⑤ 동물의 꿈이 사람과 어떻게 다른가
10. 꿈을 꿀 때 하는 행동으로 ④ 머리를 흔드는 것은 언급되지 않았다.
① 숨 빨리 쉬기　② 소리 내기　③ 다리 움직이기　⑤ 눈 움직이기

10강 실전 모의고사

1 ①	2 ②	3 ④	4 ③	05 ③
6 ④	7 ⑤	8 ⑤	9 ②	10 ⑤

1 정답 ①

남: 실례합니다. 이 의자들에 주인이 있나요?
여: 이 두 개에는 없어요.
남: 그럼 제가 하나에 앉아도 될까요?
여: <u>아, 물론이죠. 앉으세요.</u>

어휘 | mind 꺼리다, 싫어하다; 마음 **|문제|** remind A of B A에게 B를 상기시키다

문제해설 | 남자가 여자 옆의 빈 의자에 앉아도 되겠냐고 묻는 상황이므로, 이에 대한 여자의 응답으로 ①번이 가장 적절하다.
② 죄송하지만, 마음을 바꿨어요.
③ 이 의자에는 문제가 없어요.
④ 당신이 왜 저에게 그걸 상기시켜야 하는 거죠?
⑤ 죄송하지만, 그걸 가져가시면 안 돼요.

2 정답 ②

여: 안녕 Alex, 뭐하고 있니?
남: 이건 TOEIC 시험 연습 문제야. 높은 점수를 받고 싶거든.
여: 벌써 일자리에 지원하려고 생각하는 거야?
남: 응. 내년에 대학 졸업을 하잖아. 좋은 일자리 찾는 게 어려우니 좋은 자격 요건을 갖추고 싶어.
여: 높은 점수를 받는 것도 중요하지만, 난 고용주들이 고려하는 더 중요한 것들이 있다는 것을 알게 되었어.
남: 봉사 활동 같은 걸 하는 것 말이야?
여: 봉사 활동이 도움이 돼. 하지만 최적의 지원자는 다양한 삶의 경험을 갖고 있어.
남: 알겠어. 인턴사원 근무에 지원해 봐야겠다.
여: 그거 좋은 생각이다. 그런데 인턴직에만 집중하지는 마. 어떤 삶의 경험이라도 너에게 소중한 자신감과 기술을 줄 거야.
남: 그거 좋은 조언이다. 고마워.

어휘 | apply for …에 지원하다 qualifications 자격 요건 employer 고용주 applicant 지원자 a variety of 여러 가지의 internship 인턴 사원 근무 valuable 소중한 skill 기술

문제해설 | 구직활동을 위해 좋은 자격 요건을 갖추겠다는 남자에게 여자는 구직활동 시 가장 중요한 요소는 다양한 삶의 경험을 갖는 것이라고 말했다.

3 정답 ④

여: 아, 다음 주 일정은 끔찍해.
남: 무슨 문제 있어?
여: 음, 다음 주 월요일이 고등학교 축구팀 결승전이잖아.
남: 맞아. 그것 때문에 추가로 직원 몇 명을 고용하기로 되어 있잖아, 그렇지?
여: 아냐, 예정된 어떤 추가 직원도 없어. 그게 문제야.
남: 말도 안 돼! 나중에 모든 학생들이 아이스크림을 먹으러 여기 올 텐데. 어떻게 우리 둘이 그들 모두를 감당할 수 있어?
여: 우리가 매니저에게 이야기해야 할 것 같아.
남: 동의해. 매니저가 분명히 아르바이트생을 몇 명 고용할 거라고 했었는데.
여: 그는 그걸 잊은 게 틀림없어. 그가 새집으로 이사를 갈거라 최근에 매우 바쁘다고 들었거든.
남: 내가 지금 당장 그에게 말할게.

어휘 | championship 선수권 대회; *결승전 afterward 나중에, 그 후 handle 다루다, 처리하다 definitely 분명히

문제해설 | 두 사람은 다음 주 일정을 위해 추가 인력 보충을 요청하려고 매니저를 만나고자 한다.

4 정답 ③

여: 안녕하세요. 제 시계 건전지를 교체하고 싶은데요. 비용이 얼마나 들죠?
남: 건전지는 5달러입니다. 음… 이 시곗줄도 교체하시는 게 좋을 것 같네요.
여: 맞아요. 그건 너무 낡았죠. 그럼 여기 이것들은 얼마예요?
남: 금으로 된 줄들은 30달러이고, 은으로 된 줄들은 20달러예요.
여: 은으로 된 줄로 할게요.
남: 알겠습니다. 이건 단 몇 분이면 돼요. [잠시 후] 음… 이거 이상하네요.
여: 뭐가 잘못됐나요?
남: 제가 건전지를 바꿨는데도, 시계가 여전히 작동하지 않네요. 고장 난 것 같은데요.
여: 아, 이런. 그럼, 그걸 수리해야 한다는 말씀인가요?
남: 네. 수리비는 10달러입니다.
여: 알겠습니다. 수리해 주세요. 언제 가지러 오면 되나요?
남: 하루면 될 겁니다. 그때 계산하시면 돼요.
여: 고맙습니다.

어휘 | watchband 시곗줄 repair 수리하다; 수리 charge 요금

문제해설 | 건전지가 5달러, 은으로 된 시곗줄이 20달러, 시계 수리비가 10달러이므로, 여자가 지불할 금액은 35달러이다.

5 정답 ③

여: 너 괜찮니? 걱정스러워 보여.
남: 맞아. 다음 주 목요일이 우리 엄마 생신이거든.
여: 그래서? 뭐가 문제야?
남: 내가 다음 주 월요일부터 금요일까지 싱가포르에 출장을 가.
여: 알겠다. 음, 네가 꽃집에다가 어머니 생신날에 어머니께 꽃다발

을 배달해 달라고 할 수 있지.

남: 그래, 그거 좋은 생각이다. 난 떠나기 전에 꽃을 좀 주문할 수 있어. 어디 좋은 꽃집을 알고 있니?

여: 물론이지. 난 매일 퇴근길에 예쁜 꽃집을 지나거든.

남: 잘됐다. 아마 네가 나보다 꽃에 대해 더 많이 알 거야. 나랑 같이 가줄 수 있어?

여: 물론 갈 수 있지!

남: 고마워. 넌 정말 친절해.

어휘 | bunch 다발 on one's way home 집으로 돌아가는 길에

문제해설 | 남자는 어머니 생신을 위한 꽃 배달을 주문하기 위해 여자에게 꽃집에 같이 가달라고 부탁했다.

6 정답 ④

여: 와 주셔서 감사합니다, 송 선생님. 그러니까, 선생님께서 영화 투자에 관심이 있으시다고요?

남: 그렇습니다. 그렇게 하면 제 돈을 뜻깊게 사용할 것 같아서요.

여: 네. 그리고 잘만 되면 수익성도 좋을 거예요.

남: 당신이 현재 제작하고 있는 영화에 대해 제게 말씀해 주세요.

여: 음, 이것은 미래가 배경인 사랑 이야기예요. 여기 대본입니다.

남: 제가 검토해 볼게요. 당신은 정말 이런 종류의 영화가 인기 있을 거라고 생각하시나요?

여: 네. 아시다시피, 로맨틱 영화들이 요즘 극장가에서 대세잖아요.

남: 그렇죠. 배역들을 연기할 배우들은 결정하셨나요?

여: 아직이에요. 하지만 유명 연예인 몇 명과 조율 중입니다.

남: 음, 매우 관심이 가네요. 이걸 읽어본 후에 다시 얘기하도록 합시다.

어휘 | finance 자금을 대다 creative 창의적인; *뜻있는 profitable 수익성이 있는 script 대본 look over …을 살펴보다 celebrity 연예인

문제해설 | 여자는 자신이 제작하고 있는 영화에 대해 설명하고 있고, 남자는 그 영화에 자신의 돈을 투자하려는 것으로 보아, 영화감독과 투자자 사이의 대화임을 알 수 있다.

7 정답 ⑤

남: 이 새 커피숍에 날 데려와 줘서 고마워. 정말 멋져.

여: 그렇네. 실내 장식이 이렇게 현대적일 거라고 예상하지 못했어.

남: 난 저쪽에 있는 커다란 직사각형 탁자가 마음에 들어.

여: 천장에 걸려있는 샹들리에 아래에 있는 거 말하는 거야?

남: 응. 저런 널찍한 탁자는 저녁 식사 파티에 좋겠어.

여: 난 빠른 서비스도 인상적이야.

남: 음, 주문하는 계산대가 두 개인 게 도움이 되나 봐.

여: 맞아. 그건 그렇고, 우리 가야겠어.

남: 네 커피잔을 나한테 줘. 쟁반들이 쌓여 있는 저 선반 위에 손님들이 더러운 그릇들을 올려놓아야 하거든.

여: 알았어. 고마워. 난 화장실을 찾아봐야겠다.

남: 그렇게 해. 계산대 오른쪽에 케이크와 파이가 있는 진열장 옆에서 만나.

여: 좋아. 곧 돌아올게.

어휘 | rectangular 직사각형의 beneath 아래에 spacious 널찍한 shelf 선반 tray 쟁반 stack up 쌓다 display case 진열장

문제해설 | 계산대 오른쪽 진열장에는 케이크와 파이가 있다고 했으므로 ⑤번은 대화의 내용과 일치하지 않는다.

8 정답 ⑤

남: Fred와 그의 여동생 Alice는 해변에 있었다. 그들은 맨발로 해안을 따라 걷고 있었는데 그때 Alice가 비명을 질렀다. 처음에 Fred는 그녀가 장난을 치는 것이라고 생각했지만, 이내 무언가 심각하게 잘못되었다는 것을 깨달았다. Alice는 바닥에 주저앉아 그녀의 양손으로 오른쪽 발을 쥐었다. Fred는 Alice의 발에서 피가 나고 있는 것을 보았고, 모래 밖으로 깨진 유리 조각이 튀어나와 있는 것을 발견했다. Alice는 울고 있었고, Fred는 그녀가 매우 고통스럽다는 것을 알 수 있었다. Fred는 주위를 둘러봤고 멀리에 안전요원이 서 있는 것을 보았다. 이런 상황에서 Fred가 Alice에게 할 말로 가장 적절한 것은 무엇인가?

Fred: Alice, 여기서 기다려. 내가 도움을 청하러 갈게.

어휘 | barefoot 맨발로 shore 해안 scream 비명을 지르다 joke around 농담하다, 장난치다 bleed 피를 흘리다 stick out 튀어나오다 in a lot of pain 고통이 심한 lifeguard 안전요원 in the distance 먼 곳에 |문제| watch out for …을 조심하다 sharp 날카로운

문제해설 | 해변에서 산책을 하다가 여동생이 깨진 유리 조각에 발을 다쳐 피를 흘리는 상황에서 Fred가 안전요원을 발견했으므로, Fred가 할 말로 ⑤번이 가장 적절하다.
① Alice, 일어나. 계속 걷자.
② 유리를 조심해. 그건 날카로워!
③ 장난 그만해, Alice. 재미없어.
④ 넌 신발을 벗지 말았어야 했어.

9 정답 ② 10 정답 ⑤

여: 신사 숙녀 여러분, 안녕하세요. 오늘 저는 일상생활에서 우리 모두가 직면하는 문제에 대해 여러분에게 이야기하고자 합니다. 여러분이 누구이든지 간에, 여러분을 화나게 하거나 방해하는 일들이 일어납니다. 이런 스트레스를 받는 상황을 최소화하기 위해서는, 여러분의 한계를 알고 정중하게 '안됩니다'라고 말하는 법을 배우는 것이 중요합니다. 여러분이 무엇을 감당할 수 있는지에 대해 사람들에게 솔직하다고 해서 여러분이 사람들을 실망시키지는 않을 겁니다. 또한, 스트레스를 받는 상황을 피하도록 노력하세요. 예를 들어, 여러분이 항상 교통 체증을 겪게 된다면, 대체 경로를 찾아보세요. 그뿐만 아니라, 여러분의 감정을 표현하는 것이 매우 중요합니다. 여러분의 감정을 안에 숨기고 있으면, 여러분을 힘들게 하는 그 문제들은 결코 해결되지 않을 것입니다. 마지막으로, 긍정적으로 생각하려고 최선을 다하시고, 어려운 상황을 개인적인 발전의 기회로 여기도록 노력하세요. 이런 간단한 일들은 여러분이 더 행복하고, 더 평화로운 삶

을 살도록 도와줄 수 있습니다.

어휘 | face (…에) 직면하다 annoy 화나게 하다 disturb 방해하다 limit 한계 let ... down …를 실망시키다 end up 결국 (어떤 처지에) 처하게 되다 alternative 대안이 되는, 대체 가능한 issue 쟁점, 사안; *문제 resolve 해결하다 look on the bright side 긍정적으로 보다 challenging 도전적인, 힘든 **|문제|** maintain 유지하다

문제해설 | 9. 여자는 일상생활에서 스트레스를 줄이기 위한 여러 방법들을 제안하고 있다.
① 행복의 비밀
② 일상 생활에서 스트레스를 줄이는 방법
③ 감정을 표현하는 대안들
④ 타인과 좋은 관계 유지하기
⑤ 우리를 괴롭히고 방해하는 것
10. ⑤ 타인과 문제를 공유하기는 언급되지 않았다.
① 거절하는 법 배우기　　② 스트레스를 주는 상황 피하기
③ 감정 표현하기　　④ 긍정적으로 바라보기

DICTATION ANSWER　　　　pp. 44-45

1. Are these chairs taken / mind if
2. get a high score / applying for jobs / valuable confidence and skills
3. What's wrong with it / any extra workers scheduled / definitely going to hire
4. replace my watch battery / take a silver one / have it repaired
5. a business trip / order some flowers / go with me
6. financing a film / hopefully profitable / play your characters
7. A spacious table / two counters for ordering / by the display case
8. were walking barefoot / sticking out of the sand / in a lot of pain
9-10. annoy or disturb you / express your feelings / look on the bright side

---

11강 실전 모의고사　　pp. 46-47

| 1 ④ | 2 ③ | 3 ③ | 4 ⑤ | 5 ④ |
| 6 ④ | 7 ① | 8 ③ | 9 ② | 10 ④ |

1 정답 ④

여: 저 롤러코스터 높이 좀 봐!
남: 알아, 하지만 보기보다 무섭지 않아.
여: 그렇다고 해도, 난 정말 그걸 타고 싶지 않아.

남: 그럼 더 작은 놀이 기구 중 하나를 타자.

어휘 | height 높이 feel like v-ing …하고 싶다 ride 타다; 놀이 기구 **|문제|** a fear of heights 고소 공포증 horrible 끔찍한, 무서운

문제해설 | 여자가 롤러코스터가 무서워서 타고 싶지 않다고 했으므로, 이에 대한 남자의 응답으로 ④번이 가장 적절하다.
① 내게 고소 공포증이 있는 거 넌 알잖아.
② 네가 자전거를 못 타는 줄 몰랐어.
③ 올라와! 멋진 경치 좀 봐.
⑤ 그건 내가 본 것 중에 가장 무서운 거였어.

2 정답 ③

여: 한국 관광 산업에 7년 넘게 종사하면서, 저는 한 가지 체험이 대부분의 외국 관광객들의 목록들 중 1위를 차지한다는 것을 알게 되었습니다. 그 체험은 사찰 체험 프로그램인데, 사람들이 한국 불교에 대해 더 깊이 이해하도록 돕고자 고안된 문화 체험입니다. 사찰 체험에 참여하면 불교 공동체의 채식주의 식사에 참여할 수 있는 기회뿐만 아니라, 명상을 하고 염불을 할 수 있는 기회도 여러분에게 주어집니다. 여러분이 선택할 수 있는 다른 활동들로는 연등 만들기, 다도에 대해 배우기, 그리고 민속놀이 하기가 포함됩니다. 프로그램을 예약하시려면, 공식 웹사이트를 방문해 주시기 바랍니다.

어휘 | tourism industry 관광 산업 temple 절, 사찰 design 만들다, 고안하다 Buddhism 불교 practice 연습하다; *행하다, 실천하다 meditation 명상 chanting 성가; *염불 communal 공동의 vegetarian 채식주의의 lotus lantern 연등 ceremony 의식 folk game 민속놀이 reserve 예약하다

문제해설 | 여자는 한국의 사찰 체험 프로그램을 홍보하고 있다.

3 정답 ③

여: 돌아온 걸 환영해, Jim. 학회는 어땠어?
남: 괜찮았는데, 사람들과 어울리는 게 힘들었어.
여: 그게 정상이야. 나도 그런 문제가 있었어.
남: 오? 너 지금은 어떻게 어색한 분위기를 깨려고 해?
여: 난 보통 날씨에 관해 이야기하거나 다른 사람의 의상을 칭찬해.
남: 정말? 그 주제들이 약간 지루할 수 있다고 생각하지는 않니?
여: 아니. 많은 사람들은 이런 식으로 대화를 시작하는 것을 좋아해.
남: 그렇구나. 대화의 그 부분이 끝난 다음에는 무엇을 말해야 할까?
여: 음, 학회에는 항상 음식이 있을 거야. 그것에 대해 언급하고, 상대방에게 대답할 기회를 줘.
남: 그거 좋은 생각이네. 너 의사소통 전문가 같아.
여: 고마워. 두 사람 모두에게 친숙한 화제를 고르는 것만 기억해.

어휘 | have trouble v-ing …에 어려움을 겪다 socialize (사람들과) 어울리다 break the ice 어색한 분위기를 깨다 compliment 칭찬하다 comment 언급하다 communication 의사소통 expert 전문가 be familiar with …에 익숙하다

문제해설 | 두 사람은 날씨에 대해 말하거나, 다른 사람의 의상을 칭찬하는 등 어색한 분위기를 깨는 방법에 관해 이야기하고 있다.

4 정답 ⑤

남: 좋은 아침이구나, 애야. 와서 아침 먹으렴.
여: 전 먹고 싶지 않아요, 아빠. 몸이 안 좋거든요.
남: 어디가 아프니, Fiona? 창백해 보이는구나.
여: 감기에 걸린 것 같아요. 열이 나요.
남: 오, 저런. 오늘은 집에 있는 게 낫겠구나. 네가 원한다면, 너희 선생님께 전화해서 네가 너무 아프니 학교에 갈 수 없다고 말씀 드리마.
여: 아뇨, 그러실 필요 없어요. 그렇게 심하진 않아요. 감기약 좀 있어요?
남: 부엌 찬장에 좀 있단다. 앉아 있으면 내가 가져다주마.
여: 아, 고마워요, 아빠.
남: 근데 너 정말 그 약만으로 괜찮겠니? 학교 가기 전에 병원에 가는 게 어때? 내가 거기에 차로 데려다주마.
여: 아뇨, 걱정하지 마세요, 아빠. 약을 좀 먹으면 괜찮아질 거예요.
남: 알았다, 애야. 곧 돌아오마.

어휘 | pale 창백한 fever 열 cupboard 찬장

문제해설 | 남자는 감기에 걸린 여자를 위해 약을 가져다주기로 했다.

5 정답 ④

여: 안녕, Jason. 예술제 준비는 어떻게 되가?
남: 썩 좋지 않아. 우리가 주문한 현수막에 날짜가 잘못되어 있어.
여: 큰일났네. 인쇄 회사가 다시 인쇄해 줘야 하겠는데. 그들이 시간에 맞춰 새로운 축제 현수막을 인쇄할 수 있어?
남: 내가 전화했어. 시간 안에 인쇄할 수 있다는데, 또 다른 문제가 있어.
여: 뭔데?
남: 그들이 말하길 현수막을 다시 인쇄하고 싶으면, 우리가 또 비용을 지불해야 한대.
여: 왜 우리가 그들의 실수에 대해 비용을 지불해야 하는데?
남: 사실은… 내가 주문할 때 잘못된 정보를 줬거든.
여: 뭐? 내가 지난 주간 회의에서 날짜를 말해 줬잖아.
남: 알아. 내가 잘못 기억한 게 틀림없어.
여: 메모 안 하고 있었니?
남: 할 필요 없다고 생각했어.
여: 진짜 너무한다, Jason.

어휘 | preparation 준비 (사항) banner 현수막 in time 시간 맞춰 place an order 주문을 하다 misremember 부정확하게 기억하다 take notes 메모[기록]하다 unacceptable 용납할 수 없는

문제해설 | 남자가 인쇄 회사에 현수막에 들어가는 날짜를 잘못 알려줘서 현수막을 다시 인쇄해야 한다고 했다.

6 정답 ④

[휴대전화가 울린다.]
남: 여보세요?
여: 안녕, 여보. 나예요. 부탁이 있어서 전화했어요.
남: 아, 그게 뭔데요?
여: 알다시피, 내가 퇴근 후에 공항으로 당신 어머니를 모시러 가기로 했잖아요.
남: 맞아요. 당신이 못 가게 될까 봐 걱정하는 거예요?
여: 걱정하지 마요. 갈 수 있어요. 그런데 터미널 번호와 비행기 번호를 잊어버렸어요.
남: 음, 당신은 온라인에서 확인할 수 있어요.
여: 알지만 난 막 회의에 들어가려는 참이라, 시간이 없어요.
남: 그 정보가 포함된 문자 메시지를 당신에게 보내면 좋을까요?
여: 네. 그게 바로 당신한테 부탁하려던 거예요.
남: 문제없어요. 아, 그리고 제시간에 도착하도록 해요.
여: 알았어요. 그리고 가는 길에 도넛을 좀 살 거예요. 어머니께서 기내식을 싫어하시잖아요.

어휘 | be about to-v 막 …하려고 하다 contain 포함하다

문제해설 | 여자는 남자에게 터미널 번호와 비행기 번호를 확인해서 문자 메시지로 보내 달라고 부탁했다.

7 정답 ①

남: 거기가 완벽한 곳인 것 같아요. 당신이 바로 거기에 서 있으면, 내가 산을 배경으로 찍을 수 있어요.
여: 잠시만요! 내가 거기로 갈게요. [잠시 후] 여기요?
남: 아주 좋아요. 서서 정면 사진을 찍는 것부터 시작하죠.
여: 알겠어요. 이 포즈 어때요?
남: 좋아요. 재킷이 정말 잘 보이네요. 이제 옆으로 좀 돌아줄래요?
여: 이렇게요?
남: 완벽해요. 이 각도에서 사진을 몇 장 찍을게요.
여: 제가 공중에 눈을 던지는 사진을 좀 찍을까요?
남: 네, 그거 좋은 생각이네요. 그리고 정말 즐거운 것처럼 보이도록 환한 미소를 지어주세요.
여: 여전히 재킷이 보이나요?
남: 네. 회사에서 이 사진들을 아주 마음에 들어 할 거예요.
여: 분명 겨울 카탈로그 전체가 멋져 보일 거예요!

어휘 | spot 장소 background 배경 pose 자세 angle 각도 toss 던지다 bet 틀림없다

문제해설 | 남자가 여자에게 포즈를 제안하고 여자가 입고 있는 재킷을 중심으로 사진을 찍는 것으로 보아, 남자는 사진작가이고 여자는 모델임을 알 수 있다.

8 정답 ③

여: 이봐, Sam. 너 이번 여름에 인턴직에 지원할 거야?
남: 응. 실은 지금 선택할 수 있는 것들을 보고 있어.

여: 오, 넌 어떤 것에 지원하려고 하는데?

남: 아직 확실치는 않아. 난 유급직이면 좋겠어.

여: 물론이지. 그런데 네 전공과 관련된 인턴직을 하는 게 더 중요해.

남: 네 말이 맞는 것 같아. 그럼 난 아마도 광고 인턴직을 해야 할 것 같아.

여: 그리고 네가 하는 일의 종류도 중요해.

남: 음, 연구 조사를 하는 게 전화 응대를 하는 것보다 더 소중한 경험이 될 거야.

여: 그리고 지역은?

남: 시 외곽으로 통근하는 건 시간이 오래 걸릴 거야.

여: 그럼 시내에 있는 게 더 낫겠네. 그게 훨씬 더 편리할 거야.

남: 맞아. 어떤 인턴직에 지원해야 할지 알 것 같아!

어휘 | internship 인턴직 major 전공 advertising 광고 as well 또한, 역시 commute 통근하다 uptown 시 외곽에(↔ downtown)

문제해설 | 남자는 유급직이고 광고 인턴직에 관심이 있는데, 연구 조사를 하고 시내에 있는 회사에 지원하고 싶어 하므로, 남자가 지원할 인턴직은 ③번이다.

9 정답 ②

여: 안녕하세요, 학생들과 직원 여러분. 저는 다가오는 '사복의 날'에 대해 말씀드리고자 합니다. 이날은 즐거움과 기금 마련 둘 다를 위한 날입니다. 이날에는 여러분 누구도 교복을 입을 필요가 없습니다. 대신, 여러분은 사복을 입고 학교에 올 수 있습니다. 그 대가로, 여러분은 우리 학교 자선 기관인 Green Street 보육원에 상태 좋은 새 문구류 몇 점을 기부해야 합니다. 우리는 또한 오후에 장기자랑과 책 교환과 같은 몇 가지 재미있는 행사들을 할 것입니다. 선생님들 또한 참여하실 수 있다는 걸 기억하십시오! 격식을 차린 옷을 입는 대신에, 편안한 옷을 입으시기 바랍니다. 여러분 모두가 이 행사에 적극 참여하시기를 바랍니다.

어휘 | upcoming 다가오는 fundraising 모금 in return 대신에 donate 기부하다 stationery 문구류 charity 자선 단체 orphanage 보육원 swap 교환 formal 격식 차린 outfit 옷

문제해설 | ② 기금 마련을 위한 특별 공연에 대한 언급은 없다.

10 정답 ④

남: Andrea와 Danny는 결혼한 지 3년이 되었고, 둘 다 같은 마케팅 회사에서 일한다. 그들은 같이 살고 일을 하므로 종종 번갈아 운전하여 출근을 한다. 최근에 여러 번 Andrea는 그녀의 남편이 운전할 때 안전벨트를 매는 것을 잊는다는 걸 알아챘다. 반면 그녀는 항상 꼭 안전벨트를 맨다. 그녀는 사고가 났을 때 안전띠가 사람을 안전하게 해 줄 수 있기 때문에, 그렇게 하는 것이 매우 중요하다고 생각한다. 그녀는 자신의 남편이 교통사고를 당하면 벌어질 일을 걱정한다. 이런 상황에서, Andrea가 그녀의 남편에게 할 말로 가장 적절한 것은 무엇인가?

Andrea: <u>운전할 때 안전벨트 매는 것을 명심해요.</u>

어휘 | take turns 교대로 하다 occasion 때, 경우 fasten one's seat belt 안전벨트를 매다 be involved in …에 연루되다 car crash 자동차 (충돌) 사고 **|문제|** excuse 변명 illegal 불법적인 exceed 넘어서다, 초과하다 speed limit 제한 속도 freeway 고속도로

문제해설 | Andrea가 남편이 운전할 때 종종 안전벨트를 매지 않는 것에 대해 걱정하고 있는 상황이므로, 그녀가 남편에게 할 말로 ④번이 가장 적절하다.

① 우리의 낡은 차를 바꿔야 할 것 같아요.

② 불법 주차에 대해서는 변명의 여지가 없어요.

③ 내가 운전을 더 잘하니까, 내가 회사까지 운전할게요.

⑤ 고속도로에서는 제한 속도를 초과하면 안 돼요.

DICTATION ANSWER — pp. 48-49

1. as scary as / feel like riding
2. gain a deeper understanding / practice meditation / vegetarian meal / reserve your place
3. trouble socializing / a little boring / a chance to respond
4. You'd better stay home / let me get it / take some medicine
5. preparations for the art festival / in time / placed the order
6. supposed to pick up / check them online / send you a text message
7. from the front / take a few pictures / give me a big smile
8. applying for an internship / would rather get / a more valuable experience than
9. wear your own clothes / some fun events / Instead of wearing
10. take turns driving / fasten his seat belt / were involved in

12강 실전 모의고사 pp. 50-51

1 ①	2 ④	3 ②	4 ④	5 ③
6 ③	7 ③	8 ①	9 ③	10 ④

1 정답 ①

여: Sam, 일요일에 영화 보러 갈래?

남: 좋아. 지금 어떤 영화가 상영 중이야?

여: 액션 영화랑 로맨틱 코미디가 있어. 넌 어떤 걸 더 보고 싶어?

남: <u>난 둘 중 아무거나 괜찮아.</u>

어휘 | show 보여주다; *상영하다

문제해설 | 둘 중 어떤 영화를 보고 싶은지 묻는 여자의 질문에 대한 남자의 응답으로 ①번이 가장 적절하다.
② 내 시계는 30분 느려.
③ 난 혼자 영화 보는 걸 선호해.
④ 그걸 Sarah와 함께 보는 게 어때?
⑤ 미안하지만, 난 영화를 보러 갈 수 없어.

2 정답 ④

남: 이 치마를 구입하신 영수증을 가져오셨나요?
여: 네, 여기 있어요.
남: 감사합니다. 왜 환불을 원하시는지 말씀해 주시겠어요?
여: <u>색깔이 저에게 어울리지 않는 것 같아요.</u>

어휘 | receipt 영수증 get a refund 환불을 받다 |**문제**| in cash 현금으로 purchase 구입하다

문제해설 | 치마를 환불하고자 하는 이유를 묻는 남자의 질문에 대한 여자의 응답으로 ④번이 가장 적절하다.
① 그냥 현금으로 계산하고 싶어요.
② 난 전액 환불을 받아야 해요.
③ 난 그걸 신용 카드로 구입했어요.
⑤ 이 치마를 내 여동생에게 주고 싶어서요.

3 정답 ②

남: 안녕, Marcy. 난 개 한 마리를 입양할까 생각 중이야.
여: 전에 개를 키워본 적 있니?
남: 아니. 뭐 얼마나 힘들겠어? 개는 밥, 물, 운동만 필요하잖아, 그렇지?
여: 그렇지 않을 텐데. 견주가 된다는 건 할 일이 많아진다는 거야.
남: 어떤 일 말이야?
여: 개는 많은 보살핌이 필요해. 발톱을 다듬고, 매주 목욕시키고, 털과 이빨을 매일 닦는 것 같이 말이야.
남: 좋아. 그것 참 손질을 많이 해야 하는구나. 그렇지만 그렇게 나쁘게 들리진 않는데.
여: 그리고 개는 관심이 필요해. 넌 오랫동안 집을 떠나 있을 수 없어.
남: 그럼 난 매일 저녁 퇴근하고 바로 집으로 가야겠네?
여: 맞아. 너는 항상 개의 요구를 먼저 생각해야 할 거야.
남: 음, 이 일에 대해 좀더 생각해 봐야겠다.
여: 좋은 생각이야.

어휘 | adopt 입양하다 own 소유하다 dog owner 견주, 개 주인 trim 다듬다, 손질하다 nail 손톱; *발톱 fur 털 grooming 몸단장, 차림새를 단정하게 하기 attention 관심 needs 요구

문제해설 | 개를 입양할까 고려하는 남자에게 여자는 그에 따르는 많은 책임과 해야 할 일들에 대해 이야기하고 있다.

4 정답 ④

여: Mark, 뭘 보고 있니?
남: Christopher Jones가 감독한 신작 영화야. 방금 다운로드했어.
여: 우와. 그 영화를 기다리고 있었는데.
남: 나랑 같이 보지 않을래?
여: 그러고 싶은데, 내가 여기에 온 이유는 너에게 부탁을 하려고.
남: 아, 너무 시끄럽니? 소리를 줄일게.
여: 아니, 그게 아니야. 실은, 내 컴퓨터가 작동이 안 되는데 왜 그런지 모르겠어.
남: 도움이 필요하니?
여: 응. 매우 급해.
남: 알았어, 내가 도와줄게. 너도 알다시피, 난 컴퓨터에 대해 많이 알잖아.
여: 네가 최고야, Mark.

어휘 | direct 감독하다 turn down …의 소리를 줄이다 urgent 긴급한, 다급한

문제해설 | 컴퓨터가 고장 나서 도와달라고 하는 여자를 위해 남자는 컴퓨터를 수리해주기로 했다.

5 정답 ③

남: 과학자들이 유전학과 DNA에 대해 점점 더 많은 것을 계속해서 발견함에 따라, 동물들을 복제하는 과정이 점점 더 일반화되고 있습니다. 많은 사람들은 우리가 인간 복제를 시작하는 것 또한 단지 시간 문제라고 여깁니다. 하지만 저를 비롯한 많은 다른 사람들은 이것이 잘못된 방향으로 향하는, 재난을 일으키는 움직임이 될 것이라고 생각합니다. 저는 인간 복제에 몇몇 과학적 이점들이 있을 수도 있다는 것은 인정하지만, 그것까지 고려하기에는 너무 많은 위험들이 있습니다. 잠재적인 문제들이 그 이점들을 훨씬 능가하는 것처럼 보입니다.

어휘 | genetics 유전학 clone 복제하다 disastrous 재난을 일으키는 acknowledge 인정하다 benefit 이득 risk 위험 potential 잠재적인 outweigh (가치·중요성 등이) 능가하다

문제해설 | 남자는 인간 복제로 인해 발생할 문제들이 그것이 가져올 이점들을 능가하는 것처럼 보인다고 말하며, 인간 복제의 위험성에 대해 경고하고 있다.

6 정답 ③

남: 실례합니다. 여기 이 건물은 무엇인가요?
여: 아, 그건 고대 사원입니다. 3,000년이 된 것으로 추정됩니다.
남: 와, 오래됐네요. 입구 근처에 있는 저 큰 조각상들은 뭐죠?
여: 황금 사자들이에요. 그것들은 이 사원을 지키도록 되어 있죠.
남: 정말 흥미롭군요! 안으로 들어갈 수 있나요?
여: 네, 하지만 소액의 입장료가 있습니다. 그 돈은 사원을 유지하는 데 사용됩니다.

남: 그렇군요. 당신도 저희와 함께 가시나요?

여: 물론이죠. 제가 사원 안의 모든 특징들을 설명해 드릴 겁니다. 그리고 여러분이 알고 계셔야 할 몇 가지가 있습니다.

남: 아, 규칙들이 있나요?

여: 네. 사원 내부에서 사진을 찍으시면 안 됩니다. 그리고 신발을 벗으셔야 해요.

남: 알겠어요.

어휘 | ancient 고대의 temple 절, 사원 estimate 추정하다 statue 조각상 entrance 입구 guard 지키다, 보호하다 maintain 유지하다 feature 특징 be aware of …을 알다 remove 제거하다; *벗다

문제해설 | 남자는 고대 사원을 방문한 관광객이고, 여자는 관광객들을 안내해 주는 관광 안내원이다.

7 정답 ③

남: 안녕하세요. 현대 미술관에 오신 것을 환영합니다. 어떻게 도와 드릴까요?

여: 안녕하세요. 입장권이 얼마죠?

남: 성인은 10달러, 아이는 5달러입니다.

여: 알겠습니다. 성인 두 장과 아이 두 장을 사겠어요. 쿠폰도 있어요. 사용할 수 있을까요?

남: 어디 보죠… 네, 모든 입장권에 10퍼센트를 할인 받으실 수 있습니다.

여: 잘됐네요.

남: 오늘 저희가 손님 가족이 참여하실 수 있는 조각 강습회도 열고 있습니다. 찰흙을 이용해 작품을 만드실 수 있어요.

여: 그거 재미있겠네요. 입장료에 포함된 건가요?

남: 아니요. 강습회 입장권은 1인당 5달러이며, 할인은 적용되지 않습니다.

여: 알겠어요. 강습회 입장권 네 장 살게요.

남: 그러면 아이 두 명, 성인 두 명 입장권과 강습회 입장권 4장이네요?

여: 맞아요. 여기 제 카드와 쿠폰이요.

어휘 | admission 입장 hold 열다, 개최하다 sculpture 조각 workshop 워크숍, 강습회 take part in …에 참여[참가]하다 clay 찰흙, 점토 pass 입장권, 통행권

문제해설 | 성인 두 명($10x2), 아이 두 명($5x2)의 입장료에서 10% 할인을 받으면 27달러이고, 조각 강습회 입장료는 4장($5x4)은 할인이 적용되지 않는다고 했으므로, 여자가 지불할 금액은 총 47달러이다.

8 정답 ①

여: Steve는 중학생이다. 최근에, 그의 어머니는 그의 생활방식에 대해 걱정하기 시작했다. Steve는 집에서 스포츠를 보는 것과 컴퓨터 게임을 하는 것만을 즐긴다. 그는 외출하거나 운동을 하는 것을 전혀 좋아하지 않는다. 실제로, 최근에 그는 많은 화창한 날들을 소파에 앉아서 TV만 보며 지내고 있다. 그는 또한 식사 시간 사이에 감자 칩이나 막대사탕 같은 건강에 해로운 간식들을 많이 먹는다. 그의 어머니가 걱정이 되어 말을 하면, Steve는 자신이 과체중도 아니고 건강상에 문제가 있었던 적은 없다고 지적했다. 하지만 그의 어머니는 그러한 문제들이 발생하는 것은 단지 시간 문제라고 걱정한다. 이런 상황에서, Steve의 어머니가 Steve에게 할 말로 가장 적절한 것은 무엇인가?

Steve의 어머니: 건강한 습관을 시작하기에 결코 너무 이른 법은 없단다.

어휘 | mention 말하다, 언급하다 concern 관심; *걱정 point out …을 지적하다 overweight 과체중의 occur 발생하다 |문제| take it easy 쉬엄쉬엄 하다 harm 해를 끼치다

문제해설 | 운동도 안 하고 집에만 있으면서 몸에 해로운 간식들을 많이 먹는 아들에게 어머니가 할 말로 ①번이 가장 적절하다.
② 당분간은 네가 그저 쉬엄쉬엄 해야 할 것 같구나.
③ 자기 관리를 잘 하고 있다니 기쁘구나.
④ 넌 모든 돈을 먹는 데 써서는 안 된단다.
⑤ 과도한 운동은 네 건강을 해칠 수 있단다.

9 정답 ③ 10 정답 ④

남: 여성 육상인들을 위한 특별한 행사로, 매년 열리는 Peace Square Run은 모든 20대 여성들에게 열려 있습니다. 경주는 7킬로미터의 거리이며, 전 세계의 달리기 선수에게 인기가 있습니다. 이것은 2005년에 시작됐으며, 그 이래로 매년 열리고 있습니다. 작년에는 5,000명이 넘는 참가자들이 참여했습니다. 월드컵 경기장 근처의 Peace Square에서 시작하는 이 행사는 5월 26일 오후 6시 30분에 개최될 것입니다. 이 경기에 참여하는 데 관심이 있는 모든 선수들은 등록을 위해 이 행사 웹사이트에 방문하셔야 합니다. 등록비는 20달러이며, 모든 등록은 4월 16일 이전에 완료되어야 합니다. 만약 등록을 취소하기를 원하시면, 4월 30일 오후 6시 이전에 취소하셔야 합니다. 등록은 저희 웹사이트를 통해서나 행사 관계자에게 234-8282번으로 전화를 걸어서 취소할 수 있습니다. 환불이 처리되려면 취소 후 3~5일 정도의 기간이 필요합니다.

어휘 | athlete 선수; *육상 경기 선수 contestant 참가자 locate (…에) 위치하다 register 등록하다(n. registration) cancel 취소하다 (n. cancellation) coordinator 진행자 dial 전화를 걸다

문제해설 | 9. 남자는 다가오는 여성 마라톤 대회의 개최일과 등록 및 환불 방법 등의 주요 내용에 대해 공지하고 있다.
① 여성 달리기의 역사
② 행사의 일정 변경 사항
③ 마라톤 경주에 대한 정보
④ 달리기가 우리 건강에 이로운 이유
⑤ 마라톤 주자들이 준수해야 할 규칙
10. ④ 입상 상금에 대해서는 언급되지 않았다.
① 장소와 날짜
② 등록 방법
③ 등록 비용
④ 등록 취소 방법

1. go to the movies / prefer to watch
2. bring the receipt / get a refund
3. adopting a dog / away from home / your dog's needs
4. ask you a favor / can't figure out why / It's pretty urgent
5. begin cloning human beings / in the wrong direction / the potential problems
6. an ancient temple / explain all of the features / remove your shoes
7. How much are admission tickets / holding a sculpture workshop / discount doesn't apply
8. worry about his lifestyle / unhealthy snacks / such problems occur
9-10. female athletes / interested in participating in / cancel your registration / by contacting the event's coordinators

13강 FINAL TEST

pp. 56-59

1 ③	2 ②	3 ⑤	4 ④	5 ③
6 ②	7 ③	8 ⑤	9 ③	10 ③
11 ④	12 ①	13 ③	14 ④	15 ①
16 ②	17 ⑤			

1 정답 ③

W: Something is wrong with this computer.
M: I know. It shuts down whenever I try to go online.
W: What do you think the problem is?
M: I'm not sure. We need to call an expert.

여: 이 컴퓨터에 뭔가 문제가 있어요.
남: 알아요. 내가 인터넷을 하려고 할 때마다 꺼지더라고요.
여: 문제가 뭔 거 같으세요?
남: 잘 모르겠어요. 우리는 전문가를 불러야겠어요.

어휘 | shut down (기계가) 멈추다, 정지하다 **|문제|** blame (…을) 탓하다

문제해설 | 여자가 컴퓨터가 고장이 난 원인을 묻고 있으므로 이에 대한 남자의 응답으로 ③번이 가장 적절하다.
① 그게 고장 나도 날 탓하지 말아요.
② 새것은 너무 비싸기 때문이에요.
④ 당신은 비밀번호를 잘못 입력한 게 틀림없어요.
⑤ 그게 바로 요즘 사람들이 온라인 쇼핑을 선호하는 이유예요.

2 정답 ②

M: Who is going to set up the tables and chairs for the meeting?
W: Mark and Tom will do it.
M: What about distributing brochures?
W: I think Sandy is in charge of that.

남: 누가 회의를 위해 탁자와 의자를 준비할 건가요?
여: Mark와 Tom이 할 거예요.
남: 책자를 나눠주는 일은요?
여: 그건 Sandy가 맡은 것 같아요.

어휘 | distribute 나누어 주다, 배부하다 brochure (안내·광고용) 책자 in charge of …을 맡은[담당하는]

문제해설 | 남자는 누가 책자를 나눠 줄 것인지 묻고 있으므로 이에 대한 여자의 응답으로 ②번이 가장 적절하다.
① 그것들을 바꾸기에는 너무 늦었어요.
③ 그렇지만 전 회의에 참석할 수가 없어요.
④ 당신이 없었다면, 전 이 프로젝트를 해내지 못했을 거예요.
⑤ John과 Andy는 새로운 책자를 디자인하고 싶어 해요.

3 정답 ⑤

M: Good afternoon, everyone. It's a beautiful day here at the Florida Family Zoo and Wildlife Park. As you may have noticed, several of the park's birds and smaller mammals tend to gather in this area at lunchtime, hoping for a few tasty treats from visitors' lunchboxes. We ask that you please refrain from feeding them. Otherwise they will become dependent on people's offerings, and your food may even make them sick. We also ask that you carefully clear away any wrappers and other waste from the site before you leave. Such items are a danger to the animals, as they often try to eat them. Thank you for your attention.

남: 안녕하세요, 여러분. 이곳 플로리다 가족 동물원과 야생 공원의 날씨가 정말 좋습니다. 여러분께서 이미 눈치채셨을 수도 있겠지만, 공원의 새들과 작은 포유동물 여럿이 방문객들의 도시락에서 나오는 맛있는 음식들을 좀 먹으려고, 점심시간에 이 지역에 모이는 경향이 있습니다. 저희는 여러분이 동물들에게 먹이를 주는 것을 삼가시길 요청하는 바입니다. 그렇지 않으면 동물들은 사람들이 주는 먹이에 의존하게 될 것이고, 여러분이 주시는 먹이는 심지어 동물들을 아프게 만들 수도 있습니다. 저희는 또한 여러분이 떠나시기 전에 이곳에서 그 어떤 포장지나 다른 쓰레기들을 주의해서 치워주시길 부탁드립니다. 그러한 것들은 동물들이 종종 먹으려고 하기 때문에, 그들에게 위험합니다. 들어주셔서 감사합니다.

어휘 | mammal 포유동물 gather 모이다 treat 특별한 것 refrain

from v-ing …하는 것을 삼가다 feed 먹이를 주다 otherwise 그렇지 않으면 dependent on …에 의존적인 offering 제공물 clear away …을 치우다 wrapper 포장지

문제해설 | 남자는 방문객들에게 동물원의 동물들에게 먹이를 주지 말 것과 동물원을 떠나기 전에 쓰레기를 치워달라고 당부하고 있다.

4 정답 ④

M: Susan, do you know how big the Gobi Desert is?
W: No, but I heard that it's getting bigger every year.
M: That's true. Grasslands are turning into desert at an alarming rate.
W: And it's mostly caused by human activity.
M: Yes, but some people are trying to solve the problem. Have you heard of the Green Wall of China?
W: Don't you mean the "Great Wall"?
M: No, the "Green Wall." It's a 4,500-kilometer-long strip of forest being planted at the edge of the desert.
W: Is it working?
M: It's too early to say. But hopefully it will keep the Gobi Desert from getting bigger.
W: I guess it might also reduce the amount of dust affecting neighboring countries.
M: Yes, that would be another big benefit.
W: Well, I hope they're successful.

남: Susan, 너 고비 사막이 얼마나 큰지 아니?
여: 아니, 그런데 매년 더 커지고 있다고 들었어.
남: 맞아. 초원이 놀라운 속도로 사막으로 바뀌고 있어.
여: 그리고 그건 대부분 인간의 활동 때문에 일어나지.
남: 그래, 하지만 어떤 사람들은 그 문제를 해결하려고 애쓰고 있어. 너 중국의 녹색장성에 대해 들어 봤어?
여: '만리장성'을 말하는 거 아니야?
남: 아니, '녹색장성'. 그것은 그 사막 가장자리에 심어진 4,500킬로 미터 길이의 좁고 기다란 숲 지대야.
여: 그게 효과가 있어?
남: 아직 말하기에는 일러. 하지만 바라건대 그것이 고비 사막이 더 커지지 않게 해줄 거야.
여: 그게 이웃 나라들에 영향을 주는 흙먼지의 양도 줄여주겠다.
남: 응, 그건 또 다른 큰 이점이 될 거야.
여: 음, 그것들이 성공하면 좋겠어.

어휘 | desert 사막 grassland 초원 at a rate …의 비율로 alarming 놀라운 strip 좁고 기다란 땅 plant 심다 edge 가장자리 keep A from B A가 B하지 못하게 하다 dust 흙먼지 neighboring 이웃의

문제해설 | 두 사람은 사막화를 막기 위해 중국에서 시행되고 있는 프로 젝트인 '녹색장성'에 관해 이야기하고 있다.

5 정답 ③

W: Thank you for inviting me here today.
M: I'm glad you agreed to come. Why don't you tell me a bit about your past experience?
W: Well, I spent three years working for one of your competitors.
M: Did you? Why did you leave?
W: My husband got transferred, so we had to move.
M: I see. Was it a similar position to this one?
W: Yes, most of the daily tasks were identical.
M: That's excellent. What about your education?
W: I received a bachelor's degree in marketing.
M: Well, it sounds like you meet all of our requirements.
W: I'm glad to hear that.

여: 저를 오늘 이곳에 초대해 주셔서 감사합니다.
남: 오는 것에 동의해주셔서 기쁩니다. 당신의 이전 경력에 대해 말 해줄 수 있습니까?
여: 음, 저는 귀사의 경쟁사 중 한 곳에서 3년 동안 일했습니다.
남: 그러셨어요? 왜 그만두셨죠?
여: 제 남편이 전근 발령이 나서, 우리는 이사해야 했습니다.
남: 그렇군요. 이것과 비슷한 자리였습니까?
여: 네, 대부분의 일과가 같습니다.
남: 그거 정말 잘 됐군요. 어떤 교육을 받으셨나요?
여: 저는 마케팅 학사 학위가 있습니다.
남: 음, 당신이 우리의 모든 요건을 충족하는 것처럼 들리네요.
여: 그 말을 들으니 기쁘네요.

어휘 | competitor 경쟁자 get transferred 전근 발령이 나다 identical 동일한, 똑같은 bachelor's degree (대학교의) 학사 학위 meet requirements 요건을 충족시키다

문제해설 | 남자가 여자의 경력과 학력에 관해 물어본 후, 여자가 모든 요건에 충족된다고 말하고 있으므로, 남자는 면접관이고 여자는 지원자 임을 알 수 있다.

6 정답 ②

M: How's your studying going, Serena?
W: Oh, not bad. But I'll probably be up all night.
M: That's too bad. Is there anything I can do for you?
W: Well... Is there any coffee left in the pot?
M: No, it looks like you finished it all.
W: Oh, yeah. But I'm still falling asleep. Could you make some more?
M: No problem. Do you want me to make you a snack as well?
W: No thanks. I just had a couple of doughnuts from the bakery.
M: Doughnuts? They're too sugary. You need to choose

healthier snacks.

W: I know, but the sugar helps me stay awake.

M: Okay. But you'd better start taking care of yourself after this test is finished.

W: I promise I will.

남: 공부는 잘되고 있니, Serena?
여: 아, 그럭저럭요. 그런데 아마 밤을 꼬박 새워야 할 것 같아요.
남: 안됐구나. 내가 널 위해 해 줄 일이라도 있니?
여: 음… 주전자에 커피 남은 것 좀 있어요?
남: 아니, 네가 전부 다 마신 것 같은데.
여: 아, 맞아요. 그런데 전 여전히 졸려요. (커피를) 좀 더 만들어 줄 수 있으세요?
남: 물론이지. 내가 간식도 만들어 줄까?
여: 고맙지만 괜찮아요. 방금 제과점에서 산 도넛 몇 개를 먹었어요.
남: 도넛? 그건 너무 달아. 너는 몸에 더 좋은 간식을 선택해야 해.
여: 알아요, 하지만 당분은 내가 깨어 있게 도와줘요.
남: 알겠어. 하지만 이 시험이 끝난 후에 네 건강을 돌보기 시작하는 게 좋겠어.
여: 그러겠다고 약속할게요.

어휘 | be up all night 밤을 꼬박 새우다 pot 주전자 sugary 설탕이 든, 매우 단 stay awake (자지 않고) 깨어 있다

문제해설 | 여자는 졸음을 쫓기 위해 남자에게 커피를 더 만들어 줄 것을 부탁했다.

7 정답 ③

M: Honey, take a look at this wedding hall brochure.

W: Oh, it looks really nice. Maybe we should have our wedding there.

M: Yeah. I love the arch-shaped wall.

W: And the flower arrangements are beautiful.

M: They sure are. I like how they go all the way down the aisle on both sides.

W: And there are benches on both sides of the aisle, too.

M: Yes, they're quite long.

W: That's good. All of the guests will be able to get a seat.

M: That's true. And there is a grand piano up front, on the right side. We can have some nice music at the ceremony.

W: That would be nice.

M: What do you think of that curtain hanging in front of the wall?

W: I love it! Let's have our wedding here!

남: 자기, 이 예식장 책자를 봐요.
여: 오, 정말 좋아 보이네요. 우리 결혼식을 거기서 해야겠어요.
남: 네. 아치형 벽이 마음에 들어요.
여: 그리고 꽃장식도 아름다워요.
남: 정말 그렇네요. 통로를 따라 양쪽에 쭉 늘어서 있는 게 마음에 들어요.
여: 그리고 통로 양쪽에 긴 의자들도 있어요.
남: 네, 꽤 기네요.
여: 그게 좋아요. 모든 하객들이 자리에 앉을 수 있을 거예요.
남: 맞아요. 그리고 오른쪽 정면에 그랜드 피아노가 있어요. 우리는 예식에서 멋진 음악을 즐길 수 있겠어요.
여: 멋질 거예요.
남: 벽 앞에 걸린 저 커튼은 어때요?
여: 정말 좋아요! 우리 결혼식을 여기서 해요!

어휘 | arch 아치형 (구조물) arrangement 배치, 배열 aisle 통로 ceremony 의식, 예식

문제해설 | 통로 양쪽에는 둥근 탁자가 아니라 긴 의자들이 놓여 있다고 했으므로, 대화의 내용과 일치하지 않는 것은 ③번이다.

8 정답 ⑤

W: Hey, Bill. What are you doing this weekend?

M: I don't have any plans. I was going to help my friend move to a new apartment, but he decided to hire movers instead. What about you?

W: I don't have plans yet, either. But I was just thinking it would be fun to go to a baseball game.

M: Oh, well, I don't want to do that.

W: Why? Are you feeling okay?

M: Yes, I feel fine.

W: Then what's wrong? Don't you like baseball?

M: I love baseball. I think it would be fun, and the weather is going to be nice this weekend.

W: Then let's go! Why are you hesitating?

M: Well, honestly, the tickets are too expensive. But why don't you come over to my house instead?

W: Sure! Then we can watch the game on TV.

여: 이봐, Bill. 이번 주말에 뭘 할 거야?
남: 계획은 없어. 내 친구가 새 아파트로 이사 가는 걸 도우려고 했는데, 그 애가 대신 이삿짐 운송업자를 고용하기로 했어. 넌?
여: 나도 아직 계획이 없어. 그런데 야구 경기를 보러 가면 재미있겠다고 막 생각하고 있었어.
남: 오, 글쎄, 난 그러고 싶지 않아.
여: 왜? 몸은 괜찮은 거야?
남: 응, 괜찮아.
여: 그럼 뭐가 문제야? 너 야구를 좋아하지 않니?
남: 야구를 엄청 좋아하지. 재미있을 것 같고, 이번 주말에 날씨도 좋을 거야.
여: 그럼 가자! 왜 주저하는 거야?
남: 음, 솔직히, 표가 너무 비싸. 대신에 우리 집에 오는 건 어때?
여: 좋아! 그럼 경기를 TV로 볼 수 있겠다.

어휘 | hire 고용하다 mover 이삿짐 운송업자 hesitate 주저하다

문제해설 | 남자는 표가 너무 비싸서 야구 경기장에 가고 싶지 않다고 했다.

9 정답 ③

M: May I help you?

W: Yes, please. I'd like to sign up for a gym membership.

M: Sure. Basic membership is $70 per month, with various fitness classes available for an additional fee.

W: I see. What fitness classes do you offer?

M: Yoga, swimming, aerobics, and squash.

W: Hmm. I'm interested in yoga and swimming. How much are they?

M: Each class costs $10 per month.

W: So, in total I'd pay $90 per month?

M: Right. But if you sign up for three months, you save 10%. And more than six months gets you a 30% discount.

W: That's not bad, but I'll sign up for one month first with just a swimming class.

M: In that case, you won't get a discount.

W: That's fine.

남: 도와 드릴까요?

여: 네. 전 체육관 회원 등록을 하고 싶은데요.

남: 알겠습니다. 기본 회원은 한 달에 70달러이고, 추가 비용을 내면 다양한 운동 수업들을 이용할 수 있습니다.

여: 그렇군요. 어떤 운동 수업들이 있나요?

남: 요가, 수영, 에어로빅, 그리고 스쿼시요.

여: 음. 전 요가와 수영에 관심이 있어요. 그 수업들은 얼마죠?

남: 각 수업은 한 달에 10달러입니다.

여: 그럼, 전 한 달에 총 90달러를 내는 건가요?

남: 그렇습니다. 하지만 만약 고객님이 석 달을 등록하시면, 10%를 할인해 드립니다. 그리고 6개월 이상 등록하시면 30%를 할인해 드리고요.

여: 나쁘진 않지만, 전 수영 수업만 듣는 걸로 우선 한 달만 등록할게요.

남: 그렇다면, 할인을 받으실 수 없으세요.

여: 괜찮아요.

어휘 | additional 추가의 squash 스쿼시 in total 전체로서, 통틀어

문제해설 | 여자는 한 달간 회원 등록($70)을 하고 추가로 수영 수업($10)만 듣겠다고 했다. 한 달 등록에는 할인이 적용되지 않으므로, 여자가 지불할 금액은 80달러이다.

10 정답 ③

W: Have you heard about the year-end party?

M: Yeah. It sounds like it's going to be a lot of fun.

W: I heard there is going to be a big buffet.

M: That's right. There will definitely be plenty of good food to eat. I'm looking forward to the musical performance the most, though.

W: Is it true that the CEO is going to sing?

M: Yes. It's going to be very funny.

W: The location will be nice as well. Have you been to the Yacht Club before?

M: No, but I've heard it's amazing. I'm really looking forward to going there.

W: By the way, have you heard anything about the dress code?

M: Yes, I read in an email that formal dress is required.

W: I see. It's certainly going to be a memorable event!

여: 송년회에 대해 들었어요?

남: 네. 굉장히 재미있을 것 같아요.

여: 성대한 뷔페가 있을 거라고 들었어요.

남: 맞아요. 분명 맛있는 음식이 많을 거예요. 하지만 전 뮤지컬 공연이 가장 기대돼요.

여: 사장님이 노래를 부른다는 게 사실이에요?

남: 네. 정말 재미있을 거예요.

여: 장소도 근사할 거예요. 전에 Yacht Club에 가본 적 있어요?

남: 아뇨, 하지만 근사하다고 들었어요. 거기에 정말 가고 싶어요.

여: 그런데, 복장 규정에 대해서 들은 거 있어요?

남: 네, 정장을 입어야 한다고 이메일에서 읽었어요.

여: 그렇군요. 분명 기억에 남는 행사가 될 거예요!

어휘 | year-end party 송년회 dress code 복장 규정 formal 격식을 차린 memorable 기억에 남을

문제해설 | 송년회의 음식으로 뷔페가 제공되며 뮤지컬 공연이 있을 거라고 했다. 또한 송년회 장소는 Yacht Club이고 정장을 입어야 한다고 했지만, 대표 연설에 대해서는 언급되지 않았다.

11 정답 ④

W: Welcome, everybody, to the British Museum. I'd like to give you some information before you start exploring by yourselves. The British Museum is home to over seven million exhibits that illustrate the story of human culture throughout history. You can easily find your way around using the brochures distributed free to all visitors. There is also a voice-guided tour available in three languages: English, French, and Korean. Please remember that it's strictly prohibited to consume food or drinks in the museum, or to take pictures of the exhibits. Lastly, if you want to buy some souvenirs, you can visit the museum gift shop on the first floor. I hope you enjoy looking around the museum.

여: 대영 박물관에 오신 여러분 모두를 환영합니다. 여러분이 직접 답사를 시작하시기 전에 몇 가지 정보를 알려 드리고자 합니다. 대영 박물관은 전 역사에 걸쳐 인류 문화의 이야기를 보여주는 700만 점이 넘는 전시품들을 소장하고 있습니다. 여러분은 모든 방문객들에게 무료로 제공된 책자를 사용하여 길을 쉽게 찾을 수 있습니다. 또한 영어, 프랑스어, 그리고 한국어의 3개 국어로 이용 가능한 음성 안내 투어가 있습니다. 박물관 안에서는 음식물이나 음료를 섭취하는 것이나 전시물들의 사진을 찍는 것이 엄격히 금지되어 있음을 명심하십시오. 마지막으로, 만약 여러분이 기념품을 좀 구입하고 싶다면, 1층에 있는 박물관 기념품점을 방문하시면 됩니다. 박물관을 즐겁게 둘러보시길 바랍니다.

어휘 | explore 탐험하다, 답사하다 exhibit *전시품; 전시하다 illustrate 설명하다 distribute 나누어 주다 strictly 엄격히 prohibit 금지하다 consume 소비하다; *먹다, 마시다 souvenir 기념품

문제해설 | ④ 박물관 안에서 음식물이나 음료를 섭취하는 것은 금지되어 있다고 했다.

12 정답 ①

M: Good afternoon, Ms. Jones. Would you like to purchase a magazine subscription?

W: Well, I'm not sure. What are my options?

M: Take a look. There are several magazines to choose from.

W: Okay. Well, I'm not interested in economics, so I don't want that one.

M: Then how about a fashion or cooking magazine?

W: I like fashion, and my husband enjoys cooking. I guess I could choose one of those.

M: Great! And they each come with a free gift.

W: I see. I certainly don't need any flour. I just bought some last week. And my husband wouldn't want the teapot.

M: Well, there are two more options that you might like.

W: I think I will just order the cheaper one.

M: Great! You're really going to enjoy your subscription.

남: 안녕하세요, Jones 부인. 잡지 구독을 하시겠어요?

여: 음, 잘 모르겠어요. 어떤 선택 사항들이 있나요?

남: 한번 보세요. 선택할 수 있는 잡지가 여러 개 있어요.

여: 네. 음, 전 경제에는 관심이 없어서 저건 원하지 않아요.

남: 그럼 패션 잡지나 요리 잡지는 어떠세요?

여: 전 패션을 좋아하고, 제 남편은 요리를 즐겨 해요. 그것들 중 하나를 선택해야겠네요.

남: 좋아요! 게다가 그것들 모두 사은품을 함께 드립니다.

여: 그렇군요. 저는 밀가루는 정말 필요 없어요. 지난주에 좀 샀거든요. 그리고 제 남편은 찻주전자를 원하지 않을 거예요.

남: 음, 부인께서 좋아하실 만한 선택 사항이 두 개 더 있어요.

여: 전 그냥 더 저렴한 걸로 주문할게요.

남: 좋아요! 잡지 구독에 정말 만족하실 겁니다.

어휘 | subscription 구독 economics 경제학 flour 밀가루 teapot 찻주전자

문제해설 | 여자는 패션 잡지나 요리 잡지 중에서, 밀가루나 찻주전자가 아닌 사은품을 증정하고, 구독료가 더 저렴한 것으로 주문하고 싶다고 했으므로, 여자가 구독할 잡지는 ①번이다.

13 정답 ③

W: Good morning. Do you remember me?

M: Oh, yes. You came in yesterday morning, didn't you?

W: Yes, I did. I came in to get some keys made.

M: That's right. How can I help you?

W: Well, the door key you made me works fine. But the key to the gate doesn't work.

M: Are you sure?

W: Yes. I tried it several times, but it doesn't work at all.

M: Okay. Did you bring both the original and the new key?

W: Yes, here they are.

M: Thanks. I'll prepare the machine and make you another new one. Please just wait for a moment.

W: Sure. Will I be charged for the new key?

M: <u>No. I made a mistake, so this one is free.</u>

여: 안녕하세요. 저를 기억하세요?

남: 아, 네. 어제 아침에 오셨었죠, 그렇죠?

여: 네, 그랬어요. 열쇠들을 좀 만들려고 왔었어요.

남: 그랬죠. 어떻게 도와 드릴까요?

여: 음, 제게 만들어 주신 현관 열쇠는 잘 맞아요. 그런데, 대문 열쇠가 맞질 않아서요.

남: 확실한가요?

여: 네. 제가 여러 번 해 봤는데, 전혀 작동을 안 해요.

남: 알겠습니다. 원래 열쇠와 새 열쇠 둘 다 가져오셨나요?

여: 네, 여기 있어요.

남: 고맙습니다. 기계를 준비해서 다른 새것을 만들어 드리겠습니다. 잠시만 기다려 주세요.

여: 그럼요. 그런데, 새 열쇠에 대한 비용을 부담해야 하나요?

남: <u>아닙니다. 제가 실수를 했으니, 이건 무료입니다.</u>

어휘 | work 일하다; *작동하다 original 원래의 charge (비용을) 청구하다 |**문제**| spare 여분의

문제해설 | 남자가 만들어 준 열쇠가 맞지 않아서 여자가 다시 열쇠를 만들러 온 상황이므로, 새 열쇠에 대한 비용을 청구할 것인지를 묻는 여자의 물음에 대한 남자의 응답으로 ③번이 가장 적절하다.

① 열쇠가 준비되면 전화 드릴게요.

② 괜찮습니다. 당신이 서두르셔야 하는 것 압니다.

④ 물론이죠. 여분의 열쇠를 가지고 있는 것은 좋은 생각이에요.

⑤ 아니요. 유감이지만 저희는 기계가 없어요.

14 정답 ④

M: Well, I failed again today.
W: What are you talking about? Did you take a test?
M: No. My doctor said coffee is bad for my health. So I stopped drinking it last week.
W: But you had a cup this morning?
M: Two cups, actually. Every time I try to quit, I fail.
W: I see. Maybe you're just using the wrong method.
M: What do you mean?
W: Some people try to stop completely, all at once.
M: Yes, that's what I've been doing.
W: But I think it would be easier to quit gradually.
M: You might be right. But I'm not sure how to start.
W: <u>Just try to reduce the amount of coffee you drink each week.</u>

남: 있지, 나 오늘 또 실패했어.
여: 무슨 말이야? 시험이라도 봤니?
남: 아니. 의사 선생님이 커피가 건강에 나쁘다고 하셨거든. 그래서 나는 지난주에 커피 마시는 것을 그만뒀어.
여: 하지만 오늘 아침에 한 잔 마셨구나?
남: 두 잔이야, 사실. 나는 끊으려고 할 때마다 실패해.
여: 그렇구나. 아마 너는 잘못된 방법을 사용하고 있는지도 몰라.
남: 그게 무슨 말이야?
여: 어떤 사람들은 갑자기 끊으려고 해.
남: 응, 그게 내가 하고 있는 거야.
여: 하지만 내 생각엔 서서히 끊는 게 더 쉬울 것 같아.
남: 네 말이 맞을지도 몰라. 하지만 어떻게 시작할지 모르겠어.
여: <u>그냥 매주 네가 마시던 커피의 양을 줄여봐.</u>

어휘 | quit 그만두다, 끊다 method 방법 all at once 갑자기 gradually 서서히

문제해설 | 남자가 커피를 어떻게 서서히 끊어야 할지 모르겠다고 했으므로, 이에 대한 여자의 응답으로 ④번이 가장 적절하다.
① 난 대학교 1학년 때 커피를 마시기 시작했어.
② 다시 검사할 수 있는지 의사에게 물어봐야 해.
③ 네가 진실을 말한다면, 모두가 이해할 게 분명해.
⑤ 우리 집 모퉁이 근처에 아주 좋은 커피숍이 있어.

15 정답 ①

M: Marie's son will be turning 16 on Saturday. She decided to invite all of his friends over and have a big party. Her husband agreed that it was a good idea and offered to help her with the preparations. However, she was sure that she could manage on her own and thought it would be easier if she did it herself. She thanked her husband, but politely refused his offer. Her party preparations were going well until Wednesday, when her boss announced that everyone would have to work overtime for the rest of the week. Suddenly, she realized that she wouldn't have enough time to get things done. In this situation, what would Marie most likely say to her husband?
Marie: <u>I'm sorry, but can you help me out?</u>

남: Marie의 아들은 토요일에 16세가 된다. 그녀는 아들의 친구들 모두를 초대해서 성대한 파티를 열어 주기로 결심했다. 그녀의 남편은 그것이 좋은 생각이라는 데 동의했고 그녀가 (파티를) 준비하는 것을 도와주겠다고 제안했다. 하지만, 그녀는 스스로 해낼 수 있다고 확신했고, 혼자 하면 일이 더 쉬울 거라고 생각했다. 그녀는 남편에게 고맙긴 했지만, 정중하게 그의 제안을 거절했다. 그녀의 파티 준비는 수요일까지는 잘되고 있었는데, 수요일에 사장님이 이번 주 남은 기간 동안 모두 야근을 해야 할 거라고 말했다. 갑자기, 그녀는 (파티) 준비를 끝내는 데 시간이 충분하지 않으리라는 것을 깨달았다. 이런 상황에서, Marie가 남편에게 할 말로 가장 적절한 것은 무엇인가?
Marie: <u>미안하지만, 나 좀 도와줄래요?</u>

어휘 | manage 다루다, 감당하다 on one's own 혼자서 politely 공손히 refuse 거절하다 work overtime 초과근무를 하다

문제해설 | 혼자서 아들의 생일 파티를 준비하던 Marie가 갑작스러운 야근으로 인해 파티 준비할 시간이 부족하다는 것을 깨달은 상황이므로, Marie가 남편에게 할 말로 ①번이 가장 적절하다.
② 직장 상사에게 그냥 늦게까지 있을 수 없다고 말해요.
③ 파티를 위해 모든 것이 준비된 것 같아요.
④ 걱정하지 말아요. 내가 혼자서 그것을 처리할 수 있어요.
⑤ 난 너무 바빠서 파티에 갈 수 없어요.

16 정답 ②   17 정답 ⑤

W: High blood pressure can lead to heart disease, stroke, kidney failure, and other health issues. Fortunately, medications have been developed to help people maintain a healthy blood pressure. But oftentimes, changing your lifestyle can help you keep your blood pressure low without having to turn to medication. Losing weight can be a huge help. Talk to your doctor about a good weight-loss goal. Even losing just ten pounds can lower your blood pressure. Regular exercise is also important. Try to do between 30 and 60 minutes of exercise a day, and you could start seeing results in just a few weeks. Maintaining a healthy diet is also important. Be sure to eat plenty of whole grains, fruits, and vegetables. Finally, try to avoid foods that are high in sodium. In order to do this, stay away from processed foods, and don't add extra salt to your meals.

If you follow these steps, you can stay healthy without having to rely on medication.

여: 고혈압은 심장병, 뇌졸중, 신부전, 그리고 다른 건강 문제들을 일으킬 수 있습니다. 다행히, 사람들이 건강한 혈압을 유지하는 것을 돕기 위해 약물이 개발되어 왔습니다. 그러나 종종, 여러분의 생활 방식을 바꾸는 것이 약물에 의지할 필요 없이 혈압을 낮추는 데 도움이 될 수 있습니다. 체중 감량은 큰 도움이 될 수 있습니다. 적당한 체중 감량 목표에 대해 의사와 상의해 보세요. 단 10파운드를 감량하는 것만으로도 혈압을 낮출 수 있습니다. 규칙적인 운동도 또한 중요합니다. 하루에 30분에서 60분의 운동을 하도록 노력하면, 여러분은 단 몇 주 만에 효과를 보기 시작할 겁니다. 건강한 식단을 유지하는 것도 또한 중요합니다. 반드시 통곡물과 과일, 그리고 채소를 충분히 드세요. 마지막으로, 나트륨이 많이 든 음식을 피하려고 노력하세요. 이렇게 하기 위해서는, 가공식품을 멀리하고 식사에 별도의 소금을 넣지 마세요. 이 조치들을 따르면, 여러분은 약물에 의존할 필요 없이 건강을 유지할 수 있습니다.

어휘 | blood pressure 혈압 stroke 뇌졸중 kidney failure 신부전 medication 약물 turn to …에 의존하다 lower 낮추다 whole grain 통곡물 sodium 나트륨 stay away from …을 가까이하지 않다 processed food 가공식품 step 단계; *조치 rely on …에 의존하다
|문제| associated with …와 관련된 nutritional supplement 영양 보충제

문제해설 | 16. 여자는 약물을 쓰지 않고 혈압을 낮추는 여러 가지 방법들에 대해 이야기하고 있다.
① 안전하게 체중을 감량하는 방법들
② 혈압을 낮추는 방법들
③ 혈압약의 이점들
④ 고혈압과 관련된 위험들
⑤ 어떻게 의사가 당신이 더 건강한 삶을 살도록 도울 수 있는가
17. 혈압을 낮추는 방법으로 ⑤ 영양 보충제는 언급되지 않았다.
① 체중 줄이기 ② 규칙적인 운동 ③ 건강한 식단 ④ 나트륨 피하기

14강 FINAL TEST

pp. 60-63

1 ③	2 ④	3 ⑤	4 ⑤	5 ②
6 ⑤	7 ④	8 ③	9 ④	10 ①
11 ⑤	12 ①	13 ⑤	14 ②	15 ④
16 ②	17 ③			

1 정답 ③

M: Did you know that there will be a pop quiz before the midterm?
W: Yeah, I think it will help me prepare.
M: You're such an optimist! Personally, I don't think it's fair.
W: Well, it wouldn't hurt you to think positively.

남: 너 중간고사 전에 쪽지시험이 있다는 거 알았어?
여: 응, 그게 (중간고사를) 준비하는 데 도움이 될 것 같아.
남: 넌 정말 낙천주의자야! 개인적으로 난 그게 괜찮다고 생각하지 않는데.
여: 음, 긍정적으로 생각한다고 해서 너한테 해가 될 건 없어.

어휘 | pop quiz 쪽지시험 midterm 중간고사 optimist 낙관론자 personally 개인적으로 fair 공평한; *괜찮은

문제해설 | 남자가 쪽지시험에 대해 불평하고 있으므로 이에 대한 여자의 응답으로 ③번이 가장 적절하다.
① 응, 난 좋은 선택을 했어.
② 맞아. 넌 시험을 잘 볼 거야.
④ 난 중간고사에 대해 생각했어야 했어.
⑤ 난 네가 좀 더 노력해야 한다고 생각해.

2 정답 ④

W: Is this the Japanese restaurant that you mentioned before?
M: Yes! It's very famous in this area for its fresh sushi.
W: I can't wait to try it! [Pause] Oh, the restaurant is already packed.
M: I think some people are almost finished. Let's wait.

여: 여기가 네가 전에 말한 그 일식집이야?
남: 응! 이 근방에서 초밥이 신선하기로 아주 유명해.
여: 빨리 먹어 보고 싶다! [잠시 후] 아, 식당이 벌써 꽉 찼어.
남: 몇몇 사람들은 식사를 거의 끝낸 것 같아. 기다리자.

어휘 | packed 꽉 들어찬

문제해설 | 여자가 식당이 이미 꽉 찼다고 말했으므로 이에 대한 남자의 응답으로 ④번이 가장 적절하다.
① 그렇다면, 전화로 예약하자.
② 걱정하지 마. 넌 여기 초밥을 정말 좋아할 거야.
③ 실은, 난 다른 식당을 생각하고 있었어.
⑤ 이상하네. 내가 생각한 것만큼 인기 있지 않은 것 같아.

3 정답 ⑤

M: According to the laws of our city, painting graffiti in public places is illegal. However, here in our neighborhood, you can see graffiti painted on nearly every wall. Even worse, chances are high that you will never observe police officers investigating this vandalism or even trying to stop it. This is because they have been instructed by their superiors not to aggressively enforce this particular law, a decision made with the approval of the mayor. The reasoning is that it would cause too many conflicts and distract the police from more important issues. But I say that this graffiti is a serious nuisance that must be stopped, and that a law is a law.

남: 우리 시의 법에 따르면, 공공장소에 낙서하는 것은 불법입니다. 하지만, 이곳 우리 마을에서, 여러분은 거의 모든 벽에 낙서가 되어 있는 것을 볼 수 있습니다. 더욱 심각한 것은, 여러분은 결코 경찰관들이 이런 공공 기물 파손죄를 조사하거나 그것을 저지하려고 노력하는 것조차 보지 못할 가능성이 높다는 것입니다. 이것은 그들이 그들의 상관들로부터 이 특정한 법을 적극적으로 집행하지 말라는 지시를 받았기 때문인데, 이는 시장의 승인으로 이루어진 결정입니다. 그 논리는 그것이 너무 많은 갈등을 일으키고, 경찰관들이 더 중요한 문제에 집중할 수 없게 할 거라는 것입니다. 하지만 저는 이 낙서행위가 중단되어야 하는 심각한 방해 행위이며, 법은 법이라는 점을 말씀드립니다.

어휘 | graffiti (공공장소에 하는) 낙서 illegal 불법적인 investigate 조사하다 vandalism 공공 기물 파손죄 instruct 지시하다 superior 상급자, 상관 aggressively 공격적으로; *적극적으로 enforce (법을) 실시하다, 시행하다 particular 특정한 approval 인정; *승인 mayor 시장 reasoning 추론, 이론 conflict 갈등 distract 산만하게 하다 nuisance 골칫거리; *방해 행위

문제해설 | 남자는 공공장소에 낙서하는 것이 불법임에도 불구하고 적극적인 단속이 이루어지지 않는 상황을 비판하며 더욱 적극적인 단속을 요구하고 있다.

4 정답 ⑤

W: Nicolas, how is your business these days?
M: It is doing very well. I am thinking about opening a second location.
W: That's great news. I would really like to open my own business.
M: It is a lot of work but very rewarding.
W: That's exactly what a famous businessman said in an interview. I have been trying to learn how successful people built their businesses.
M: It is great to study other people's businesses, but you shouldn't only focus on people's successes.
W: Why not? I don't want to make an unsuccessful business.
M: Of course not. But people often make the same mistakes when starting a business.
W: I see. So learning about other people's mistakes can help me avoid them?
M: Right. That is the best way to start planning a business.

여: Nicolas, 요즘 네 사업은 어때?
남: 아주 잘되고 있어. 2호점을 낼까 생각 중이야.
여: 정말 잘됐다. 나도 내 소유의 사업을 시작하고 싶어.
남: 일이 굉장히 많지만 아주 보람 있어.
여: 그게 바로 유명한 사업가가 인터뷰에서 했던 말이야. 난 성공한 사람들이 어떻게 그들의 사업을 일으켰는지 배우려고 하고 있거든.
남: 다른 사람들의 사업체를 연구하는 것도 좋지만, 사람들의 성공에만 집중하지는 말아야 해.
여: 왜? 나는 사업에 실패하고 싶지 않은데.
남: 물론 아니지. 그런데 사람들은 사업을 시작할 때 흔히 같은 실수를 저질러.
여: 알겠어. 그러니까 다른 사람들의 실수에 대해서 배우면 내가 그런 실수를 피하는 데 도움이 될 수 있다는 거지?
남: 맞아. 그게 사업 계획을 시작하는 최선의 방법이야.

어휘 | location 지점 rewarding 보람이 있는, 수익이 좋은

문제해설 | 사업을 하고 싶어 하는 여자에게 남자는 다른 사업가의 성공에만 집중할 것이 아니라, 사업을 시작할 때 흔히 저지르는 실수에서 배우는 것이 좋은 방법이라고 이야기하고 있다.

5 정답 ②

W: Hi, nice to meet you.
M: Hello. My name's Michael. I'm a big fan of your work.
W: Thank you, Michael. Here, let me sign your copy of my book.
M: Here it is. I can't wait to read it. Actually, I've read all your other books.
W: I'm happy to hear that. Which was your favorite?
M: I particularly enjoyed *Under the Rain Clouds*, your novel about Bolivia.
W: Really? That's one of my favorites, too.
M: Actually, I've read that book more than three times. Whenever I read it, I can picture the landscape so clearly. You're an amazing writer.
W: Well, I'm flattered.
M: Actually, I'm trying to become a writer myself.
W: Really? That's great. My advice is to keep on writing and never give up.
M: Thank you. I'm so glad to have met you.

여: 안녕하세요, 만나서 반가워요.
남: 안녕하세요. 제 이름은 Michael입니다. 전 당신 작품의 열렬한 팬이에요.
여: 고마워요, Michael. 자, 당신이 가지고 있는 제 책에 사인해 드릴게요.
남: 여기 있어요. 전 그걸 빨리 읽고 싶어요. 사실, 전 당신의 다른 책들을 모두 읽었거든요.
여: 그 말을 들으니 기쁘네요. 당신이 가장 좋아했던 책은 뭔가요?

남: 전 볼리비아에 관한 소설인 「Under the Rain Clouds」를 특히 즐겨 읽었어요.
여: 정말요? 그건 제가 가장 좋아하는 책들 중 하나이기도 해요.
남: 사실, 전 그 책을 세 번 넘게 읽었어요. 그걸 읽을 때마다, 배경을 아주 선명하게 상상할 수 있어요. 당신은 굉장한 작가예요.
여: 음, 과찬이세요.
남: 사실, 전 작가가 되려고 노력하는 중이에요.
여: 정말요? 멋지네요. 제 조언은 계속 글을 쓰시고 절대 포기하시지 말라는 거예요.
남: 고마워요. 당신을 만나게 돼서 정말 기뻐요.

어휘 | copy (같은 책의) 권, 부 particularly 특히 novel 소설 picture (마음에) 그리다, 상상하다 landscape 풍경 be flattered (어깨가) 으쓱해지다

문제해설 | 남자가 여자의 팬이며 그녀의 책들을 모두 읽었다고 하면서 여자를 굉장한 작가라고 하는 것으로 보아, 여자는 소설가이고 남자는 독자임을 알 수 있다.

6 정답 ⑤

[*Telephone rings.*]
M: Hello, Mighty Sportswear.
W: Hi, Tony. It's me. I called you to check if everything is prepared for the store opening.
M: No problem. Is there anything special I should check?
W: Did you make sure to hang up all the T-shirts?
M: Yes. I also put up the 30% off sign.
W: Great. Did you put our new running shoes on the top shelf?
M: Yes. I also put a basketball, a soccer ball, and a volleyball under them.
W: Good. Did you change the mannequin into summer clothes?
M: Of course. It's wearing our brand new shorts and a short-sleeved shirt.
W: Everything sounds perfect. Good job!

[전화벨이 울린다.]
남: 여보세요, Mighty 스포츠웨어입니다.
여: 안녕, Tony. 나예요. 가게 개업을 위해 모든 것이 준비되었는지 확인하려고 전화했어요.
남: 문제없습니다. 제가 확인해야 할 특별한 것이 있나요?
여: 모든 티셔츠들을 걸어 놓았나요?
남: 네. 30% 할인 표지판도 두었어요.
여: 잘했어요. 새로운 운동화들은 상단 진열대에 두었죠?
남: 네. 그 아래에 농구공, 축구공, 배구공도 두었습니다.
여: 좋아요. 마네킹은 여름옷으로 갈아입혔나요?
남: 물론이죠. 그건 저희 신상품인 반바지와 반소매 셔츠를 입고 있어요.
여: 모든 게 완벽한 것 같네요. 잘했어요!

어휘 | sportswear 운동복 put up …을 게시하다 mannequin 마네킹 brand new 완전 새것인

문제해설 | 남자는 마네킹에 반바지와 반소매 옷을 진열했다고 했으므로 대화의 내용과 일치하지 않는 것은 ⑤번이다.

7 정답 ④

W: Hey, what just happened?
M: The lights went out. And look, all the electrical appliances went off.
W: There must have been a power outage. Wow, the whole street is dark.
M: Well, we can't watch our favorite drama tonight.
W: Maybe the power will come back on soon.
M: Last year, the power stayed out for six hours while the power company struggled to repair the lines.
W: That's right. Well, I don't want to sit in the dark for six hours.
M: Why don't we go downtown, then? We can catch a movie there instead.
W: Good.
M: Wait a minute. I'll report the problem to the power company first.
W Okay.
M: Oh, my cell phone battery is dead. Can you find the number of the power company with your cell phone?
W: No problem.

여: 얘, 방금 무슨 일이 있었니?
남: 불이 나갔어. 그리고 봐, 모든 전기 기구들이 다 꺼졌어.
여: 정전이 된 게 틀림없어. 와, 길 전체가 어두워.
남: 음, 우리는 오늘 밤에 우리가 제일 좋아하는 드라마를 못 보겠네.
여: 아마 곧 전기가 다시 들어올 거야.
남: 작년에, 전력 회사가 전선들을 고치려고 애쓰는 동안 여섯 시간이나 전기가 나갔었잖아.
여: 맞아. 음, 난 여섯 시간 동안 어두운 데 앉아 있기는 싫은데.
남: 그럼, 시내로 가는 게 어때? 우리는 대신 거기서 영화를 볼 수 있어.
여: 좋아.
남: 잠깐만 기다려. 내가 먼저 전력 회사에 이 문제를 신고할게.
여: 그래.
남: 아, 휴대전화 배터리가 나갔네. 네 휴대전화로 전력 회사 전화번호를 찾아 줄 수 있니?
여: 당연하지.

어휘 | electrical appliance 전기 기구 go off (불·전기 등이) 나가다 outage 정전 struggle 애쓰다 report 알리다, 전하다

문제해설 | 남자가 여자에게 휴대전화로 전력 회사 전화번호를 찾아 달

라고 부탁하자, 여자는 그렇게 하겠다고 했다.

8 정답 ③

W: There you are, Jake!
M: Hey, Jennifer!
W: I tried to call you several times, but you didn't answer your phone.
M: Oh, sorry. I didn't know that you called me.
W: Did you leave your phone at home again?
M: No, I didn't leave it at home.
W: Then why didn't you answer? Did your battery die?
M: No, my battery was running low when I was at the library with my friend, so I plugged it in to recharge it.
W: Well, why didn't you call me back?
M: I couldn't. Someone stole my phone when I was away!
W: Really? That's awful. You haven't found it yet?
M: No, but I reported that it has been stolen.
W: I hope you can get it back soon.

여: 너 여기 있었구나, Jake!
남: 어, Jennifer!
여: 너에게 여러 번 전화했는데, 네가 전화를 받지 않았어.
남: 아, 미안해. 네가 전화했는지 몰랐어.
여: 너 또 집에 전화기를 두고 왔니?
남: 아니, 전화기를 집에 놓고 오지는 않았어.
여: 그럼 왜 전화를 안 받았어? 배터리가 다 닳았어?
남: 아니, 친구랑 도서관에 있을 때 배터리가 떨어져 가서 충전하려고 플러그를 꽂아 놨어.
여: 그럼 왜 내게 다시 전화하지 않았어?
남: 할 수가 없었어. 내가 없는 사이에 누가 내 전화기를 훔쳐 갔어!
여: 정말? 끔찍하다. 전화기는 아직 못 찾았어?
남: 응, 하지만 그것을 도난당했다고 신고했어.
여: 네가 빨리 그걸 되찾으면 좋겠다.

어휘 | run low 고갈되다, 다 (떨어져) 가다 plug in …에 플러그를 꽂다 recharge 충전하다 awful 끔찍한

문제해설 | 남자는 도서관에서 휴대전화를 도난당해 여자에게 전화를 할 수가 없었다.

9 정답 ④

[*Telephone rings.*]
M: Hello, this is the Lakehouse Hotel. How may I help you?
W: Hi. I'd like to book a room for two for this Friday.
M: All right. We have a standard room available for $80.
W: I see. Does it have a view of the lake?
M: No, but we have a deluxe room with a view for $30 more.
W: I see. Is breakfast included in that price?
M: No, breakfast is $10 per person.
W: Actually, I'll be accompanied by my son. He's only seven. Does he have to pay the full price for breakfast?
M: No, he doesn't. Breakfast is half-price for children under 12.
W: Then I'll take the deluxe room and breakfast for the two of us.
M: Certainly. Will you be staying for just a single night?
W: That's correct.
M: All right. Your room has been reserved.

[전화벨이 울린다.]
남: 여보세요, Lakehouse 호텔입니다. 어떻게 도와 드릴까요?
여: 안녕하세요. 이번 주 금요일에 2인용 객실 하나를 예약하고 싶은데요.
남: 네. 80달러에 이용 가능한 스탠다드 룸이 있습니다.
여: 그렇군요. 호수 경치가 보이나요?
남: 아니요, 그렇지만 30달러를 추가하여 경치가 보이는 디럭스 룸이 있습니다.
여: 알겠습니다. 그 가격에 조식이 포함되어 있나요?
남: 아니요, 조식은 1인당 10달러입니다.
여: 실은, 저는 아들과 같이 갈 거예요. 겨우 일곱 살이죠. 그 애도 조식에 전액을 지불해야 하나요?
남: 아닙니다. 12살 미만의 아동은 조식이 반값입니다.
여: 그럼 2인 조식으로 디럭스 룸으로 하겠습니다.
남: 알겠습니다. 1박만 머무르실 건가요?
여: 그렇습니다.
남: 네. 고객님의 방이 예약되었습니다.

어휘 | be accompanied by …를 동반하다[동행하다]

문제해설 | 여자는 아들과 함께 디럭스 룸($110)에서 하루 묵을 예정인데, 1인 조식비($10)와 12세 미만인 아들의 조식비($5)를 합쳐, 여자가 지불할 금액은 총 125달러이다.

10 정답 ①

M: Hi, Amanda. How was your weekend?
W: Hi, George. It was good. I went with Martin to the international furniture expo.
M: That sounds interesting. Did you have a good time?
W: Yeah, it was great. There were over 30 different furniture companies from around the world there.
M: Did they have any office furniture there, or was it mostly home furnishings?
W: It was mostly home furnishings, but there was some office furniture, too.
M: Cool. Did they have any special activities?
W: Yes. Actually, they had a do-it-yourself booth where we made picture frames.

M: That sounds fun.

W: It was. I made one as a gift for my mother.

M: How nice! I should have joined you.

W: Why don't we go together next time? The tickets are only $10 each!

남: 안녕, Amanda. 주말 잘 보냈어?

여: 안녕, George. 잘 보냈어. Martin과 국제 가구 박람회에 갔어.

남: 재미있었겠다. 즐거운 시간 보냈어?

여: 응, 정말 좋았어. 거기에 전 세계에서 온 각양각색의 가구 회사들이 30개도 넘게 있었거든.

남: 거기에 사무용 가구도 있었니, 아니면 대부분 가정용 가구였니?

여: 거의 가정용 가구였지만, 사무용 가구도 좀 있었어.

남: 멋지다. 특별한 행사도 있었어?

여: 응. 사실, 우리가 사진 액자를 만드는 D.I.Y. 부스가 있었어.

남: 재미있었겠네.

여: 그랬어. 난 엄마한테 선물로 드리려고 하나 만들었어.

남: 정말 근사한데! 나도 너희들과 함께 갔어야 했는데.

여: 다음에 함께 가는 게 어때? 표는 장당 10달러밖에 안 해!

11 정답 ⑤

W: Attention please, students. As you know, we are going on a field trip tomorrow to the National Art Museum. Everyone needs to meet at the school tomorrow morning at 8 a.m. Do not be late. You must bring your own lunch, since we will be eating outdoors at a park near the museum. Bring an umbrella in case of rain, and also bring a pen and paper so you can work on your reports. Everyone must hand in a report about the field trip next Monday. The school has already gotten everyone passes to the art museum, so there's no need to bring a lot of money. Dress appropriately; this is a school event. Don't wear makeup or anything you would not wear to school. I'll see all of you tomorrow!

여: 학생 여러분, 주목해 주세요. 아시다시피, 우리는 내일 국립 미술관으로 현장 학습을 갑니다. 여러분 모두 내일 아침 8시에 학교에서 만나야 합니다. 늦지 마십시오. 우리는 미술관 근처 공원에서 야외에서 식사할 것이기 때문에 각자 자신의 점심을 가져와야 합니다. 비가 올 때를 대비하여 우산을 가져오시고, 보고서 작성을 할 수 있도록 펜과 종이도 가져오십시오. 여러분 모두 현장 학습에 관한 보고서를 다음 주 월요일에 제출해야 합니다. 학교에서 이미 여러분 모두의 미술관 입장권을 구입했으므로, 돈을 많이 가져올 필요는 없습니다. 이것은 학교 행사이므로, 옷을 적절하게 입으시기 바랍니다. 화장을 하거나 학교에 올 때 입어서는 안 되는 것들을 입지는 마십시오. 여러분 모두 내일 뵙겠습니다!

12 정답 ①

M: Do you want to have a look at the cars on this website now, dear?

W: Sure. Is there a good selection?

M: Yes. There are several options. How about getting an SUV? They're very safe.

W: Yes, I'd like that. We should get one even though they're more expensive.

M: I agree. Would you like a sunroof?

W: It would be nice to have one, but I don't think we really need one.

M: Okay. How about a navigation system?

W: Oh, that's definitely necessary. It's so easy to get lost without one.

M: Good point. Well, it looks like we have a few options.

W: Hmm… I really don't want to spend more than $28,000.

M: All right. Then I think I know which car is right for us.

남: 지금 이 웹사이트에 있는 차들을 한번 볼래요, 여보?

여: 그럼요. 물건은 다양하게 있나요?

남: 네. 여러 가지 선택 사항이 있어요. SUV를 구입하는 건 어때요? 그건 매우 안전하잖아요.

여: 네, 그러고 싶어요. SUV가 더 비싸도 우리는 그게 필요해요.

남: 동의해요. 당신은 선루프를 원해요?

여: 있으면 좋겠지만, 우리에게 꼭 필요한 것 같지는 않아요.

남: 알겠어요. 내비게이션 시스템은요?

여: 오, 그건 꼭 필요해요. 그게 없으면 길을 잃기 아주 쉽잖아요.

남: 좋은 지적이에요. 음, 선택지가 몇 개 있는 것 같네요.

여: 흠… 전 28,000달러 이상은 정말 쓰고 싶지 않아요.

남: 알겠어요. 그럼 우리에게 어떤 차가 제격인지 알겠네요.

13 정답 ⑤

W: Hey, Ian. How did you do on the biology final?
M: I didn't do very well. It was too hard.
W: Really? What was your score?
M: Well... I got an 88.
W: Oh, that's not bad. I heard a lot of students didn't do well at all.
M: I heard that, too. But I'm not satisfied with my grade. I studied hard for that exam.
W: Don't be too disappointed. A lot of other people probably feel the same way.
M: I guess so. Anyway, how did you do, Rachel?
W: Well, I got a 97.
M: Wow, that's incredible! Now I understand why you were smiling when we found out our grades.
W: I couldn't believe it. I even heard it was the best score in the class.
M: <u>Maybe next time I should prepare for the exam with you.</u>

여: 저기, Ian. 생물 기말고사 잘 봤니?
남: 아주 잘 보진 못했어. 너무 어려웠거든.
여: 정말? 몇 점인데?
남: 음… 88점을 받았어.
여: 오, 나쁘지 않네. 많은 학생들이 시험을 정말 못 봤다고 하던데.
남: 나도 그거 들었어. 그런데 난 내 성적이 만족스럽지 않아. 그 시험을 위해서 열심히 공부했거든.
여: 너무 실망하지 마. 다른 많은 사람들도 아마 같은 생각을 할 걸.
남: 그럴 것 같아. 그건 그렇고, Rachel, 넌 어떻게 봤어?
여: 음, 난 97점을 받았어.
남: 와, 대단해! 우리가 성적을 확인할 때 네가 왜 미소 짓고 있었는지 이제야 알겠어.
여: 나도 믿기지가 않아. 심지어 반에서 최고 점수라고 하더라.
남: <u>다음에는 너와 함께 그 시험을 준비해야겠다.</u>

어휘 | biology 생물학 final 기말고사 incredible 믿기 힘든, 굉장한 **|문제|** nonsense 터무니없는 말

문제해설 | 어려웠던 시험에서 여자가 반에서 가장 높은 점수를 받았다고 했으므로, 이에 대한 남자의 응답으로 ⑤번이 가장 적절하다.
① 내 기분을 이해해 줘서 고마워.
② 넌 반드시 더 열심히 공부해야 할 거야.
③ 글쎄, 네 점수를 내게 말할 필요는 없었는데.
④ 난 네 말에 동의하지 않아. 그건 완전히 터무니없는 말이야.

14 정답 ②

W: Hi. Can I help you?
M: Yes. There is a problem with my camera. I need to have it repaired.
W: All right. Do you have it with you?
M: Yes. Here it is.
W: What's the problem with it?
M: This piece is broken, and the batteries keep falling out.
W: Oh, I see. Well, we can definitely fix this, but it will take some time because there are several jobs ahead of yours.
M: That's fine. When can I pick it up?
W: You can come back on Wednesday. It will be ready by then.
M: Great. Oh, by the way, I bought this camera this year, so it should still be under warranty.
W: Okay. Do you have the warranty form?
M: Yes, but I left it at home.
W: <u>You can bring it when you pick up your camera.</u>

여: 안녕하세요. 도와 드릴까요?
남: 네. 제 카메라에 문제가 있어서요. 그걸 수리하고 싶어요.
여: 알겠습니다. 카메라를 가지고 계시나요?
남: 네. 여기 있어요.
여: 카메라에 무슨 문제가 있는 건가요?
남: 이 부분이 부서져서 배터리가 계속 빠져요.
여: 오, 알겠습니다. 음, 저희가 이걸 고칠 수 있는 건 분명한데, 고객님 앞에 여러 일들이 있어서 시간이 좀 걸릴 겁니다.
남: 괜찮아요. 제가 언제 가져갈 수 있을까요?
여: 수요일에 오세요. 그때까지 준비가 될 거예요.
남: 좋아요. 오, 그런데 이 카메라는 올해 산 거라 아직 품질 보증 기간일 거예요.
여: 네. 품질 보증서를 가지고 계세요?
남: 네, 그런데 집에 놓고 왔어요.
여: <u>카메라를 찾아가실 때 그걸 가져오세요.</u>

어휘 | piece 일부, 부분 fall out …가 떨어져 나가다 ahead of …앞에 under warranty 품질 보증 기간인 **|문제|** notify 알리다

문제해설 | 남자가 품질 보증서를 집에 놓고 왔다고 했으므로 이에 대한 여자의 응답으로는 ②번이 가장 적절하다.
① 걱정하지 마세요. 당신은 새 것을 살 필요가 없어요.
③ 언제 찾아가실 수 있는 준비가 되는지 알려드릴게요.
④ 유감스럽게도, 고객님의 카메라는 제시간 내에 준비가 안 될 거예요.
⑤ 죄송하지만, 저희는 이 제품에 대해 품질 보증을 해드리지 않아요.

15 정답 ④

M: Greg played sports in high school, but since starting university he hasn't made time for regular exercise. Worried about being out of shape and gaining weight, he has decided to get back in the habit of exercising. He has asked his friend Mandy if he can join her each day for her morning exercises, and she has welcomed him. However, when his alarm clock goes off each morning, he usually feels too tired to get out of bed. Disappointed about being unable to keep his resolution, he tells Mandy about the hard time he is having. She wants to say something that will encourage him to keep trying. In this situation, what would Mandy most likely say to Greg?

Mandy: If you keep getting up early, it will get easier soon.

남: Greg는 고등학교 때는 운동을 했지만, 대학 생활을 시작한 이후로 규칙적인 운동을 할 시간을 갖지 못하고 있다. 몸매가 안 좋아지고 체중이 느는 것이 걱정되어, 그는 운동하는 습관을 되찾기로 결심했다. 그는 친구인 Mandy에게 매일 그녀의 아침 운동에 함께 해도 되는지를 물었고, 그녀는 그를 환영했다. 하지만, 매일 아침 알람 시계가 울리면, 그는 대개 너무 피곤해서 침대에서 일어날 수가 없다. 자신의 결심을 지키지 못하는 것에 실망해서, 그는 Mandy에게 자신이 겪고 있는 힘든 시간에 대해 이야기한다. 그녀는 그가 계속 시도하도록 격려할 무언가를 말해주고 싶다. 이런 상황에서, Mandy가 Greg에게 할 말로 가장 적절한 것은 무엇인가?

Mandy: 네가 계속 일찍 일어난다면, 곧 더 쉬워질 거야.

어휘 | out of shape 건강이 안 좋은, 몸매가 엉망인 go off (시계가) 울리다 resolution 결심 **|문제|** keep in shape 몸매를 유지하다

문제해설 | Greg는 건강을 위해서 Mandy와 함께 매일 아침 운동을 하려고 결심했지만 실천하는 데 어려움을 겪고 있으므로, Mandy가 Greg에게 할 말로 ④번이 가장 적절하다.
① 왜 헬스클럽에서 운동을 해 왔니?
② 난 요즘 네가 살쪘다고 생각하지 않아.
③ 네가 결심을 지켜서 매우 자랑스러워.
⑤ 난 학기 중에는 몸매를 관리하기가 어렵다는 걸 알았어.

16 정답 ② 17 정답 ③

W: You might think that all inventions are made by following a careful plan. However, many are created completely by accident. Potato chips, for example, were invented by a chef named George Crum. He wasn't trying to perfect a recipe, though. He was angry that one of his customers kept saying that his French fried potatoes were not crispy enough. He sliced the potatoes very thin and fried them until they were extra crispy. To Crum's surprise, the customer loved them, and that's how potato chips were born. Ice cream cones are another example. They were created when an ice cream stall ran out of plates. They decided to borrow waffles from a neighboring stand and roll them up to serve the ice cream. Also, when a Swiss engineer went on a hunting trip with his dog and noticed seeds sticking to his pet's fur, he copied this effect to produce Velcro. Lastly, when eleven-year-old Frank Epperson accidentally left homemade soda water outside, it froze with a spoon in it during the cold night. This gave him the idea to make flavored ice on a stick, which would later be known as the Popsicle.

여: 여러분은 모든 발명품들이 세심한 계획에 따라 만들어졌다고 생각할지 모릅니다. 그러나, 많은 발명품들은 아주 우연히 만들어집니다. 예를 들어, 감자 칩은 George Crum이라는 요리사에 의해 발명되었습니다. 하지만 그는 완벽한 요리법을 만들려던 것이 아니었습니다. 그는 고객 중 한 명이 계속 그의 감자 튀김이 충분히 바삭하지 않다고 말해서 화가 났습니다. 그는 감자를 아주 얇게 썰어서 그것들이 더 바삭해질 때까지 튀겼습니다. Crum이 놀랄 정도로, 그 고객은 그것들을 정말 좋아했고, 그것이 감자 칩이 생기게 된 계기입니다. 아이스크림콘은 또 다른 예시입니다. 그것은 아이스크림 가판대에서 그릇이 동났을 때 만들어졌습니다. 그들은 이웃 좌판에서 와플을 빌려 그것들을 둘둘 말아 아이스크림을 내어 주기로 정했습니다. 또한, 한 스위스인 기술자가 개와 함께 사냥 여행을 가서 씨앗이 그의 애완동물의 털에 붙는 것을 발견했을 때, 그는 이 효과를 모방하여 벨크로를 만들었습니다. 마지막으로, 11살이었던 Frank Epperson이 우연히 집에서 만든 탄산수를 밖에 놓아 두었을 때, 추운 밤 동안 그 안에 있던 숟가락과 함께 그것이 얼었습니다. 이것으로 그는 막대기 위에 풍미가 더해진 얼음을 만들겠다는 발상을 하게 됐는데, 이는 나중에 아이스바로 알려지게 되었습니다.

어휘 | by accident 우연히 recipe 요리법 crispy 바삭바삭한 slice 썰다 stall 가판대(= stand) neighboring 이웃의 stick to …에 달라붙다 effect 효과 flavored 향을 첨가한

문제해설 | 16. 여자는 여러 가지 구체적인 예시를 통해 우연히 만들어진 발명품들에 대해 이야기하고 있다.
① 역사상 가장 위대한 몇몇 발명가들
② 우연히 만들어진 발명품들
③ 유용한 것을 발명하는 비결
④ 발명 시 필요한 세심한 계획
⑤ 많은 인기를 얻은 발명품들
17. ③ 와플은 아이스크림콘을 만들기 위해 사용한 도구이지, 우연히 만들어진 발명품은 아니다.
① 감자 칩 ② 아이스크림콘 ④ 벨크로(찍찍이) ⑤ 아이스바

<table>
<tr><td colspan="6">15강 FINAL TEST   pp. 64-67</td></tr>
<tr><td>1 ③</td><td>2 ⑤</td><td>3 ④</td><td>4 ④</td><td>5 ⑤</td></tr>
<tr><td>6 ③</td><td>7 ④</td><td>8 ⑤</td><td>9 ①</td><td>10 ④</td></tr>
<tr><td>11 ④</td><td>12 ③</td><td>13 ⑤</td><td>14 ①</td><td>15 ⑤</td></tr>
<tr><td>16 ②</td><td>17 ③</td><td></td><td></td><td></td></tr>
</table>

1 정답 ③

M: May I help you, ma'am?
W: Yes. I'm looking for a T-shirt for my brother.
M: We have a pink striped one and a blue polka-dotted one. Which do you prefer?
W: I don't like either of them.

남: 도와 드릴까요, 손님?
여: 네. 제 남동생에게 줄 티셔츠를 찾고 있어요.
남: 분홍색 줄무늬 티셔츠와 파란색 물방울무늬 티셔츠가 있어요. 어떤 것이 더 좋으세요?
여: 전 둘 다 별로예요.

어휘 | striped 줄무늬가 있는 polka-dotted 물방울무늬(의) **|문제|** suit 어울리다 exchange 교환하다

문제해설 | 직원이 두 가지 티셔츠 중에 어느 것이 더 마음에 드는지 물었으므로 이에 대한 여자의 응답으로 ③번이 가장 적절하다.
① 그 애는 티셔츠를 좋아하지 않아요.
② 전 남성용 바지를 선호해요.
④ 이 노란색 티셔츠는 제게 어울리지 않아요.
⑤ 이 분홍색 줄무늬 티셔츠를 교환하고 싶어요.

2 정답 ⑤

W: Tony! You are so tanned!
M: Yeah, I went to Hawaii for vacation.
W: When did you get back from your vacation?
M: I just came back on Sunday evening.

여: Tony! 너 엄청 탔구나!
남: 응, 휴가 동안 하와이에 갔었거든.
여: 휴가 갔다가 언제 돌아온 거야?
남: 일요일 저녁에 막 돌아왔어.

어휘 | tanned 햇볕에 탄 **|문제|** souvenir 기념품 exhausted 지친

문제해설 | 여자가 휴가에서 언제 돌아왔는지 물었으므로 이에 대한 남자의 응답으로 ⑤번이 가장 적절하다.
① 난 거기에서 5일 동안 머물렀어.
② 난 몇 주 후에 돌아올 거야.
③ 널 위해 기념품을 좀 샀어.
④ 난 이번 여행으로 완전히 녹초가 됐어.

3 정답 ④

W: Good afternoon, parents. I'm here to talk to you about a few things concerning your children. Many children are injured each Halloween, and this happens primarily due to a lack of parental attention. So how can you help your children have a safe and fun Halloween? The most important thing to remember is children should not go out "trick or treating" unaccompanied by an adult. Also, they should not have costume swords or knives that are sharp. They should not wear baggy or oversized costumes that could cause them to trip, either. They should always stay on the sidewalk and be especially careful when crossing the street. Please follow these tips, and have a good time with your kids!

여: 안녕하세요, 학부모님들. 저는 여러분의 자녀들에 관한 몇 가지 사항들을 말씀드리기 위해 이 자리에 섰습니다. 많은 아이들이 핼러윈 때마다 다치는데, 이것은 주로 부모님들의 주의 부족 때문에 일어납니다. 그럼 어떻게 하면 여러분의 자녀들이 안전하고 재미있는 핼러윈을 보낼 수 있도록 도울 수 있을까요? 기억하셔야 할 가장 중요한 것은, 아이들이 어른을 동반하지 않은 채 'trick or treating'을 하러 나가서는 안 된다는 것입니다. 또한, 그들은 의상에 어울리는 날카로운 검이나 칼을 지니면 안 됩니다. 그들을 걸려 넘어지게 할 수 있는 헐렁하거나 너무 큰 의상을 입어도 안 됩니다. 그들은 항상 인도 위에 있어야 하고, 특히 길을 건널 때에는 조심해야 합니다. 이 조언들을 따르셔서, 여러분의 자녀들과 즐거운 시간 보내십시오!

어휘 | concerning (…에) 관하여 primarily 주로 parental 부모의 trick or treating (핼러윈 풍습으로) 과자를 받으려고 이웃집에 방문하여 '과자를 안 주면 장난칠 거예요'라고 말하는 행위 unaccompanied 동행자가 없는 costume 의상 baggy 헐렁한 oversized 너무 큰 trip 여행; *걸려 넘어지다

문제해설 | 여자는 아이들이 다치지 않고 핼러윈을 보낼 수 있도록 부모들이 알아야 할 안전수칙을 알려주고 있다.

4 정답 ④

W: Sorry I'm late, Dan.
M: Hi, Mary. Did you oversleep?
W: No. I got up at 7:00 a.m. Actually, I spent a lot of time putting on clothes and makeup.
M: For what? I don't remember you saying you have any reason to dress up.
W: I didn't. I don't have any special plans today.
M: Then why do you care about how you look?
W: I am always thinking about what other people are going to think of me, so sometimes I change my outfit several times before going out.
M: Really? I don't think people pay that much attention to the clothes that others are wearing.
W: Regardless, I want to present myself as best as I can.
M: Well, the best way to do that is to be yourself and show up on time!
W: I know. But it's not easy to change my mind or my bad habits.

여: 늦어서 미안해, Dan.

남: 안녕, Mary. 늦잠 잤어?

여: 아니. 아침 7시에 일어났어. 실은 옷 입고 화장하느라 시간이 많이 걸렸어.

남: 뭣 때문에? 네가 옷을 갖춰 입을 이유가 있다고 말한 기억은 없는데.

여: 그런 말 안 했어. 오늘 특별한 계획은 없어.

남: 그럼 왜 네가 어떻게 보이는지에 대해 신경을 쓰는 거야?

여: 난 항상 다른 사람들이 나에 대해 어떻게 생각할지에 대해 신경을 써서, 종종 외출하기 전에 옷을 여러 번 바꿔 입거든.

남: 정말? 난 사람들이 남들이 입고 있는 옷에 그렇게 많이 신경 쓴다고 생각하지 않아.

여: 아무튼, 난 가능한 한 가장 좋은 모습을 보이고 싶어.

남: 음, 그렇게 하는 최고의 방법은 있는 그대로의 모습을 보이면서 제시간에 나타나는 거야!

여: 알아. 그런데 내 생각이나 나쁜 습관을 고치는 게 쉽지 않아.

어휘 | oversleep 늦잠 자다 dress up 옷을 갖춰 입다 outfit 옷, 복장 regardless 상관하지 않고, 여하튼

문제해설 | 남자는 사람들은 남의 옷차림에 크게 신경을 쓰지 않으며, 있는 그대로의 모습으로 약속 장소에 늦지 않게 오는 것이 더 중요하다고 했으므로, 타인의 시선을 신경 쓰지 말라는 것이 남자의 의견임을 알 수 있다.

5 정답 ⑤

W: Excuse me, sir. Can you roll down the window, please?

M: Of course. Is there something wrong?

W: Yes, there is. Can I ask why you're not wearing your seat belt?

M: Oh. I, um... I took it off after you pulled me over.

W: Well, I saw you weren't wearing it when you drove past.

M: I'm sorry. I guess I just forgot. It's the first time I haven't worn it.

W: You should keep in mind that your seat belt can save your life.

M: All right. I promise I won't make the same mistake again.

W: Even so, you've got to pay a fine. A rule is a rule.

M: Oh, I really wish I had worn it.

W: Well, I hope you remember from now on.

여: 실례합니다, 선생님. 창문 좀 내려 주시겠습니까?

남: 물론이죠. 뭐가 잘못됐나요?

여: 네. 왜 안전벨트를 안 매고 계신지 여쭤봐도 될까요?

남: 아. 전, 음…당신이 차를 길가에 대라고 한 뒤에 벨트를 풀었어요.

여: 글쎄요, 전 선생님이 차를 몰고 지나가실 때 안전벨트를 매지 않으신 걸 봤는데요.

남: 죄송합니다. 깜박했나 봐요. 안전벨트를 안 맨 건 이번이 처음이에요.

여: 안전벨트가 선생님의 생명을 구할 수도 있다는 사실을 명심하셔야 합니다.

남: 네. 다시는 똑같은 실수를 하지 않겠다고 약속합니다.

여: 그래도, 벌금을 내셔야 합니다. 규칙은 규칙이니까요.

남: 아, 안전벨트를 매고 있었다면 정말 좋았을 텐데.

여: 음, 이제부터 명심하시길 바랍니다.

어휘 | roll down …을 내리다[열다] pull ... over …에게 차를 길 한쪽에 대게 하다 past (…을) 지나서 fine 벌금 from now on 이제부터

문제해설 | 안전벨트를 매지 않은 채로 운전하는 남자를 발견하고, 여자가 차를 세운 뒤 벌금을 부과하는 것으로 보아, 여자는 경찰관이고 남자는 운전자이다.

6 정답 ③

M: I've finished decorating the stage for the play. What do you think?

W: Well, the sofa is in the center of the stage. That's good.

M: And I put the bookshelf in the left-hand corner, just like you asked.

W: Thank you. But where's the round table?

M: Over there, next to the sofa. I put a flower vase on it.

W: Oh, okay. But why did you put the stereo directly behind the sofa? I wanted it on the right side.

M: I know, but I thought it looked better underneath the landscape painting.

W: Oh! You hung the painting on the back wall.

M: Yes. That seemed to be the ideal spot for it.

W: Hmm… Yes, I guess you're right. Everything looks fantastic.

M: I'm glad to hear that!

남: 연극을 위한 무대 장식을 다 마쳤어. 어떻게 생각해?

여: 음, 소파가 무대 중앙에 있네. 그거 괜찮다.

남: 그리고 네가 요청한 대로 왼쪽 구석에 책장을 두었어.

여: 고마워. 그런데 원탁은 어디 있어?

남: 저기 소파 옆에. 내가 꽃병도 올려 놨어.

여: 오, 알겠어. 그런데 왜 스테레오를 소파 바로 뒤에 뒀어? 난 그게 오른쪽에 있길 바랐는데.

남: 알지만, 그게 풍경화 아래에 있는 게 더 보기 좋다고 생각했어.

여: 오! 너 뒤쪽 벽에 그림을 걸어 놨구나.

남: 응. 거기가 그 그림에 이상적인 장소인 것 같았어.

여: 음… 그래, 네 말이 맞는 것 같아. 모든 게 멋져 보인다.

남: 그 말을 들으니 좋네!

어휘 | decorate 꾸미다 stereo 스테레오(음악 재생 장치) underneath …의 아래에 landscape painting 풍경화 ideal 이상적인

7 정답 ④

M: Excuse me, may I help you?

W: Yes, please. I'm looking for some comfortable sandals.

M: I see. What do you think of these?

W: They're pretty. Can I try on a size six?

M: Sure. Here you go.

W: Well, they're a little tight. Do you have any that are one size bigger?

M: Actually, that size is out of stock. Do you want to try on some other sandals instead?

W: No, thanks. I really like these. The style and color are perfect.

M: Well, I could order them for you.

W: When would I be able to pick them up?

M: They'd be here by Thursday. Do you want me to do that?

W: Yes, please. Here's my card. Please call me when they arrive.

남: 실례합니다, 도와 드릴까요?

여: 네. 전 편한 샌들을 좀 찾고 있어요.

남: 알겠습니다. 이건 어떠신가요?

여: 예쁘네요. 사이즈 6을 신어볼 수 있을까요?

남: 물론이죠. 여기 있어요.

여: 음, 약간 끼네요. 더 큰 게 있나요?

남: 사실, 그 사이즈는 품절입니다. 대신 다른 샌들을 좀 신어 보시 겠어요?

여: 아뇨, 됐어요. 전 이게 정말 마음에 들어요. 스타일과 색상이 완 벽해요.

남: 그럼, 제가 고객님을 위해 그 샌들을 주문해 드릴 수 있어요.

여: 언제 가지러 오면 될까요?

남: 이곳에 목요일까지는 도착할 겁니다. 그렇게 해 드릴까요?

여: 네. 여기 제 명함이에요. 샌들이 도착하면 전화해 주세요.

어휘 | comfortable 편안한 tight 꼭 끼는 out of stock 품절된

문제해설 | 남자는 여자를 위해 한 사이즈 더 큰 샌들을 주문하기로 했다.

8 정답 ⑤

W: Can I talk to you for a minute, Steve?

M: Sure, Megan. What's up?

W: Well, I have been thinking about leaving my job.

M: Really? Are you not getting along with your coworkers?

W: It's not that. My coworkers are fine.

M: Well, I know you have been working long hours recently. You must be under a lot of stress.

W: I am. But my boss always encourages me and appreciates my hard work, so I don't mind it too much.

M: Then what's the problem? Is it the long commute?

W: No. My salary isn't high enough. I feel like I deserve a lot more than I get.

M: I see. Have you tried asking for a raise?

W: Yes, but I was told that the company can't afford it right now.

여: 잠깐 이야기할 수 있을까요, Steve?

남: 그럼요, Megan. 무슨 일이에요?

여: 음, 제가 퇴사를 할까 생각 중이에요.

남: 정말요? 동료들과 잘 어울리지 못하나요?

여: 그건 아니에요. 제 동료들은 좋아요.

남: 음, 최근에 당신이 장시간 근무하고 있다는 걸 알아요. 틀림없이 스트레스가 많았을 거예요.

여: 네. 하지만 제 상사께서 항상 저를 격려해 주시고, 제가 열심히 일하는 것을 알아주셔서, 그건 크게 신경 쓰지 않아요.

남: 그럼 문제가 뭔가요? 통근 거리가 먼가요?

여: 아뇨. 제 급여가 충분히 많지 않아요. 전 지금 받는 것보다는 훨 씬 더 많이 받을 자격이 있다고 생각해요.

남: 알겠어요. 급여 인상을 요청해 봤나요?

여: 네, 그런데 회사가 지금 당장은 올려 줄 수 없다고 들었어요.

어휘 | encourage 격려하다 appreciate 인정하다 commute 통근 (거리) deserve (…할) 자격이 있다 raise 인상 afford (…할) 형편이 되다

문제해설 | 여자는 급여가 충분치 않다고 생각하여 퇴사를 고려하고 있 다고 했다.

9 정답 ①

W: Hi, Scott. Are you buying something online?

M: Yes. I'm ordering new uniforms for my soccer team.

W: Wow, they look great. How much are they?

M: They're $20 each, and I need to get 14 of them.

W: That's not bad. How about shipping charges?

M: That's an extra $15, unless the order is more than $250. Then, it's free.

W: Hmm... Your order will be more than that, won't it?

M: I think so. But I also get a discount, since I'm a member of this site.

W: Cool. So how much is the discount?

M: It's 10%. So I need to do the math to see if I have to pay for shipping.

W: Well, can you add one more for my younger brother?

M: Sure, no problem!

여: 안녕, Scott. 너 온라인으로 뭘 사는 거야?

남: 응. 우리 축구팀을 위해 새 유니폼을 주문하는 중이야.

여: 와, 멋져 보인다. 그것들은 얼마야?
남: 한 벌에 20달러인데, 난 14벌을 사야 해.
여: 나쁘지 않네. 배송비는 어때?
남: 250달러 이상 주문하지 않으면, 15달러가 추가돼. 그 이상이면
　　무료야.
여: 음… 네 주문은 그것보단 많겠네, 그렇지?
남: 그럴 것 같아. 그런데 난 이 사이트의 회원이라서 할인도 받아.
여: 좋다. 그럼 얼마나 할인받는데?
남: 10%야. 그래서 내가 배송비를 지불해야 할지 보려면 계산을 해
　　봐야 해.
여: 음, 내 남동생을 위해 하나만 더 추가해 줄 수 있니?
남: 물론이지, 문제없어!

어휘 | shipping charge 배송료　do the math 계산하다

문제해설 | 남자는 여자의 남동생 것까지 포함하여 유니폼을 총 15벌 사
기로 했으며($20×15), 10%를 할인받고, 총 주문액이 250달러 이상
이어서 배송비가 무료이므로 지불할 금액은 270달러이다.

10　정답 ④

M: Good morning, Shelley.
W: Good morning, Mr. Reed.
M: I saw you drive in with Olivia.
W: Yes, we're carpooling these days.
M: I see. Is it convenient?
W: Yes, it is. It saves money on gas and helps the
　　environment at the same time. And some mornings I
　　can just enjoy being a passenger instead of driving.
M: It seems like a good idea.
W: Well, there are some disadvantages. For example, I
　　have to leave my house earlier than usual so that I don't
　　delay the others.
M: So, it's not just you and Olivia that carpool together?
W: No, we usually pick up Ryan and Debbie, too.
M: I see. I suppose carpooling also gives you the chance to
　　get to know your coworkers a little better.
W: Right. That's another advantage.

남: 안녕하세요, Shelley.
여: 안녕하세요, Reed 씨.
남: 당신이 Olivia와 함께 차로 오는 걸 봤어요.
여: 네, 우리는 요즘 카풀을 하고 있어요.
남: 그렇군요. 그거 편리한가요?
여: 네. 기름값도 아끼고 동시에 환경에 도움이 되거든요. 그리고 어
　　떤 날 아침에는 운전하는 대신 그냥 승객이 되는 걸 즐길 수 있
　　어요.
남: 좋은 생각인 것 같아요.
여: 음, 단점이 좀 있어요. 예를 들면, 다른 사람들을 기다리게 하지
　　않도록 평소보다 좀 더 일찍 집에서 나와야 해요.
남: 그럼, 카풀을 함께 하는 건 당신과 Olivia만이 아닌가요?

여: 네, 우린 보통 Ryan과 Debbie도 태워요.
남: 그렇군요. 카풀을 하는 건 또한 동료들을 좀 더 잘 알 수 있게 해
　　주는 기회도 주겠네요.
여: 맞아요. 그게 또 다른 이점이죠.

어휘 | convenient 편리한　disadvantage 단점(↔ advantage)
delay 미루다; *지연시키다　suppose 생각하다, 추정하다

문제해설 | 카풀을 하면 편리하고, 연료비를 아낄 수 있고, 환경에 도움
이 되고, 함께 하는 동료들을 잘 알 수 있게 된다고 했지만, 출근 시간 단
축은 언급되지 않았다.

11　정답 ④

M: Cricket and baseball might look pretty similar, but they
　　are actually quite different. For instance, in baseball,
　　the non-batting team has nine players on the field,
　　but in cricket, it has eleven. Cricket is a more popular
　　sport than baseball in Britain. Many people wonder
　　where cricket's strange name came from, but no one
　　is completely sure of its origins. It was being played as
　　early as 1598, so it's actually much older than baseball.
　　At that time, it was called "creckett." This name could
　　have come from the Old English word "cryce", which
　　meant "stick." And even though most people believe
　　that cricket is an English game, some have suggested
　　that it actually began in a region of northern Europe
　　called Flanders.

남: 크리켓과 야구는 매우 유사하게 보일 수 있지만 사실은 아주 다
　　릅니다. 예를 들어, 야구에서 공격하지 않는 팀의 선수는 경기장
　　에 9명이 있지만, 크리켓에서는 11명이 있습니다. 크리켓은 영
　　국에서 야구보다 더 인기 있는 스포츠입니다. 많은 사람들이 크
　　리켓의 이상한 이름이 어디서 유래했는지 궁금해하지만, 아무도
　　그것의 기원에 대해서는 정확히 모릅니다. 그것은 일찍이 1598
　　년도에 행해지고 있었으므로 사실상 야구보다 훨씬 더 오래되
　　었습니다. 그 당시에 그것은 'creckett'라고 불렸습니다. 이 이
　　름은 '막대기'를 뜻하는 고대 영어 단어인 'cryce'에서 왔을 수
　　도 있습니다. 그리고 대부분의 사람들이 크리켓이 영국 경기라
　　고 믿고 있지만, 어떤 사람들은 그것이 사실 Flanders라고 불
　　린 북유럽 지역에서 시작되었다고 말합니다.

어휘 | batting 【스포츠】 타격; *공격　completely 완전히, 전적으로
origin 기원　suggest (넌지시) 말하다　region 지역

문제해설 | ④ 크리켓이라는 이름은 '막대기'라는 의미의 고대 영어 단어
인 cryce에서 온 것으로 추정된다고 했다.

12　정답 ③

M: Karen, look at this advertisement. There's a big sale on
　　sofas.

W: Really? We should buy one. Ours is old.

M: And uncomfortable. Which sofa should we buy?

W: Well, we need enough room for at least four people to sit.

M: Right. So our whole family can sit together.

W: How much money do you think we can spend?

M: We can't afford anything over $900.

W: Okay. There are several models in our budget.

M: I prefer leather sofas. Fabric doesn't look as nice.

W: I like leather too. That leaves us with two options.

M: Which color do you like? What about white?

W: Hmm, that doesn't match our other furniture.

M: You're right. I didn't think about that. Let's choose the other one.

W: Great! Let's go to the webpage and order it now.

남: Karen, 이 광고 좀 봐요. 대대적인 소파 세일을 하네요.

여: 그래요? 우리 하나 사야겠어요. 우리 것은 낡았잖아요.

남: 그리고 불편하죠. 어떤 소파를 살까요?

여: 음, 최소한 네 명이 앉을 만한 공간이 필요해요.

남: 맞아요. 그러면 우리 가족 모두가 함께 앉을 수 있어요.

여: 우리가 얼마를 쓸 수 있을 것 같아요?

남: 900달러 이상은 쓸 수 없어요.

여: 알겠어요. 우리 예산 안에 몇 개의 모델이 있어요.

남: 난 가죽소파를 선호해요. 천은 그렇게 좋아 보이지 않거든요.

여: 나도 가죽이 좋아요. 그럼 우리에게 두 가지 선택지가 남네요.

남: 어떤 색이 좋아요? 흰색은 어때요?

여: 음, 그건 다른 가구와 어울리지 않아요.

남: 맞아요. 그건 생각 못했어요. 나머지 남은 한 가지를 고릅시다.

여: 좋아요! 우리 지금 웹사이트에 가서 주문해요.

어휘 | advertisement 광고 room 공간 afford (…할 금전적) 형편이 되다 budget 예산 leather 가죽 fabric 천 match 어울리다

문제해설 | 4인용 이상, 900달러 이하의, 가죽으로 만들어졌고, 흰색이 아닌 소파는 ③번이다.

13 정답 ⑤

M: Eileen, may I talk with you for a minute?

W: Sure, Howard. Is there something wrong?

M: Well, I feel I need to speak to you about your temper.

W: My temper? What about my temper?

M: Some of your coworkers have complained that you're short-tempered.

W: Really? I thought I was getting along well with everyone.

M: Yes, you are. But when you get stressed out, you tend to get angry.

W: Well, maybe a little. But it's not a big deal.

M: What about last Friday? What happened between you and Douglas?

W: Oh. He made a mistake on a report, and I yelled at him. But just a little.

M: So you don't think there's anything wrong with your behavior?

W: Well, if people are complaining, I guess I should watch my temper.

남: Eileen, 잠시 이야기 좀 해도 될까요?

여: 물론이죠, Howard. 무슨 문제가 있나요?

남: 음, 전 당신의 성격에 대해 말해야 할 것 같아요.

여: 제 성격이요? 제 성격에 대해서 무엇을요?

남: 당신의 동료 중 몇몇이 당신이 성미가 급하다고 불평을 해서요.

여: 정말요? 전 모두와 잘 지내고 있다고 생각했었는데요.

남: 네, 그래요. 하지만 스트레스를 받으면 당신은 화를 내는 경향이 있어요.

여: 음, 약간 그럴 수도 있죠. 하지만 그건 별거 아니에요.

남: 지난 금요일에는요? 당신과 Douglas 사이에 무슨 일이 있었나요?

여: 아. 그가 보고서에 실수를 해서, 제가 그에게 소리를 질렀어요. 하지만 그냥 조금이었어요.

남: 그래서 당신의 행동에 문제가 없다고 생각하는 건가요?

여: 음, 사람들이 불평을 한다면, 화를 내는 걸 조심해야겠네요.

어휘 | temper (걸핏하면 화를 내는) 성질, 성미 short-tempered 성미가 급한, 화를 쉽게 내는 yell at …에게 소리치다 **|문제|** scold 꾸짖다

문제해설 | 스트레스를 받으면 동료들에게 화를 내는 여자의 행동을 남자가 지적하며 그런 행동에 문제가 없다고 생각하는지 물었으므로, 이에 대한 여자의 응답으로 ⑤번이 가장 적절하다.

① 전 꾸지람을 들어서 약간 화가 났어요.

② 실수를 덜 하도록 노력하겠다고 약속해요.

③ 제가 일찍 떠난 것에 대해서 제 동료에게 사과할게요.

④ 사람들이 저에게 소리를 지르면, 전 스트레스를 받아요.

14 정답 ①

W: Hey, Kurt, what's wrong? You look concerned about something.

M: I am. I lost my cell phone on my way to school.

W: What? How?

M: I'm not sure. But I think I left it on the subway, since I remember calling my mom before I got off.

W: Did you try calling your number?

M: Of course. I tried many times, but there was no answer. I think the battery went dead, so I may never find it.

W: Oh, that's too bad. Wait, did you check the lost and found in the subway station?

M: No, I didn't.

W: You might find it there. They keep all the items lost on the subway.

M: Okay. Do you know where it is located?
W: Yes, it is near the entrance to City Hall station.
M: <u>Thank you for the useful information.</u>

여: 저기, Kurt, 무슨 일이야? 너 뭔가에 대해 걱정하는 것 같은데.
남: 맞아. 학교에 오는 길에 휴대전화를 잃어버렸어.
여: 뭐? 어떻게?
남: 잘 모르겠어. 하지만 지하철에 두고 온 것 같은 게, 내리기 전에 우리 엄마에게 전화한 걸 기억하거든.
여: 네 번호로 전화해 봤니?
남: 물론이지. 여러 번 해 봤는데, 응답이 없었어. 배터리가 다 되어서, 절대 찾을 수 없을 것 같아.
여: 아, 그거 정말 안됐다. 잠깐만, 너 지하철역의 분실물 보관소는 확인했어?
남: 아니, 안 했는데.
여: 그곳에서 찾을 수도 있어. 거기는 지하철에서 잃어버린 물품들을 전부 보관하거든.
남: 알았어. 그게 어디에 있는지 아니?
여: 응, 시청역 입구 근처에 있어.
남: <u>유용한 정보 고마워.</u>

어휘 | concerned 걱정하는, 염려하는 get off (차에서) 내리다 lost and found 분실물 보관소 entrance 입구 **|문제|** grateful 고마워하는

문제해설 | 지하철에서 휴대전화를 잃어버린 남자에게 여자가 지하철역의 분실물 보관소를 확인해보라는 말과 함께 위치를 알려준 상황이므로, 이에 대한 남자의 응답으로 ①번이 가장 적절하다.
② 난 분실물 보관소 직원에게 너무 고마워.
③ 내가 너라면, 새로운 휴대전화를 살 거야.
④ 그렇게 큰 실수를 저질러서 정말 미안해.
⑤ 그래, 넌 지금 당장 분실물 신고를 해야 해.

15 정답 ⑤

W: Lucy started working at a company six months ago. During that time, she and the woman sitting next to her, Tara, have become close friends. This morning, Tara gave Lucy an invitation to her wedding. Lucy was thrilled by the invitation until she noticed the date of the wedding. Unfortunately, the ceremony is to be held on the same date as a high-school reunion she has been looking forward to for months. Although she would love to attend the wedding, she cannot pass up the rare chance to meet up with all her old school friends. In this situation, what would Lucy most likely say to Tara?
Lucy: <u>I'm so sorry, but I have prior engagement that day.</u>

여: Lucy는 6개월 전에 한 회사에서 일하기 시작했다. 그동안 그녀와 그녀 옆자리에 앉은 여자인 Tara는 친한 친구가 되었다. 오늘 아침, Tara는 Lucy에게 그녀의 결혼식 초대장을 주었다. Lucy는 결혼식 날짜를 알기 전까진 그 초대에 기뻐했다. 유감스럽게도, 결혼식은 그녀가 몇 달간 고대해 왔던 고등학교 동창회와 같은 날에 열릴 예정이다. 비록 그녀는 결혼식에 참석하고 싶긴 하지만, 그녀의 오랜 학교 친구들을 모두 만날 수 있는 흔치 않은 기회를 놓칠 수는 없다. 이런 상황에서, Lucy가 Tara에게 할 말로 가장 적절한 것은 무엇인가?
Lucy: 정말 미안하지만, 난 그날 선약이 있어.

어휘 | thrilled 흥분한, 신이 난 ceremony 의식, 식 reunion 동창회 pass up (기회를) 놓치다 rare 드문 prior engagement 선약

문제해설 | Lucy는 친한 동료인 Tara의 결혼식 초대를 받았지만 같은 날에 예정된 동창회에 참석해서 옛날 친구들을 모두 만나고 싶어하므로, Lucy가 Tara에게 할 말로 ⑤번이 가장 적절하다.
① 걱정하지 마. 넌 괜찮을 거야.
② 난 이미 네게 학교 동창회에 대해 이야기했어.
③ 네 결혼식에 참석하게 되어서 너무 기뻐.
④ 너의 고등학교 친구들이 네 결혼식에 참석할 거야.

16 정답 ②   17 정답 ③

W: Good morning, everyone. Currency comes in many forms in the modern world, from physical cash to digital currency that we can transfer using bank cards and online applications. But what did people do before currency was invented? In the past, when people needed goods and services, they would barter for them. This means they would trade something they already had for whatever they wanted. At first, it was as simple as one farmer trading one of his chickens for a basket of another farmer's apples. Eventually, some cultures started using seashells to barter with instead of actual items. The more seashells you had, the wealthier you were. Around 650 B.C., people began to use precious metals for the same purpose, shaping gold and silver into flat disks that became the first coins. This practice eventually spread all around the world and was adopted by most cultures. Hundreds of years later, the Chinese started using paper for the same purpose.

여: 안녕하세요, 여러분. 현대 사회에서 화폐는 물리적인 현금에서 우리가 은행 카드와 온라인 어플리케이션을 이용하여 이체할 수 있는 전자 화폐에 이르기까지 다양한 형태로 존재합니다. 그러나 화폐가 고안되기 전에 사람들은 무엇을 사용했을까요? 과거에는 사람들이 상품과 서비스가 필요할 때, 그것들을 물물 교환하곤 했습니다. 이는 이미 가지고 있는 것을 그들이 원하는 어떤 것과 교환했다는 것을 의미합니다. 처음엔, 한 농부가 자기 닭을 다른 농부의 사과 한 바구니와 교환하는 것처럼 단순했습니다. 결국, 어떤 문화권들은 실제 물건들 대신에 물물 교환을 하기 위해 조개껍데기를 사용하기 시작했습니다. 조개껍데기를 더 많이 가질수록, 더 부유했습니다. 기원전 650년경, 사람들은 같은 목

적으로 귀금속들을 사용하기 시작했는데, 금과 은을 최초의 동전이 된 납작한 원반형으로 만들었습니다. 이 관습은 결국 전 세계로 퍼졌고 대부분의 문화권들에 의해 채택되었습니다. 수백 년 후, 중국인들이 같은 목적으로 종이를 사용하기 시작했습니다.

어휘 | currency 통화, 화폐 physical 물리적인 cash 현금 digital currency 디지털 통화, 전자 화폐 transfer 옮기다; *이체하다 goods 상품 barter 물물 교환하다 trade A for B A를 B와 교환하다 seashell 조개껍데기 wealthy 부유한 precious metal 귀금속 shape (어떤) 모양으로 만들다 flat 납작한 disk (납작한) 원반 practice 관습 spread 퍼지다 adopt 채택하다

문제해설 | 16. 과거에는 물물 교환을 통해 필요한 상품과 서비스를 얻었지만, 점차 조개껍데기, 금속, 종이 등의 대표 수단을 통해 물건을 사게 되었다는 내용이므로 화폐가 어떻게 발달해왔는가에 관해 이야기하고 있다.
① 물물 교환의 문제점
② 시간이 지남에 따라 화폐가 어떻게 발달했는가
③ 상품을 직접 물물 교환하는 것의 이점
④ 전자 화폐 사용의 이점
⑤ 귀금속을 동전으로 사용하게 된 이유
17. 물물 교환이나 화폐로 사용된 물건으로 ③ 돌은 언급되지 않았다.
① 사과 ② 조개껍데기 ④ 금속 ⑤ 종이

16_강 FINAL TEST

pp. 68-71

1 ①	2 ④	3 ②	4 ⑤	5 ①
6 ③	7 ⑤	8 ④	9 ④	10 ③
11 ④	12 ②	13 ②	14 ①	15 ④
16 ①	17 ④			

1 정답 ①

M: Excuse me. Could you help me find a book?
W: Sure. Can you tell me what the book is about?
M: It's about the famous artist Pablo Picasso.
W: <u>It should be at the end of this aisle.</u>

남: 실례합니다. 책 찾는 것을 도와주실 수 있나요?
여: 물론이죠. 무엇에 관한 책인지 말씀해 주시겠어요?
남: 유명한 화가 Pablo Picasso에 관한 책이에요.
여: <u>그건 이 통로 끝에 있을 거예요.</u>

어휘 | aisle 통로 **|문제|** shelf 선반, 책꽂이

문제해설 | 남자가 Pablo Picasso에 관한 책이 어디 있는지 물었으므로, 이에 대한 여자의 응답으로 ①번이 가장 적절하다.

② 당신은 정말 독서를 좋아하네요, 그렇죠?
③ 네. 그는 제가 매우 좋아하는 화가 중 한 명이에요.
④ 당신이 Pablo Picasso를 좋아할 거라고 예상하지 못했어요.
⑤ 좋아요. 이 책을 책꽂이 맨 위에 꽂아주시겠어요?

2 정답 ④

W: Hi, Jake! I haven't seen you in ages.
M: I know. It's been a long time. I heard you won the employee of the year award.
W: That's right. I can't believe it.
M: <u>Congratulations! Everybody thinks you deserve it.</u>

여: 안녕, Jake! 오랜만이야.
남: 그러게. 오랜만이다. 네가 올해의 직원상을 받았다고 들었어.
여: 맞아. 믿기지 않아.
남: <u>축하해! 모두들 네가 그걸 받을 자격이 있다고 생각해.</u>

어휘 | award 상 **|문제|** deserve (…할) 자격이 있다

문제해설 | 여자가 올해의 직원상을 받은 것이 믿기지 않는다고 말했으므로, 이에 대한 남자의 응답으로 ④번이 가장 적절하다.
① 글쎄, 난 올해 정말 열심히 일했어.
② 널 마지막으로 본 게 언제인지 기억이 안 나.
③ 넌 열심히 노력했잖아. 아마 내년에는 네가 상을 탈 거야.
⑤ 올해 신입 사원이 좀 들어오면 좋을 거야.

3 정답 ②

W: Good afternoon, may I have your attention, please? Flight D567 has almost finished boarding. However, some passengers have not yet boarded. Passengers Gibson, Silvers, and Morris, traveling to Melbourne on flight D567, please make your way immediately to Gate 11, where your plane is awaiting departure. This is the final boarding call for passengers Gibson, Silvers, and Morris on flight number D567 to Melbourne. This flight is scheduled to depart in ten minutes. Failure to arrive at Gate 11 with your passport and boarding pass within the next ten minutes will result in your luggage being removed from the plane. Thank you.

여: 안녕하세요, 주목해 주시겠습니까? D567편 비행기가 탑승을 거의 마쳤습니다. 하지만, 몇몇 승객분들이 아직 탑승하지 않으셨습니다. D567편으로 멜버른으로 가시는 승객 Gibson 씨, Silvers 씨, 그리고 Morris 씨는 여러분의 비행기가 출발하려고 대기 중인 11번 게이트로 즉시 와 주시기 바랍니다. 이 것은 D567편 멜버른행 승객 Gibson 씨, Silvers 씨, 그리고 Morris 씨에게 전하는 마지막 탑승 안내 방송입니다. 이 비행기는 10분 후에 출발할 예정입니다. 앞으로 10분 이내에 여러분의 여권과 탑승권을 가지고 11번 게이트에 도착하지 못하시면 여러분의 수하물은 비행기에서 내려지게 될 것입니다. 감사

합니다.

어휘 | board 탑승하다 make one's way 나아가다 immediately 즉시 await 기다리다 departure 출발(*v*. depart) boarding call 탑승 안내 방송 boarding pass 탑승권 luggage 수하물

문제해설 | 여자는 10분 후에 출발하는 비행기에 아직 탑승하지 않은 세 명의 승객들에게 탑승을 촉구하는 안내 방송을 하고 있다.

4 정답 ⑤

W: Michael! What's wrong? Your face is so red.
M: I am so angry at my friend.
W: What happened? Did you have a fight?
M: No. But he canceled our plans at the last minute.
W: I am sorry to hear that. I hope you two can talk about this later.
M: I would rather not. I just want to forget it.
W: So you just want to hold your emotions inside?
M: Yes. That is the best way. I don't like fighting with my friends.
W: You don't have to fight. You can calmly explain why you are angry to your friend.
M: I see. Maybe that would prevent this from happening again.
W: It might. It would also help you feel better.
M: That is a good point. I don't feel good right now.

여: Michael! 뭐가 잘못된 거야? 네 얼굴이 엄청 빨개.
남: 내 친구에게 무지 화가 나.
여: 무슨 일이 있었어? 싸운 거야?
남: 아니. 하지만 걔가 막판에 우리 계획을 취소했어.
여: 안됐구나. 난 너희 둘이 이 일에 대해 나중에 이야기 나눴으면 좋겠어.
남: 안 하는 게 낫겠어. 난 그냥 그것을 잊고 싶어.
여: 그러면 네 감정을 그냥 속에 담아두고 싶은 거야?
남: 맞아. 그게 최선이야. 난 친구들과 싸우는 걸 싫어해.
여: 넌 싸우지 않아도 돼. 네가 왜 친구에게 화가 났는지 차분히 설명할 수 있어.
남: 알겠어. 어쩌면 그게 이런 일이 되풀이되지 않게 막을 수도 있겠구나.
여: 아마도. 네 기분이 나아지는 데 도움이 될 수도 있지.
남: 좋은 말이구나. 난 지금 기분이 좋지 않아.

어휘 | at the last minute 마지막 순간에, 막판에 would rather do (차라리) …하겠다 calmly 침착하게, 차분히 prevent A from v-ing A가 …하지 못하게 막다

문제해설 | 친구에게 화가 난 남자에게 여자는 불편한 감정을 속에 담아두지 말고 친구에게 화난 이유를 차분히 설명하라고 한다.

5 정답 ①

W: So, how do you feel about winning this award?
M: I'm thrilled. And I'm truly honored to be up here.
W: Congratulations. Now, on behalf of your coworkers, I'll ask you a few things. When did you first become interested in buildings?
M: Well, I used to make fantasy cities with blocks when I was young. Then, as I got older, my parents encouraged me to make my fantasy designs come true.
W: Wonderful. Why do you love designing buildings?
M: It allows me to make a difference in the world. I particularly love designing beautiful structures that remind city dwellers of nature.
W: I see. One final question: What are you currently working on?
M: I'm currently working on a museum that will be built in Taipei.
W: Wow, good luck with that. And thank you for answering my questions.
M: You're welcome.

여: 자, 이 상을 받으신 소감이 어떤가요?
남: 황홀해요. 그리고 이 자리에 있게 되어 정말 영광입니다.
여: 축하드립니다. 이제, 동료들을 대신해서 제가 몇 가지 질문을 하겠습니다. 언제 처음 건축에 관심을 가지게 되었나요?
남: 음, 전 어렸을 때 블록으로 상상의 도시를 만들곤 했어요. 그 후 나이가 들면서 부모님께서 제가 상상 속의 디자인을 실현해 보도록 격려해 주셨죠.
여: 멋지네요. 왜 건물을 설계하는 걸 좋아하세요?
남: 그건 제가 세상을 변화시킬 수 있게 해 줘요. 전 특히 도시 거주자들에게 자연을 떠올리게 하는 아름다운 구조물을 설계하는 것을 아주 좋아해요.
여: 그렇군요. 마지막 질문인데, 현재 어떤 작업을 하고 계신가요?
남: 저는 현재 Taipei에 지어질 박물관을 작업하고 있어요.
여: 와, 그 작업에 행운이 있길 바랍니다. 그리고 질문에 답해 주셔서 감사드립니다.
남: 천만에요.

어휘 | thrilled 황홀한, 아주 흥분한 honored 영광인, 명예로운 on behalf of …을 대신하여 fantasy 상상의, 공상의 come true 실현하다 structure 구조물 dweller 거주민

문제해설 | 남자에게 언제부터 건축에 관심이 있었는지, 왜 건물을 설계하는 일을 좋아하는지, 현재 하는 작업은 무엇인지 등을 여자가 묻고, 남자가 대답하는 것으로 보아 기자와 건축가 간의 대화임을 알 수 있다.

6 정답 ③

W: Honey, this restaurant is so romantic!
M: It sure is. Although it's kind of expensive, it's worth it

for our first wedding anniversary.

W: Thank you for bringing me here. I really like the nice view of the sunset.

M: I'm glad to hear that. Actually, I chose this place because of the ocean. It is so beautiful.

W: And what about the decorations with flowers below the window? They are so pretty.

M: But they are not as pretty as you!

W: Oh! Thank you, dear! Hmm… These wooden chairs are a little uncomfortable, though.

M: I agree! It's the only thing wrong with this restaurant. I wish we were sitting on a soft sofa.

W: Let's not focus on that. I still like it here. The lamp next to me is lovely.

M: It sure is! It goes well with the atmosphere here.

W: This is such a fabulous place.

여: 여보, 이 식당은 정말 로맨틱해요!

남: 진짜 그렇네요. 좀 비싸기는 하지만, 우리의 첫 결혼기념일을 보낼 만한 가치가 있어요.

여: 여기에 데려와 줘서 고마워요. 일몰이 보이는 멋진 전망이 정말 마음에 들어요.

남: 그 말을 들으니 좋네요. 사실 바다 때문에 이곳을 선택했어요. 아주 아름다워요.

여: 게다가 창문 아래에 있는 꽃장식은 어떻고요? 정말 예뻐요.

남: 그래도 당신만큼 예쁘지는 않아요!

여: 오! 고마워요, 여보! 음… 그런데 이 나무 의자는 좀 불편해요.

남: 동의해요! 그게 이 식당에서 유일하게 마음에 안 드는 거예요. 부드러운 소파에 앉으면 좋을 텐데요.

여: 그것에 집중하지 말아요. 그래도 전 여기가 좋아요. 제 옆에 있는 전등도 멋져요.

남: 진짜 그렇네요! 여기 분위기와 잘 어울려요.

여: 여긴 정말 환상적인 곳이에요.

어휘 | sunset 일몰 atmosphere 분위기 fabulous 기막히게 멋진

문제해설 | 창문 아래에 전구 장식이 아닌 꽃장식이 있다고 했으므로 대화의 내용과 일치하지 않는 것은 ③번이다.

7 정답 ⑤

W: Excuse me. Do you work here?

M: Yes, I do. I'm the head lifeguard at this pool.

W: Oh, great. This is my first time here. Can I ask you a question about lessons?

M: Sure. What do you want to know?

W: Are they at different times of the day?

M: Yes. The schedule is posted on that door right there.

W: Okay. And are they free for members?

M: Yes, ma'am. There's no extra charge for members.

W: Great!

M: No problem. But there is one thing—you need to put on a swimming cap.

W: Oh, okay. But I'm not actually in the pool yet.

M: I know. But the rules say you have to wear one when you're in the pool area.

W: Okay, no problem. I've got one right here.

여: 실례합니다. 여기서 일하시나요?

남: 네, 그렇습니다. 전 이 수영장의 수석 인명 구조원입니다.

여: 아, 잘됐네요. 전 여기에 처음 왔는데요. 강좌에 관해 질문을 하나 해도 될까요?

남: 물론이죠. 뭘 알고 싶으신가요?

여: 하루에 강좌 시간대가 다양한가요?

남: 네. 시간표는 바로 저쪽 문에 게시되어 있습니다.

여: 알겠습니다. 그리고 그 강좌들은 회원들에게는 무료인가요?

남: 네, 회원님. 회원들에게는 추가 비용이 없습니다.

여: 잘됐네요!

남: 그럼요. 그런데 한가지, 회원님은 수영 모자를 쓰셔야 합니다.

여: 아, 알겠습니다. 하지만 전 아직 실제로 수영장 안에 있는 건 아니잖아요.

남: 아닙니다. 하지만 규칙에 따르면 수영장 구역에 있을 때는 수영 모자를 쓰셔야 해요.

여: 알겠어요, 그러죠. 바로 여기에 가지고 있거든요.

어휘 | head (단체·조직의) 책임자 lifeguard (수영장의) 인명 구조원 extra charge 추가 비용

문제해설 | 남자가 여자에게 수영장 구역에서는 수영 모자를 써야 한다고 했으므로, 여자는 수영 모자를 쓸 것이다.

8 정답 ④

[*Telephone rings.*]

M: Hello?

W: Hi, Phil. It's Susanne.

M: Oh, hi, Susanne. I was about to call you.

W: Are you ready to go shopping?

M: Sorry. But I don't think I can go shopping with you today.

W: What? Did you forget about our plan?

M: No. I still need to buy new clothes, but today isn't good.

W: Why not? Are you trying to save money?

M: It's not that. I just came down with a bad cold, so I would rather not go out today.

W: I see. Then why don't I come over? We can shop online together.

M: That's okay. I would rather go with you to the mall some other time.

W: All right, Phil. I hope you feel better soon.

[전화벨이 울린다.]
남: 여보세요?
여: 안녕, Phil. 나 Susanne야.
남: 오, 안녕, Susanne. 너에게 막 전화하려던 참이었어.
여: 쇼핑 갈 준비가 되었니?
남: 미안하지만 난 오늘 너랑 쇼핑을 못 갈 것 같아.
여: 뭐라고? 우리 계획을 잊었어?
남: 아니. 여전히 새 옷을 사야 하는데, 오늘은 안 될 것 같아.
여: 왜 안 되는데? 돈을 모으려고 그래?
남: 그건 아니야. 그냥 독감에 걸려서, 오늘은 외출을 안 하는 게 나
  을 것 같아.
여: 그렇구나. 그럼 내가 너네 집에 갈까? 함께 온라인 쇼핑을 할 수
  있어.
남: 괜찮아. 언제 한번 너랑 쇼핑몰에 가는 게 나을 것 같아.
여: 알겠어, Phil. 빨리 낫길 바라.

9 정답 ④

M: Good morning, ma'am. How can I help you?
W: I'd like to get some pork.
M: Okay. What is it for?
W: I'm going to grill it because my friends are coming over
  tonight.
M: Then how about this? This pork is the best grade, and
  it's on sale for $10 per pack.
W: It looks great. I'll take four packs.
M: Good choice. Don't you need some sauce for your
  pork?
W: Actually, I do. How much is this garlic sauce?
M: It's $6, but if your total is more than $50, I'll offer it to
  you at half price.
W: Then, I'll take one more pork pack.
M: Great! How would you like to pay?
W: By cash. Here it is.

남: 안녕하세요, 손님. 어떻게 도와 드릴까요?
여: 돼지고기를 좀 사고 싶어요.
남: 네. 뭐 하는 데 쓰실 건가요?
여: 오늘 밤 제 친구들이 놀러 올 거라서 고기를 좀 구우려고요.
남: 그럼 이건 어떠세요? 이 돼지고기는 최상급이고, 한 팩당 10달
  러에 판매 중이에요.
여: 좋아 보이네요. 네 팩 살게요.
남: 좋은 선택이에요. 돼지고기에 쓸 소스는 좀 필요하지 않으세요?
여: 사실, 필요해요. 이 마늘 소스는 얼마인가요?
남: 6달러인데, 손님이 주문한 것이 모두 50달러를 넘기면, 반값에
  드릴게요.
여: 그럼, 돼지고기 한 팩을 더 살게요.

남: 좋아요! 어떻게 계산하시겠어요?
여: 현금으로요. 여기 있어요.

10 정답 ③

M: Hi, Carol. I heard you've finished another novel.
  Congratulations!
W: Thanks! I'm looking forward to releasing it.
M: I can't wait to read it. I absolutely loved your last book.
W: It's nice of you to say so. By the way, would you like to
  come to the release party?
M: Sure! That sounds interesting.
W: Yes. I am going to read the first chapter of the book
  and sign copies for whoever buys one.
M: Cool! Where will it be held?
W: Downtown, at the Tenth Street Bookstore.
M: I know where that is. Are you going to have a Q-and-A
  session?
W: Yes, and there will also be lots of nice food.
M: Excellent!
W: Also, I will pick five people at random to receive a free
  copy of my book.
M: All right! I hope I win!

남: 안녕, Carol. 네가 또 다른 소설을 다 끝냈다고 들었어. 축하해!
여: 고마워! 그게 출간되기를 손꼽아 기다리고 있어.
남: 나도 빨리 그걸 읽고 싶어. 난 네 지난번 책이 정말 좋았어.
여: 그렇게 말해주니 고마워. 그건 그렇고, 출간 기념 파티에 올래?
남: 물론이지! 재미있겠다.
여: 응. 내가 책의 첫 장을 낭독하고 책을 구매하는 모든 분들의 책
  에 사인해 줄 거야.
남: 멋지다! 어디서 열려?
여: 시내에 있는 Tenth Street 서점에서.
남: 거기가 어디에 있는지 알아. 질의응답 시간을 가질 거니?
여: 응, 그리고 근사한 음식이 많이 있을 거야.
남: 훌륭해!
여: 게다가, 5명을 무작위로 뽑아서 내 책을 한 권씩 무료로 증정할
  거야.
남: 좋다! 내가 뽑히면 좋겠다!

명을 뽑아 책을 증정하는 추첨 행사가 있을 거라고 했지만, 기자 간담회
에 대해서는 언급되지 않았다.

11 정답 ④

M: Hello, and welcome to the third annual North City Art
Festival. Each year, our city celebrates local artists by
displaying their work over a two-day period. Several
downtown streets have been closed off to traffic,
allowing festival-goers to safely stroll from exhibit to
exhibit. This year, we've added local dance teams and
musicians to the schedule, allowing them to perform
alongside the displays of paintings and sculptures.
Many of the pieces on display are also on sale, so if
you're an art collector, be sure to bring your wallet.
The festival will conclude with a wonderful fireworks
display on Sunday evening.

남: 안녕하세요, 그리고 제3회 연례 North 시 예술 축제에 오신 것
을 환영합니다. 매년, 저희 시는 이틀에 걸쳐 지역 예술가들의
작품을 전시함으로써 그들을 세상에 알립니다. 시내의 몇몇 도
로들은 차량 통행이 통제되어, 축제에 오신 분들이 안전하게 여
러 전시장을 돌아보실 수 있도록 했습니다. 올해, 저희는 지역
댄스팀과 음악가들을 일정에 추가하여, 그들이 그림과 조각품
전시 옆에서 공연할 수 있게 했습니다. 또한 전시된 작품들 중
다수는 판매 중이므로, 만일 여러분이 예술품 수집가이시면, 지
갑을 꼭 가져오십시오. 축제는 일요일 저녁에 멋진 불꽃놀이와
함께 막을 내릴 것입니다.

어휘 | celebrate 축하하다; *세상에 알리다 display 전시하다; 전
시 close off …을 차단하다 stroll 거닐다, 산책하다 exhibit 전시품
alongside (…의) 옆에서 collector 수집가 conclude 끝나다, 마치다
firework 불꽃놀이

문제해설 | ④ 지역 댄스팀과 음악가들이 공연할 예정이라고 했다.

12 정답 ②

M: Which one of these hotels do you think we should
book for our trip to Korea?
W: Well, it would be nice to stay in Gimpo because it's
close to the airport.
M: But we will spend most of our time in Seoul. Don't
you think we should stay there?
W: Hmm… I guess you're right.
M: And some of the Seoul hotels have a shuttle service.
That should make it easy to get to and from the airport.
W: All right. Then we should definitely stay in a hotel with
a shuttle service.
M: How about this one? They offer free breakfast.
W: It's $300 a night, though. Don't you think that's awfully

expensive?
M: I guess we can just get breakfast on our own.
W: Yeah, it will be more fun that way.
M: All right. Then let's reserve a room in this hotel.
W: Great!

남: 우리의 한국 여행을 위해 이 호텔 중 어느 곳으로 예약해야 한다
고 생각해?
여: 음, 공항에서 가까우니까 김포에 머무는 게 좋을 것 같은데.
남: 하지만 우리는 대부분의 시간을 서울에서 보낼 거야. 거기에 머
물러야 하지 않을까?
여: 음… 네 말이 맞는 것 같네.
남: 그리고 어떤 서울 호텔은 셔틀버스 서비스를 제공해. 그게 공항
에 오고 가는 걸 수월하게 해 줄 거야.
여: 좋아. 그럼 우리는 반드시 셔틀버스 서비스를 제공하는 호텔에
머물러야겠네.
남: 여기는 어때? 조식을 무료로 주네.
여: 근데 1박에 300달러야. 그건 너무 비싸다고 생각하지 않아?
남: 그냥 우리가 알아서 아침을 먹을 수 있을 것 같아.
여: 응, 그렇게 하는 게 더 재미있을 거야.
남: 좋아. 그럼 이 호텔 방을 예약하자.
여: 좋아!

어휘 | awfully 정말, 몹시 on one's own 스스로

문제해설 | 두 사람은 서울에 있고 셔틀버스 서비스를 제공하며 무료 조
식을 제공하지 않는 호텔을 선택하기로 했으므로, 두 사람이 머무를 호
텔은 ②번이다.

13 정답 ②

M: What's wrong? You look so worried.
W: I'm taking my driver's test tomorrow.
M: That's great! I'm sure you'll pass. After all, you did so
well on the written test.
W: Thanks for your encouragement. But still, I'm nervous
about the road test.
M: Don't worry. You've taken a lot of lessons, and you've
practiced a lot.
W: Yes, and I feel comfortable driving with my instructor
next to me. But I'm nervous about driving by myself.
M: Oh, don't worry about that. Just imagine that he's right
next to you.
W: I'll try. Do you have any other good advice for passing
the test?
M: Just try to have more confidence in yourself.

남: 무슨 일 있니? 걱정스러워 보여.
여: 내일 운전면허 시험을 보거든.
남: 그거 멋진데! 난 네가 통과할 거라 확신해. 어쨌든, 넌 필기시험
을 아주 잘 봤잖아.

여: 격려해 줘서 고마워. 하지만 아직도, 도로주행 시험은 두려워.

남: 걱정하지 마. 넌 수업을 많이 받았고, 연습도 많이 했잖아.

여: 응, 그런데 난 옆에 강사가 있는 상태로 운전하면 편안해. 하지만 혼자서 운전하는 건 떨려.

남: 아, 그건 걱정하지 마. 그냥 강사가 바로 네 옆에 있다고 상상해 봐.

여: 해 볼게. 시험에 통과하기 위한 또 다른 좋은 충고가 있니?

남: <u>스스로에 대해 더 자신감을 갖도록 노력해 봐.</u>

어휘 | encouragement 격려 instructor 강사 **|문제|** confidence 자신감 public transportation 대중교통

문제해설 | 도로주행 시험을 앞두고 초조해하는 여자가 남자에게 또 다른 충고를 해달라고 했으므로, 이에 대한 남자의 응답으로 ②번이 가장 적절하다.

① 넌 운전 강습을 좀 더 받았어야 했어.

③ 네가 원한다면 다른 강사를 선택할 수 있어.

④ 대신에 대중교통을 이용하는 게 어때?

⑤ 그냥 천천히 그리고 신중하게 네 답을 적으렴.

14 정답 ①

M: Hi, Meg. Sorry I'm late. I almost forgot about our meeting.

W: Didn't you write it down in your daily planner?

M: Actually, I don't even have one. I usually just write things on scraps of paper.

W: Don't you ever lose them?

M: Sometimes. But it's not a real problem.

W: Well, I guess everyone is different. Anyway, are you ready to work on our report?

M: Sure. I brought photocopies of the pages you said we needed.

W: Let me see. [*Pause*] This is only the first 10 pages. We need the first 20.

M: Twenty pages? I thought you said just the first 10 pages.

W: Oh, boy. Do you at least still have the book?

M: No, I returned it to the library. I'm really sorry about this.

W: <u>You should get more organized.</u>

남: 안녕, Meg. 늦어서 미안해. 하마터면 우리 만나는 걸 잊을 뻔했어.

여: 약속을 일정 수첩에 안 적어 놓았니?

남: 실은, 수첩도 없어. 난 보통 종이 쪽지에 적어놔.

여: 그걸 잃어버리지 않니?

남: 가끔. 하지만 그건 큰 문제는 아니야.

여: 음, 사람마다 다르니까. 어쨌든, 보고서를 작업할 준비 됐니?

남: 물론이지. 우리가 필요하다고 말한 페이지들을 복사해 왔어.

여: 어디 보자. [*잠시 후*] 이건 앞에 10페이지뿐이잖아. 우리는 앞에

20페이지가 필요해.

남: 20페이지라고? 네가 앞에 10페이지만이라고 말했던 것 같은데.

여: 아, 이런. 그래도 아직 그 책을 가지고 있는 거지?

남: 아니, 도서관에 반납했어. 이렇게 돼서 정말 미안해.

여: <u>넌 좀 더 조직적일 필요가 있어.</u>

어휘 | planner 일정 계획표, 수첩 scrap 조각 photocopy 복사(물) at least 적어도, 최소한 **|문제|** organized 조직적인, 체계적인 copy 복사하다

문제해설 | 메모하는 습관이 없는 남자가 약속도 잊을 뻔하고, 복사를 제대로 해 오지 않은 데다, 봐야 할 책도 도서관에 반납해 버린 상황이므로, 이에 대한 여자의 응답으로 ①번이 가장 적절하다.

② 넌 책을 가져오는 걸 잊은 것 같아.

③ 네가 20페이지 전부를 복사한 것 같지 않은데.

④ 그게 바로 우리가 보고서를 작성해야 하는 이유야.

⑤ 네가 일정 수첩을 마련할 거라는 걸 알게 되어 기뻐.

15 정답 ④

W: Becky plays on her school soccer team. Last month, the team's goalkeeper injured herself during practice. With a big game approaching, the coach asked Becky if she would be the goalkeeper. Becky didn't want to miss this great opportunity to play in a game, so she agreed without hesitation. For several weeks, Becky worked really hard, learning how to be an effective goalkeeper. Just a few days before the big game, however, the team's original goalkeeper announced that she was healthy enough to play. Becky complained that she had worked hard for nothing. In this situation, what would the coach most likely say to Becky?

Coach: <u>Eventually, you'll have a chance to display your skills.</u>

여: Becky는 학교 축구팀에서 활동한다. 지난달에 팀의 골키퍼가 연습 도중에 부상을 당했다. 중요한 경기를 앞두고 코치는 Becky에게 골키퍼를 하겠느냐고 물었다. Becky는 경기에서 뛸 이렇게 좋은 기회를 놓치고 싶지 않아서, 망설임 없이 동의했다. 몇 주 동안, Becky는 유능한 골키퍼가 되는 방법을 배우면서, 정말 열심히 연습했다. 하지만, 그 중요한 경기 바로 며칠 전에, 팀의 원래 골키퍼가 시합을 해도 충분할 만큼 자신이 건강해졌다고 알렸다. Becky는 괜히 열심히 연습했다고 불평을 했다. 이런 상황에서, 코치가 Becky에게 할 말로 가장 적절한 것은 무엇인가?

코치: <u>언젠가는, 네 실력을 보여줄 기회가 올 거란다.</u>

어휘 | injure 부상을 입히다 approach 다가오다 hesitation 주저, 망설임 effective 유능한 for nothing 헛되이 **|문제|** do one's best 최선을 다하다 eventually 결국, 언젠가는 display 드러내다

문제해설 | 골키퍼가 되기 위해 몇 주 동안 열심히 연습한 Becky가 경

기에 나갈 수 없게 되어 불평하고 있는 상황이므로, 코치가 Becky에게 할 말로 ④번이 가장 적절하다.
① 최고의 선수들조차도 때로는 경기에서 진단다.
② 넌 좋은 결과를 얻기 위해서 최선을 다해야 해.
③ 만약 네가 다치지 않았더라면, 넌 잘할 수 있었을 거야.
⑤ 다음 번에는, 결정을 내리기 전에 나에게 물어봐야 해.

16 정답 ① 17 정답 ④

M: Scientists have discovered that our brains are able to adapt and change even in old age. This is good news for all of us, as it means that growing old doesn't necessarily have to bring about mental decline. There are several ways to keep our brains fit and improve our memory as we age. First, get regular exercise. Exercise increases the amount of oxygen that goes to your brain. This can help reduce the risk of disorders that lead to memory loss. It is also essential to get enough sleep. If you deprive yourself of sleep, your brain can't undergo an important process for strengthening new memories and your memory can be harmed. Diet is also important. Scientists have discovered that the omega-3 fatty acids found in fish are particularly good for your brain. Lastly, doing activities that require you to use your hands is also helpful. This includes everything from juggling to playing a musical instrument.

남: 과학자들은 우리의 뇌가 노년에도 상황에 적응하고 변화할 수 있다는 것을 발견했습니다. 이것은 우리 모두에게 좋은 소식인데, 나이가 든다는 것이 반드시 정신적인 쇠퇴를 가져오지는 않는다는 것을 의미하기 때문입니다. 나이가 듦에 따라 우리의 뇌를 건강하게 유지하고 기억을 향상시키는 여러 가지 방법들이 있습니다. 첫째로, 규칙적인 운동을 하세요. 운동은 여러분의 뇌로 가는 산소의 양을 증가시킵니다. 이것은 기억 상실에 이르게 하는 질병의 위험을 감소시키는 데 도움이 될 수 있습니다. 또한 충분한 수면을 취하는 것이 필수적입니다. 여러분에게 잠이 부족하면, 여러분의 뇌는 새로운 기억들을 강화하는 중요한 과정을 경험할 수 없어 기억력이 나빠질 수 있습니다. 식단도 중요합니다. 과학자들은 생선에서 발견되는 오메가3 지방산이 여러분의 뇌에 특히 좋다는 것을 발견했습니다. 마지막으로, 여러분의 손을 사용하게 하는 활동들을 하는 것 또한 도움이 됩니다. 저글링을 하는 것에서 악기를 다루는 것까지 모든 것이 해당됩니다.

어휘 | adapt 적응하다 not necessarily 반드시 …한 것은 아닌 bring about 야기하다, 초래하다 mental 정신적인 decline 쇠퇴 fit 건강한 oxygen 산소 disorder 질병 memory loss 기억 상실 essential 필수적인 deprive A of B A에게서 B를 빼앗다 undergo 겪다 strengthen 강화하다 fatty acid 지방산 musical instrument 악기
|문제| aging 나이 먹음, 노화

문제해설 | 16. 남자는 뇌를 건강하게 유지하는 방법에 대해 이야기하고 있다.
① 뇌를 건강하게 유지하는 방법
② 식단과 운동의 중요성
③ 노화 과정에서 뇌의 역할
④ 젊게 느끼도록 도와줄 수 있는 활동들
⑤ 노화에 대한 최근의 과학적 발견들
17. 뇌를 건강하게 유지하는 방법으로 ④ 이상적인 체중 유지하기에 대해서는 언급되지 않았다.
① 규칙적인 운동하기　　　　② 충분한 수면 취하기
③ 오메가3 지방산이 든 음식 먹기　　④ 손으로 하는 활동들

10분 만에 끝내는 영어 수업 준비!

NE Tutor

NE Tutor는 NE능률이 만든 대한민국 대표 영어 티칭 플랫폼으로
영어 수업에 필요한 모든 콘텐츠와 서비스를 제공합니다.

www.netutor.co.kr

NE Tutor
- 튜터 Mall
- 교재/수업자료
- 커리큘럼
- 스마트 문제뱅크
- E-Book
- 스마트 클래스

· 전국 영어 학원 선생님들이 뽑은 **NE Tutor 서비스 TOP 4!** ·

교재 수업자료 ELT부터 초중고까지 수백여 종 교재의 부가자료, E-Book, 어휘 문제 마법사 등 믿을 수 있는 영어 수업 자료 제공

커리큘럼 대상별/영역별/수준별 교재 커리큘럼 & 영어 실력에 맞는 교재를 추천하는 레벨테스트 제공

한국 교육과정 기반의 IBT 영어 테스트 어휘+문법+듣기+독해 영역별 영어 실력을 정확히 측정하여, 전국 단위 객관적 지표 및 내신/수능 대비 약점 처방

문법 문제뱅크 NE능률이 엄선한 3만 개 문항 기반의 문법 문제 출제 서비스, 최대 50문항까지 간편하게 객관식&주관식 문제 출제

NE_Tutor